EARTH'S MIGHTIEST HEROES

THE AVENGERS

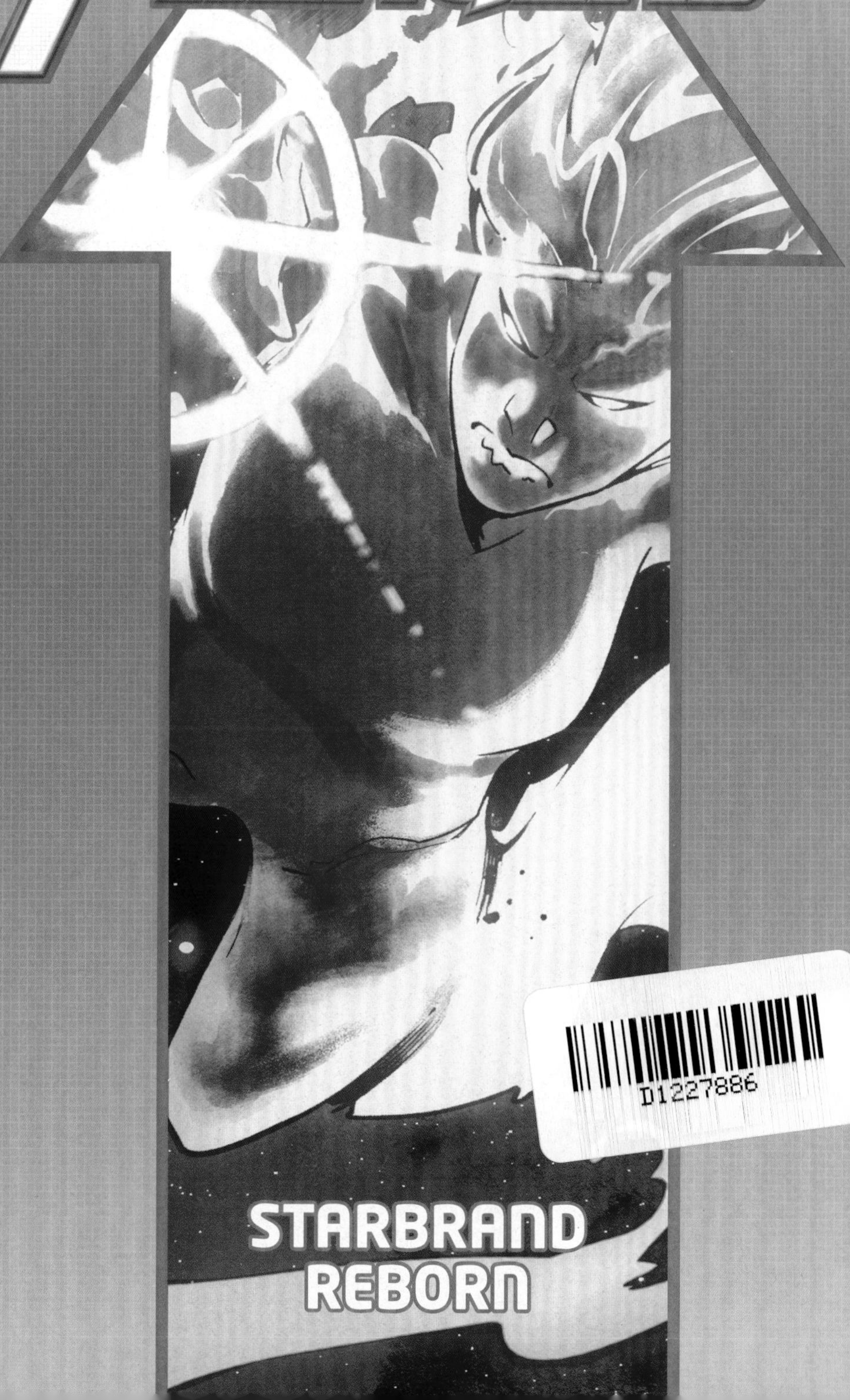

STARBRAND REBORN

ON A DAY UNLIKE ANY OTHER, A DARK CELESTIAL INVASION LED IRON MAN, THOR AND CAPTAIN AMERICA TO RE-FORM THE AVENGERS, ADDING BLACK PANTHER, CAPTAIN MARVEL, SHE-HULK AND GHOST RIDER TO THEIR RANKS.

SINCE THE DAWN OF TIME, THE PLANETARY DEFENSE MECHANISM KNOWN AS THE STARBRAND HAS BEEN WIELDED BY A VARIETY OF PEOPLE, GRANTING THEM VIRTUALLY INFINITE POWER. OVER THE YEARS, THE STARBRAND MANIFESTED IN SEVERAL HOSTS, AND THE FIRST WALKED THE EARTH OVER ONE MILLION YEARS AGO…

COLLECTION EDITOR **JENNIFER GRÜNWALD**
ASSISTANT MANAGING EDITOR **MAIA LOY**
ASSISTANT MANAGING EDITOR **LISA MONTALBANO**
EDITOR, SPECIAL PROJECTS **MARK D. BEAZLEY**

VP PRODUCTION & SPECIAL PROJECTS **JEFF YOUNGQUIST**
BOOK DESIGNERS **SALENA MAHINA** & **ADAM DEL RE**
SVP PRINT, SALES & MARKETING **DAVID GABRIEL**
EDITOR IN CHIEF **C.B. CEBULSKI**

AVENGERS BY JASON AARON VOL. 6: STARBRAND REBORN. Contains material originally published in magazine form as AVENGERS (2018) #26-30. First printing 2020. ISBN 978-1-302-92094-4. Published by MARVEL WORLDWIDE, INC., a subsidiary of MARVEL ENTERTAINMENT, LLC. OFFICE OF PUBLICATION: 1290 Avenue of the Americas, New York, NY 10104. © 2020 MARVEL No similarity between any of the names, characters, persons, and/or institutions in this magazine with those of any living or dead person or institution is intended, and any such similarity which may exist is purely coincidental. **Printed in Canada.** KEVIN FEIGE, Chief Creative Officer; DAN BUCKLEY, President, Marvel Entertainment; JOHN NEE, Publisher; JOE QUESADA, EVP & Creative Director; TOM BREVOORT, SVP of Publishing; DAVID BOGART, Associate Publisher & SVP of Talent Affairs; Publishing & Partnership; DAVID GABRIEL, VP of Print & Digital Publishing; JEFF YOUNGQUIST, VP of Production & Special Projects; DAN CARR, Executive Director of Publishing Technology; ALEX MORALES, Director of Publishing Operations; DAN EDINGTON, Managing Editor; SUSAN CRESPI, Production Manager; STAN LEE, Chairman Emeritus. For information regarding advertising in Marvel Comics or on Marvel.com, please contact Vit DeBellis, Custom Solutions & Integrated Advertising Manager, at vdebellis@marvel.com. For Marvel subscription inquiries, please call 888-511-5480. Manufactured between 3/13/2020 and 4/14/2020 by SOLISCO PRINTERS, SCOTT, QC, CANADA.

10 9 8 7 6 5 4 3 2 1

EARTH'S MIGHTIEST HEROES

THE AVENGERS

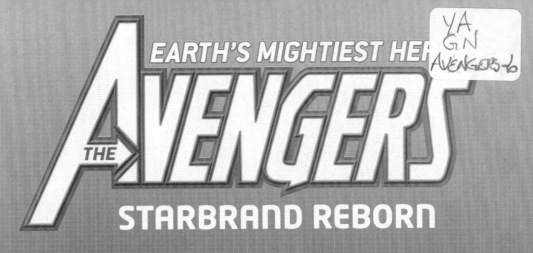

STARBRAND REBORN

JASON AARON
WRITER

DALE KEOWN (#26), ANDREA SORRENTINO (#26),
ED McGUINNESS (#27-30), PACO MEDINA (#29)
& FRANCESCO MANNA (#30)
PENCILERS

JOE WEEMS (#26), CAM SMITH (#26), CRAIG YEUNG (#26),
ANDREA SORRENTINO (#26), MARK MORALES (#27-30),
ED McGUINNESS (#29), PACO MEDINA (#29)
& FRANCESCO MANNA (#30)
INKERS

JASON KEITH
WITH ERICK ARCINIEGA (#26, #28)
& JAY DAVID RAMOS (#26)
COLOR ARTISTS

VC's CORY PETIT
LETTERER

DALE KEOWN & JASON KEITH (#26);
ED McGUINNESS & VAL STAPLES (#27);
ED McGUINNESS & JASON KEITH (#28-29)
AND MICO SUAYAN & RAIN BEREDO (#30)
COVER ART

SHANNON ANDREWS BALLESTEROS
ASSISTANT EDITOR

TOM BREVOORT
EDITOR

AVENGERS CREATED BY STAN LEE & JACK KIRBY

26 AS STRONG AS THE STARS

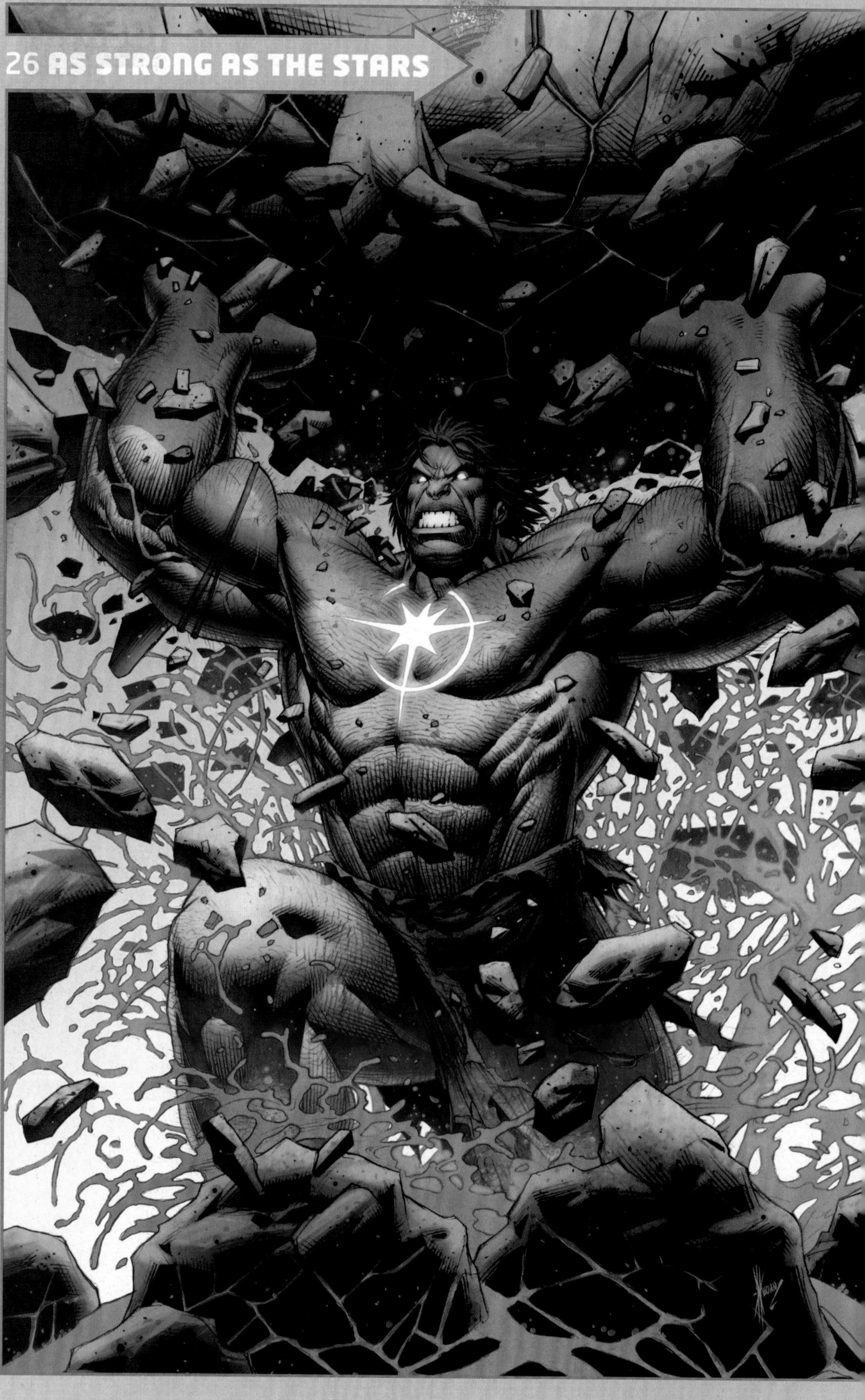

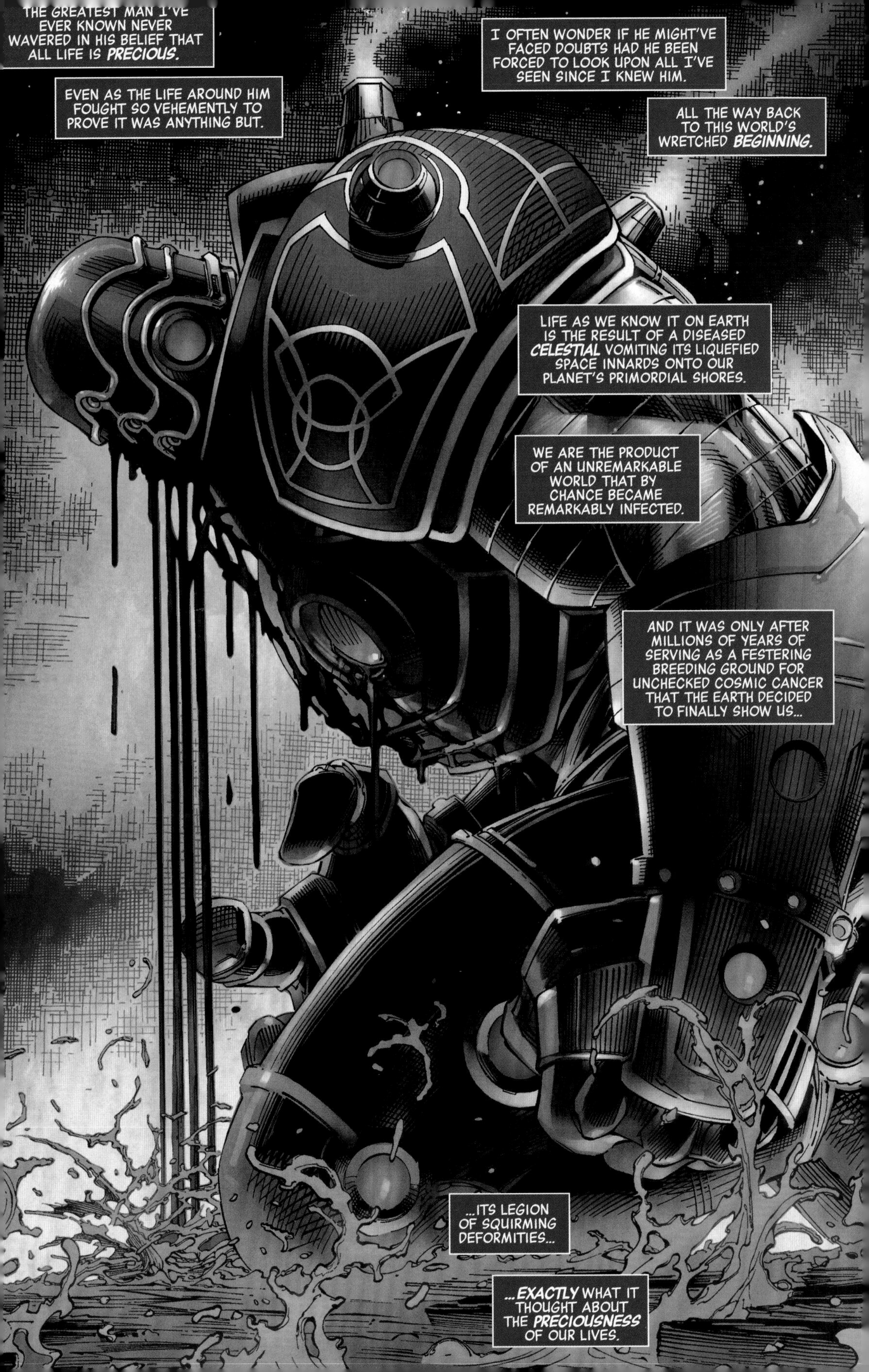
THE GREATEST MAN I'VE EVER KNOWN NEVER WAVERED IN HIS BELIEF THAT ALL LIFE IS PRECIOUS.
EVEN AS THE LIFE AROUND HIM FOUGHT SO VEHEMENTLY TO PROVE IT WAS ANYTHING BUT.
I OFTEN WONDER IF HE MIGHT'VE FACED DOUBTS HAD HE BEEN FORCED TO LOOK UPON ALL I'VE SEEN SINCE I KNEW HIM.
ALL THE WAY BACK TO THIS WORLD'S WRETCHED BEGINNING.
LIFE AS WE KNOW IT ON EARTH IS THE RESULT OF A DISEASED CELESTIAL VOMITING ITS LIQUEFIED SPACE INNARDS ONTO OUR PLANET'S PRIMORDIAL SHORES.
WE ARE THE PRODUCT OF AN UNREMARKABLE WORLD THAT BY CHANCE BECAME REMARKABLY INFECTED.
AND IT WAS ONLY AFTER MILLIONS OF YEARS OF SERVING AS A FESTERING BREEDING GROUND FOR UNCHECKED COSMIC CANCER THAT THE EARTH DECIDED TO FINALLY SHOW US...
...ITS LEGION OF SQUIRMING DEFORMITIES...
...EXACTLY WHAT IT THOUGHT ABOUT THE PRECIOUSNESS OF OUR LIVES.

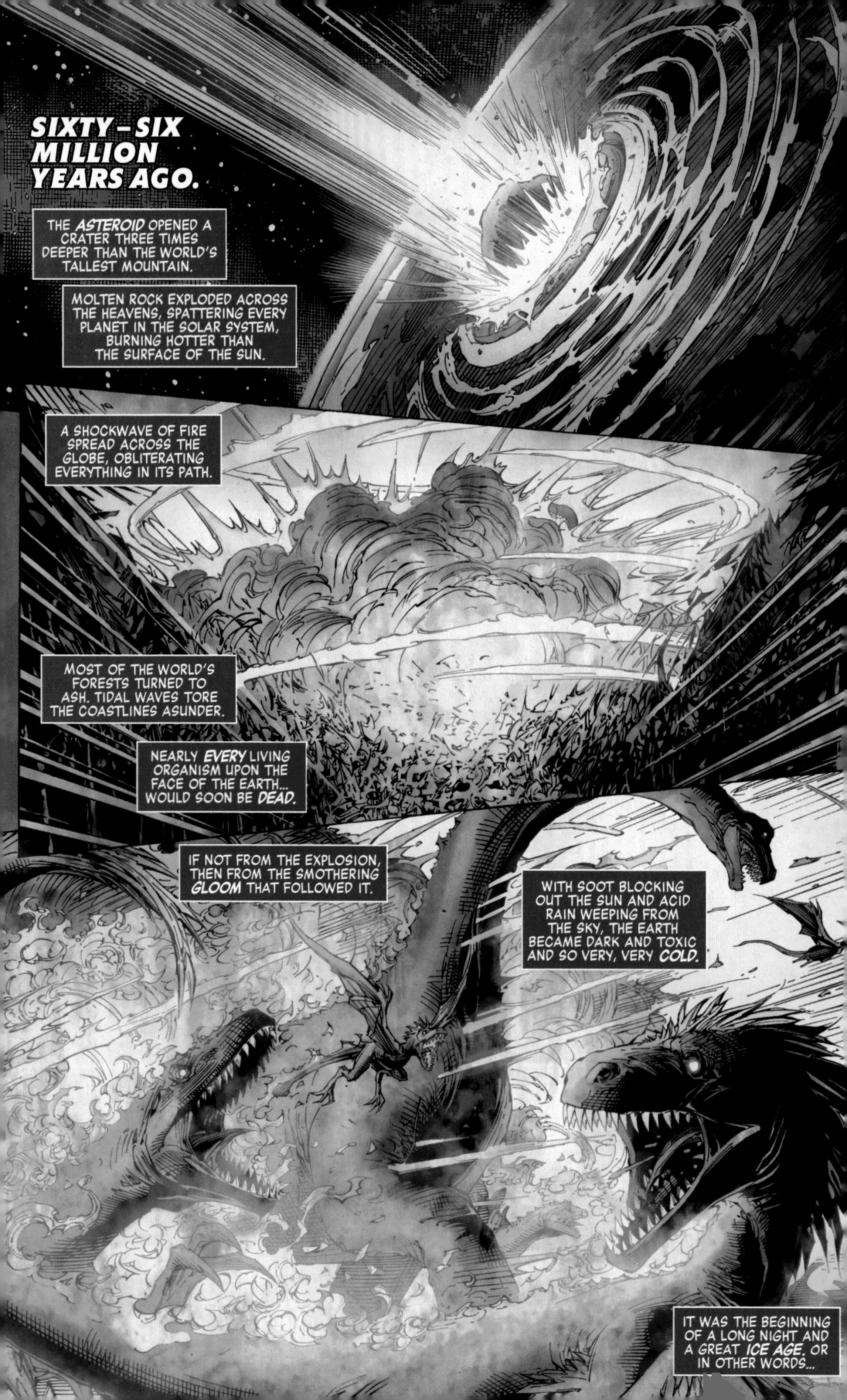
SIXTY-SIX MILLION YEARS AGO.
THE ASTEROID OPENED A CRATER THREE TIMES DEEPER THAN THE WORLD'S TALLEST MOUNTAIN.
MOLTEN ROCK EXPLODED ACROSS THE HEAVENS, SPATTERING EVERY PLANET IN THE SOLAR SYSTEM, BURNING HOTTER THAN THE SURFACE OF THE SUN.
A SHOCKWAVE OF FIRE SPREAD ACROSS THE GLOBE, OBLITERATING EVERYTHING IN ITS PATH.
MOST OF THE WORLD'S FORESTS TURNED TO ASH. TIDAL WAVES TORE THE COASTLINES ASUNDER.
NEARLY EVERY LIVING ORGANISM UPON THE FACE OF THE EARTH... WOULD SOON BE DEAD.
IF NOT FROM THE EXPLOSION, THEN FROM THE SMOTHERING GLOOM THAT FOLLOWED IT.
WITH SOOT BLOCKING OUT THE SUN AND ACID RAIN WEEPING FROM THE SKY, THE EARTH BECAME DARK AND TOXIC AND SO VERY, VERY COLD.
IT WAS THE BEGINNING OF A LONG NIGHT AND A GREAT ICE AGE. OR IN OTHER WORDS...

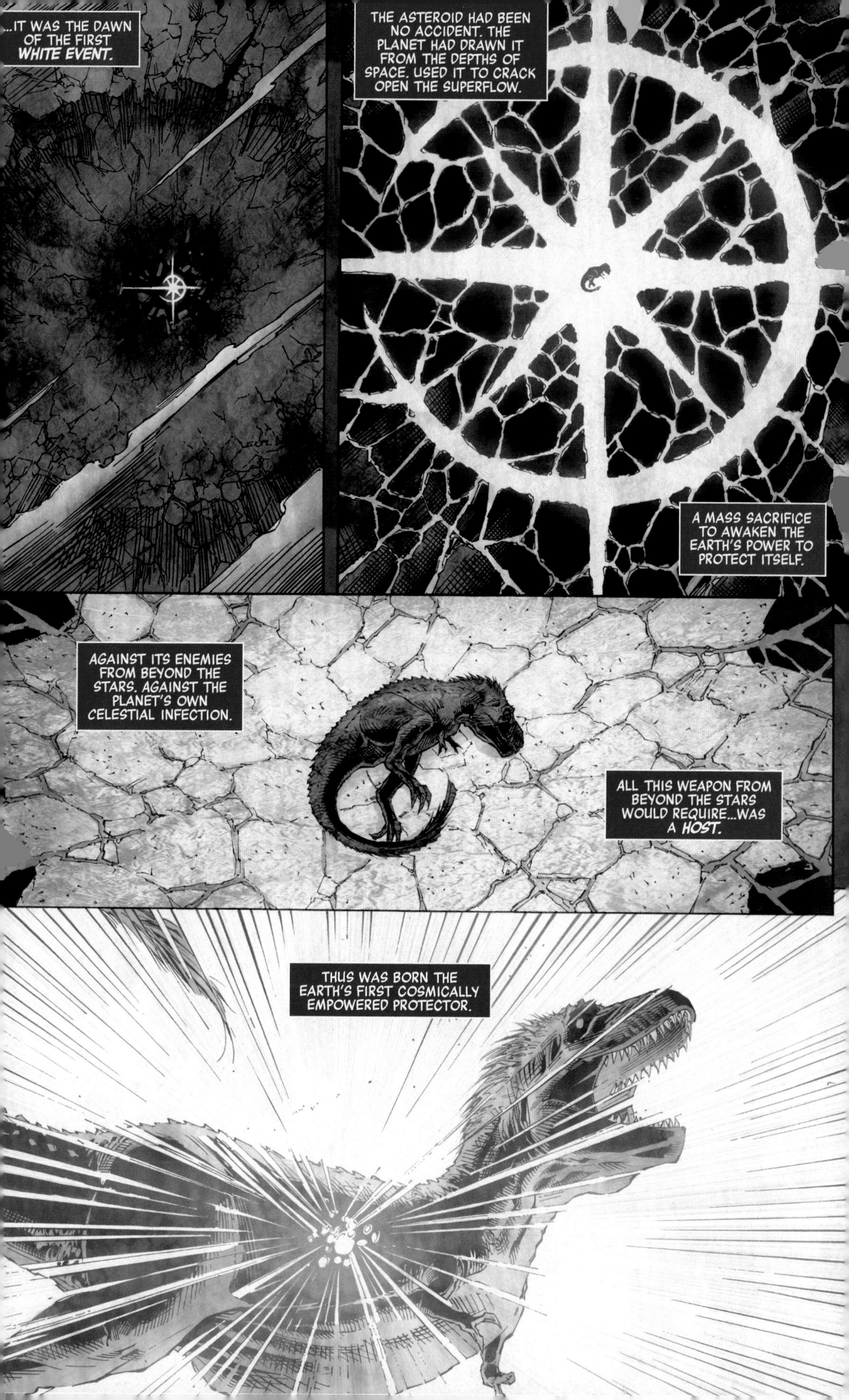
...IT WAS THE DAWN OF THE FIRST WHITE EVENT.
THE ASTEROID HAD BEEN NO ACCIDENT. THE PLANET HAD DRAWN IT FROM THE DEPTHS OF SPACE. USED IT TO CRACK OPEN THE SUPERFLOW.
A MASS SACRIFICE TO AWAKEN THE EARTH'S POWER TO PROTECT ITSELF.
AGAINST ITS ENEMIES FROM BEYOND THE STARS. AGAINST THE PLANET'S OWN CELESTIAL INFECTION.
ALL THIS WEAPON FROM BEYOND THE STARS WOULD REQUIRE...WAS A HOST.
THUS WAS BORN THE EARTH'S FIRST COSMICALLY EMPOWERED PROTECTOR.

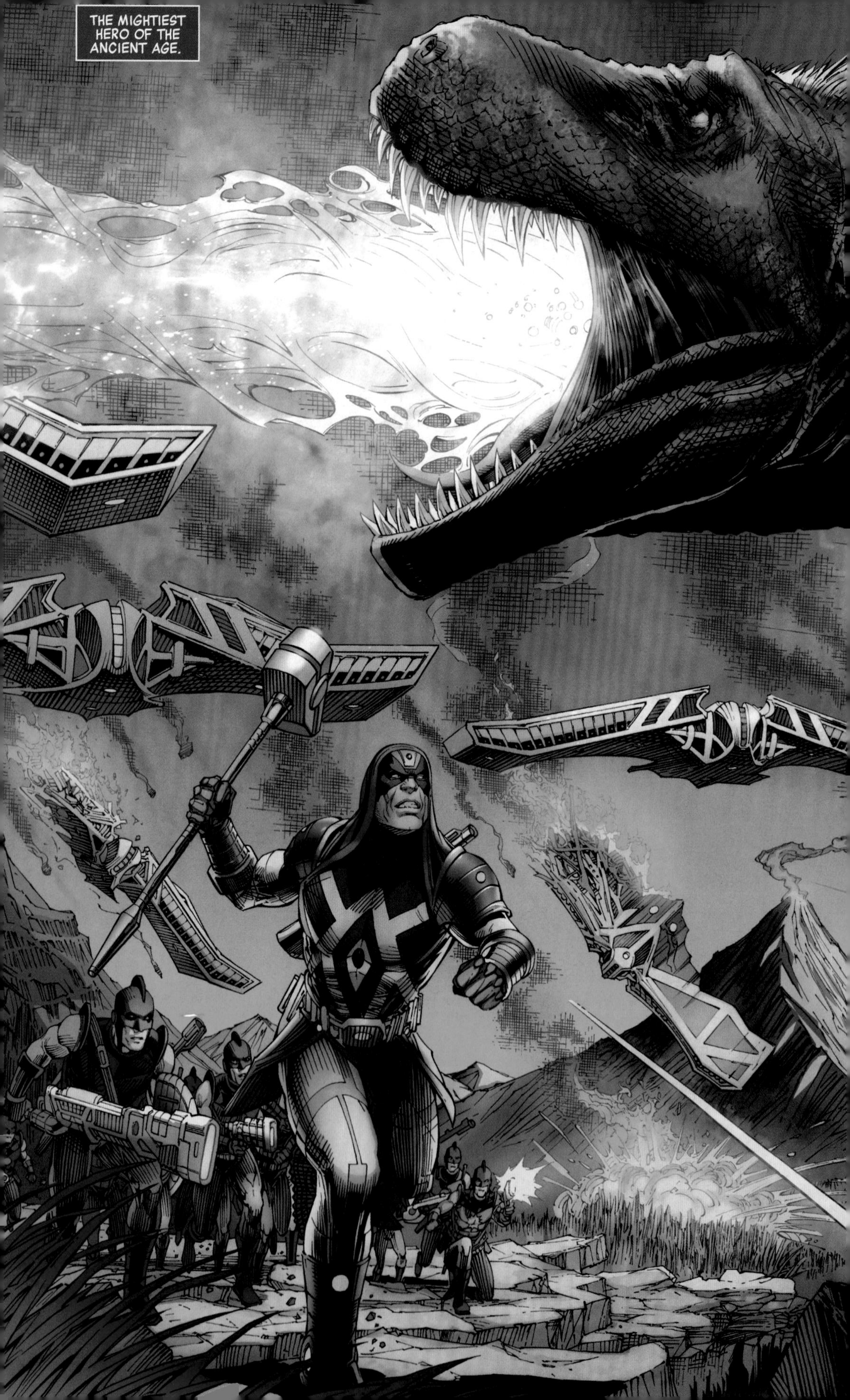
THE MIGHTIEST HERO OF THE ANCIENT AGE.

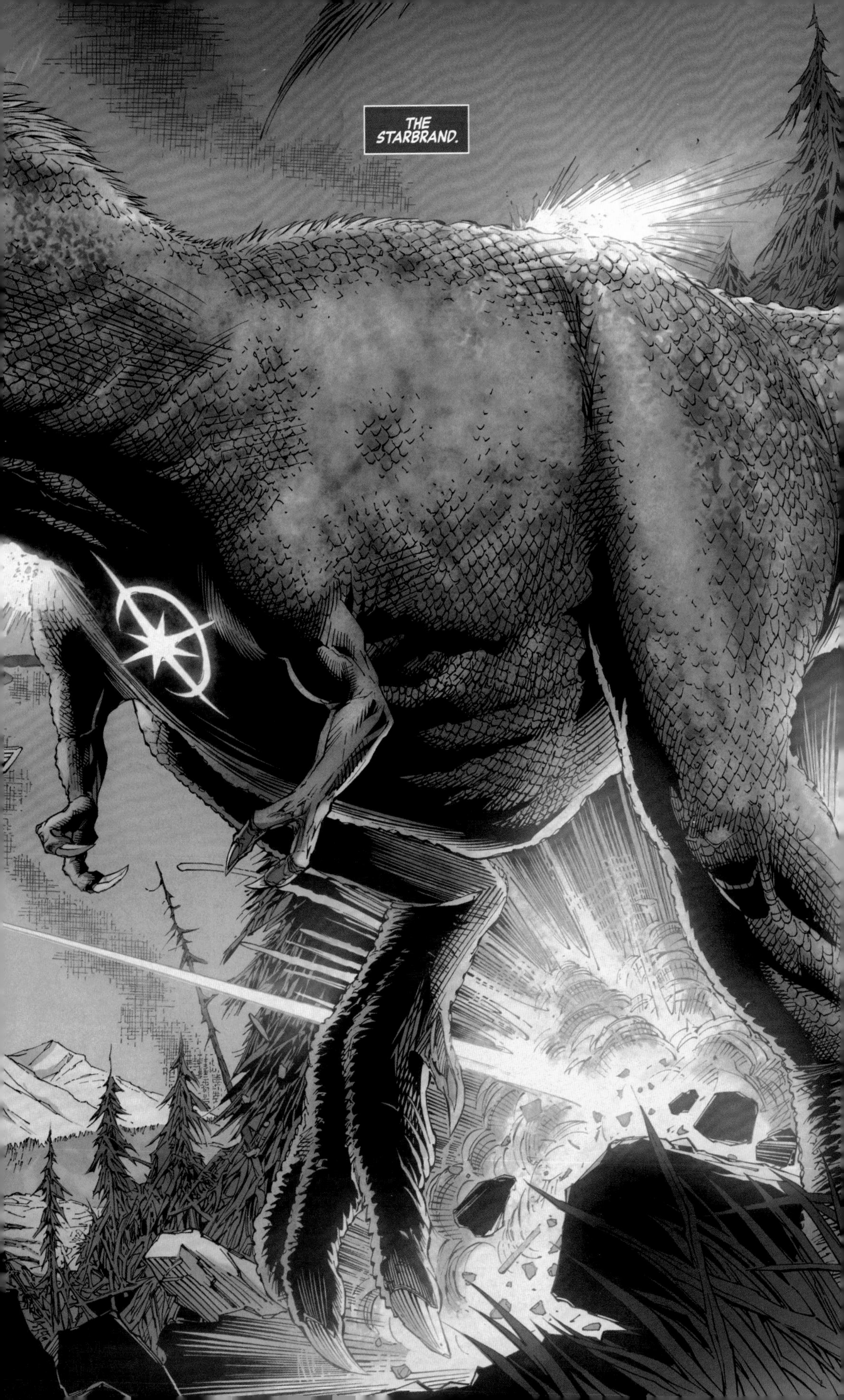
THE STARBRAND.

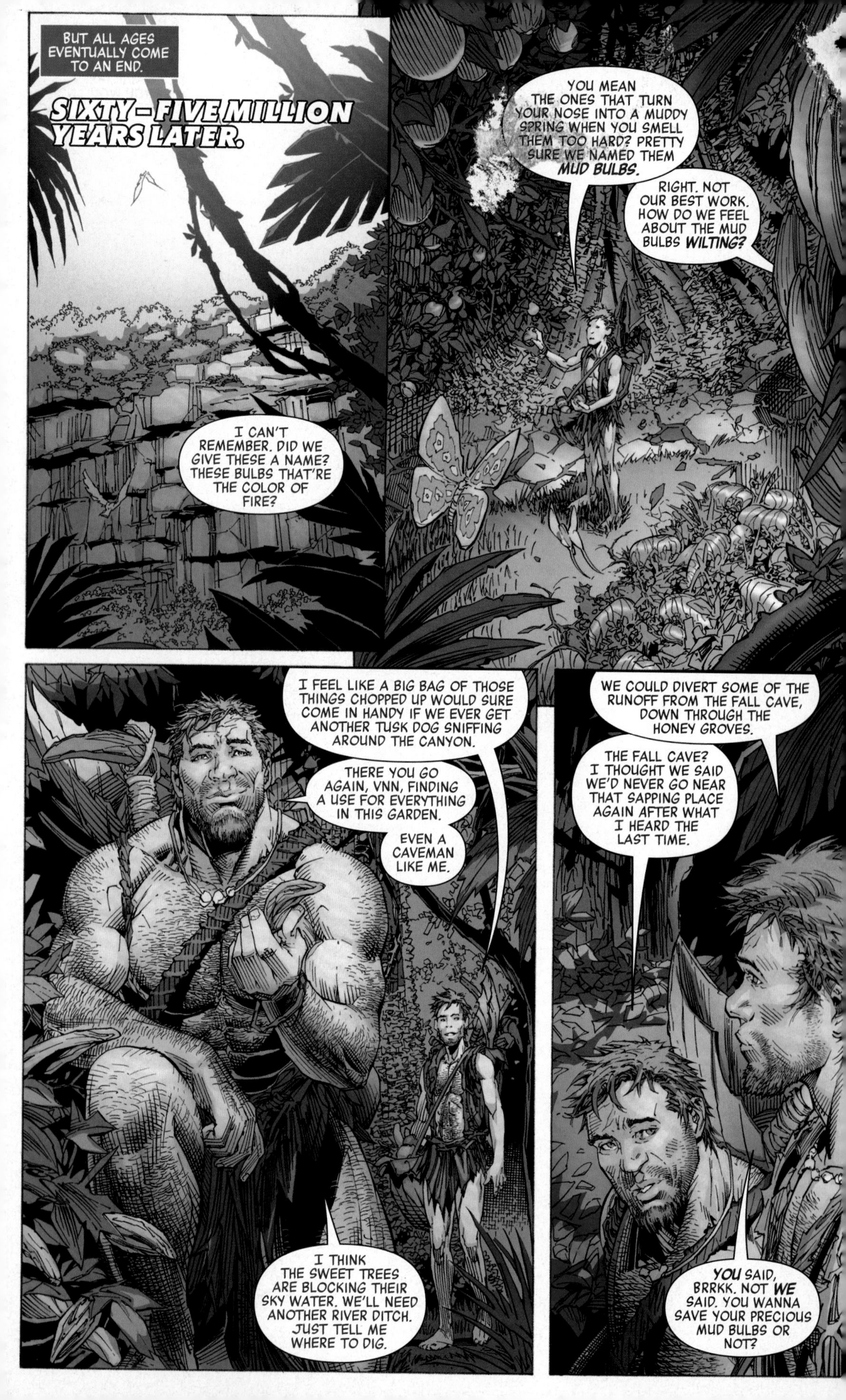
BUT ALL AGES EVENTUALLY COME TO AN END.
SIXTY-FIVE MILLION YEARS LATER.
I CAN'T REMEMBER. DID WE GIVE THESE A NAME? THESE BULBS THAT'RE THE COLOR OF FIRE?
YOU MEAN THE ONES THAT TURN YOUR NOSE INTO A MUDDY SPRING WHEN YOU SMELL THEM TOO HARD? PRETTY SURE WE NAMED THEM MUD BULBS.
RIGHT. NOT OUR BEST WORK. HOW DO WE FEEL ABOUT THE MUD BULBS WILTING?
I THINK THE SWEET TREES ARE BLOCKING THEIR SKY WATER. WE'LL NEED ANOTHER RIVER DITCH. JUST TELL ME WHERE TO DIG.
I FEEL LIKE A BIG BAG OF THOSE THINGS CHOPPED UP WOULD SURE COME IN HANDY IF WE EVER GET ANOTHER TUSK DOG SNIFFING AROUND THE CANYON.
THERE YOU GO AGAIN, VNN, FINDING A USE FOR EVERYTHING IN THIS GARDEN.
EVEN A CAVEMAN LIKE ME.
WE COULD DIVERT SOME OF THE RUNOFF FROM THE FALL CAVE, DOWN THROUGH THE HONEY GROVES.
THE FALL CAVE? I THOUGHT WE SAID WE'D NEVER GO NEAR THAT SAPPING PLACE AGAIN AFTER WHAT I HEARD THE LAST TIME.
YOU SAID, BRRKK. NOT WE SAID. YOU WANNA SAVE YOUR PRECIOUS MUD BULBS OR NOT?

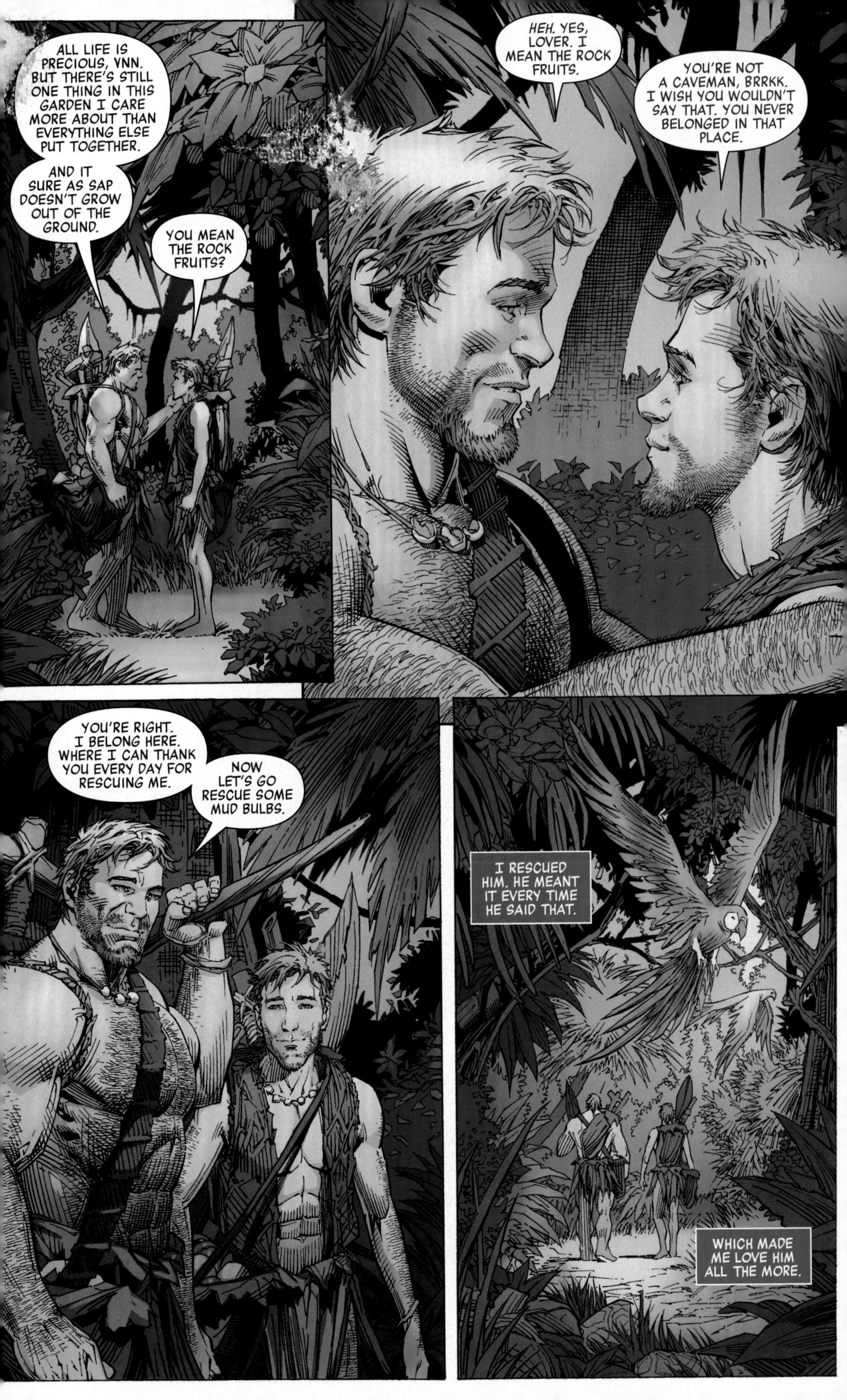
ALL LIFE IS PRECIOUS, VNN. BUT THERE'S STILL ONE THING IN THIS GARDEN I CARE MORE ABOUT THAN EVERYTHING ELSE PUT TOGETHER.
AND IT SURE AS SAP DOESN'T GROW OUT OF THE GROUND.
YOU MEAN THE ROCK FRUITS?
HEH. YES, LOVER. I MEAN THE ROCK FRUITS.
YOU'RE NOT A CAVEMAN, BRRKK. I WISH YOU WOULDN'T SAY THAT. YOU NEVER BELONGED IN THAT PLACE.
YOU'RE RIGHT. I BELONG HERE. WHERE I CAN THANK YOU EVERY DAY FOR RESCUING ME.
NOW LET'S GO RESCUE SOME MUD BULBS.
I RESCUED HIM. HE MEANT IT EVERY TIME HE SAID THAT.
WHICH MADE ME LOVE HIM ALL THE MORE.

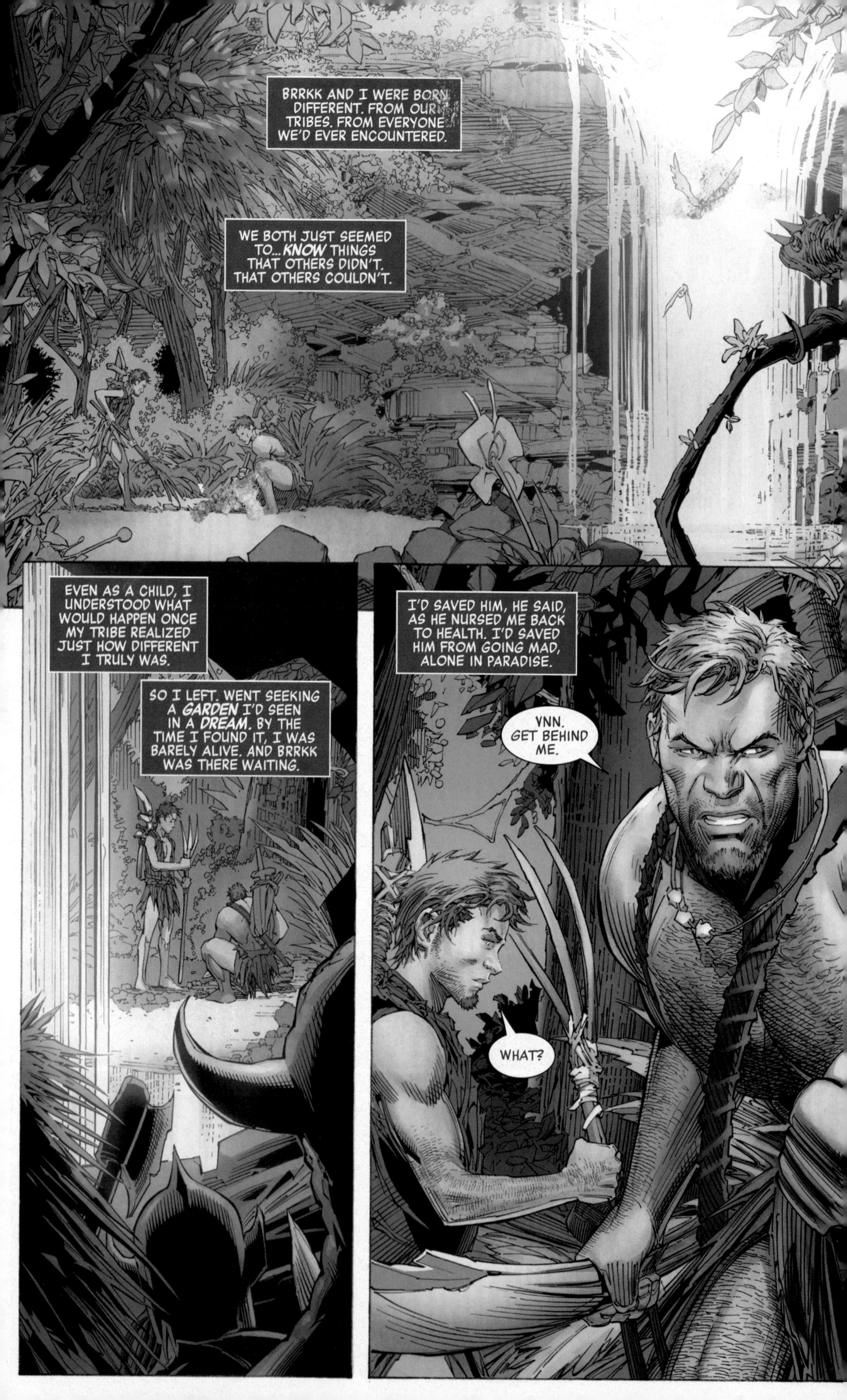

BRRKK AND I WERE BORN DIFFERENT. FROM OUR TRIBES. FROM EVERYONE WE'D EVER ENCOUNTERED.
WE BOTH JUST SEEMED TO... KNOW THINGS THAT OTHERS DIDN'T. THAT OTHERS COULDN'T.
EVEN AS A CHILD, I UNDERSTOOD WHAT WOULD HAPPEN ONCE MY TRIBE REALIZED JUST HOW DIFFERENT I TRULY WAS.
SO I LEFT. WENT SEEKING A GARDEN I'D SEEN IN A DREAM. BY THE TIME I FOUND IT, I WAS BARELY ALIVE. AND BRRKK WAS THERE WAITING.
I'D SAVED HIM, HE SAID, AS HE NURSED ME BACK TO HEALTH. I'D SAVED HIM FROM GOING MAD, ALONE IN PARADISE.
VNN. GET BEHIND ME.
WHAT?

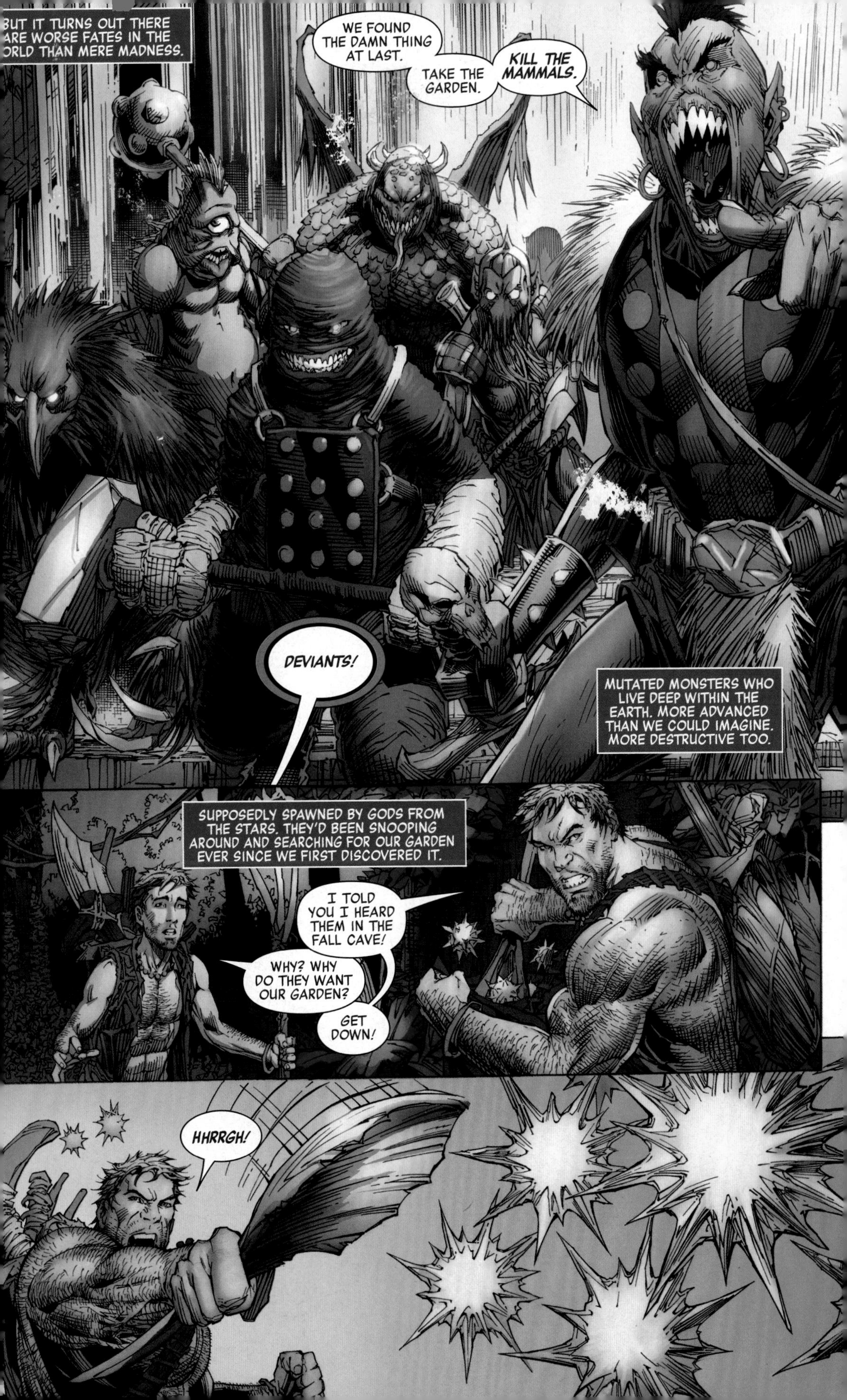

BUT IT TURNS OUT THERE ARE WORSE FATES IN THE WORLD THAN MERE MADNESS.
WE FOUND THE DAMN THING AT LAST.
TAKE THE GARDEN.
KILL THE MAMMALS.
DEVIANTS!
MUTATED MONSTERS WHO LIVE DEEP WITHIN THE EARTH. MORE ADVANCED THAN WE COULD IMAGINE. MORE DESTRUCTIVE TOO.
SUPPOSEDLY SPAWNED BY GODS FROM THE STARS. THEY'D BEEN SNOOPING AROUND AND SEARCHING FOR OUR GARDEN EVER SINCE WE FIRST DISCOVERED IT.
I TOLD YOU I HEARD THEM IN THE FALL CAVE!
WHY? WHY DO THEY WANT OUR GARDEN?
GET DOWN!
HHRRGH!

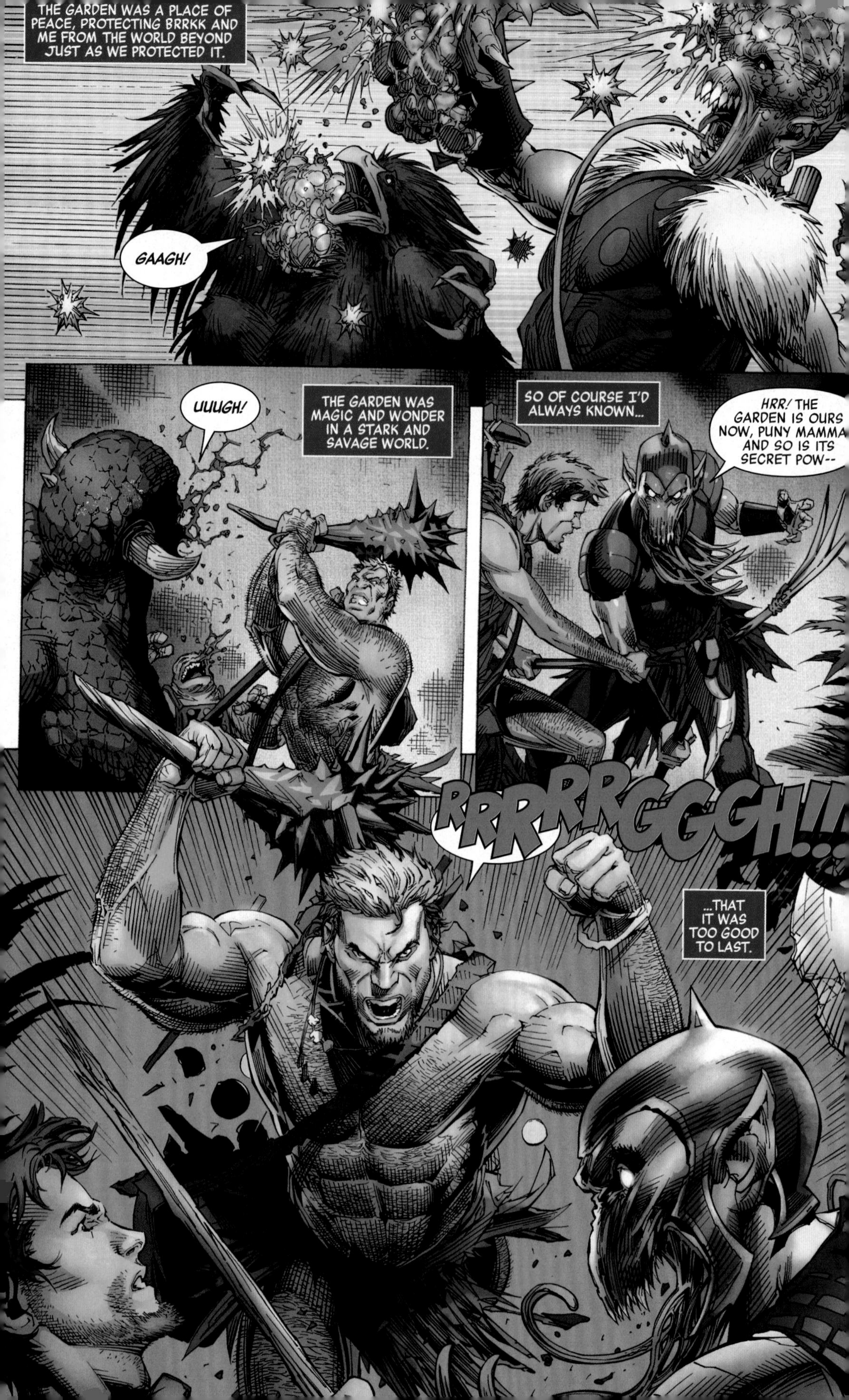
THE GARDEN WAS A PLACE OF PEACE, PROTECTING BRRKK AND ME FROM THE WORLD BEYOND JUST AS WE PROTECTED IT.
GAAGH!
UUUGH!
THE GARDEN WAS MAGIC AND WONDER IN A STARK AND SAVAGE WORLD.
SO OF COURSE I'D ALWAYS KNOWN...
HRR! THE GARDEN IS OURS NOW, PUNY MAMMA AND SO IS ITS SECRET POW--
RRRRRGGGH!!!
...THAT IT WAS TOO GOOD TO LAST.

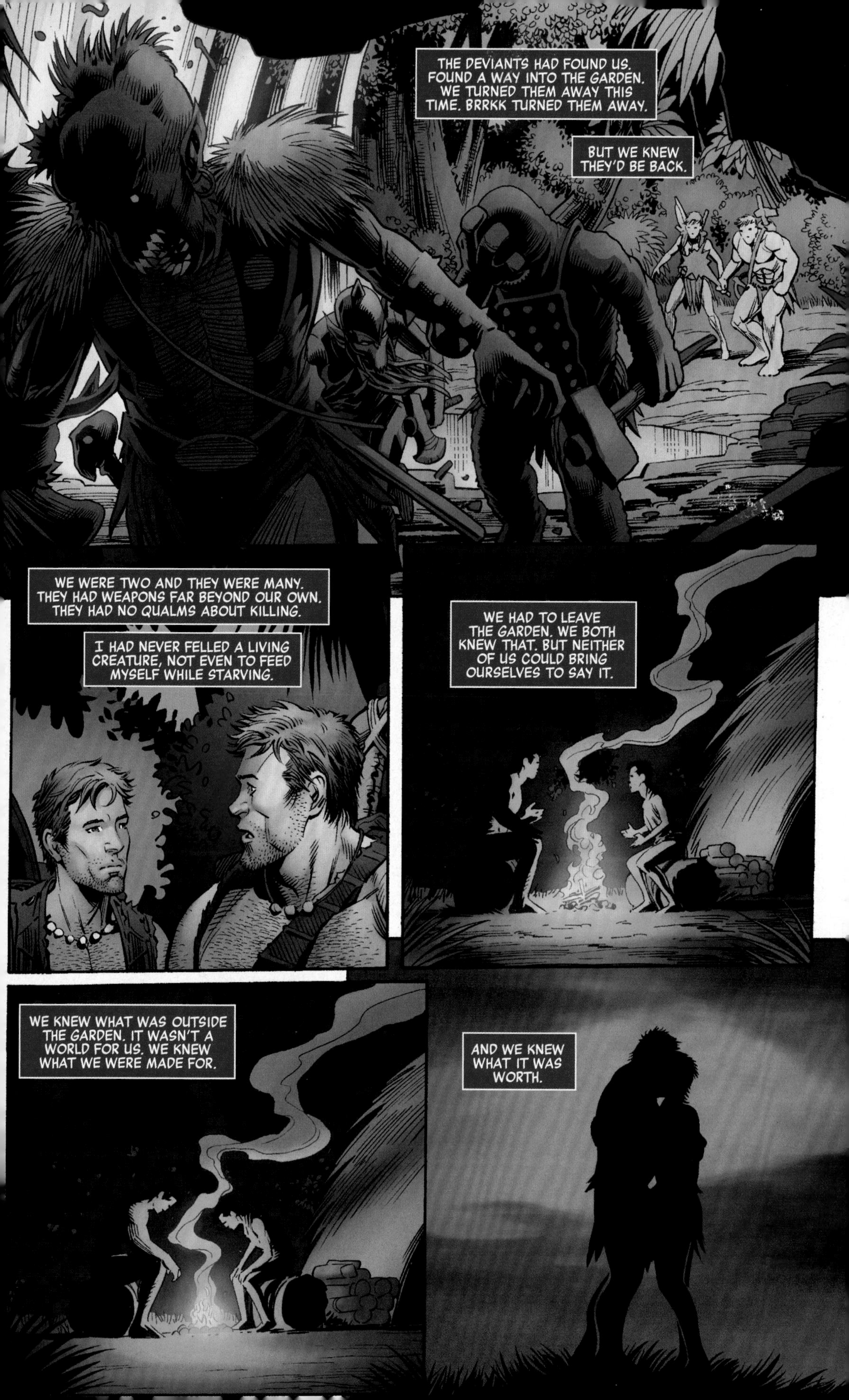
THE DEVIANTS HAD FOUND US. FOUND A WAY INTO THE GARDEN. WE TURNED THEM AWAY THIS TIME. BRRKK TURNED THEM AWAY.
BUT WE KNEW THEY'D BE BACK.
WE WERE TWO AND THEY WERE MANY. THEY HAD WEAPONS FAR BEYOND OUR OWN. THEY HAD NO QUALMS ABOUT KILLING.
I HAD NEVER FELLED A LIVING CREATURE, NOT EVEN TO FEED MYSELF WHILE STARVING.
WE HAD TO LEAVE THE GARDEN. WE BOTH KNEW THAT. BUT NEITHER OF US COULD BRING OURSELVES TO SAY IT.
WE KNEW WHAT WAS OUTSIDE THE GARDEN. IT WASN'T A WORLD FOR US. WE KNEW WHAT WE WERE MADE FOR.
AND WE KNEW WHAT IT WAS WORTH.

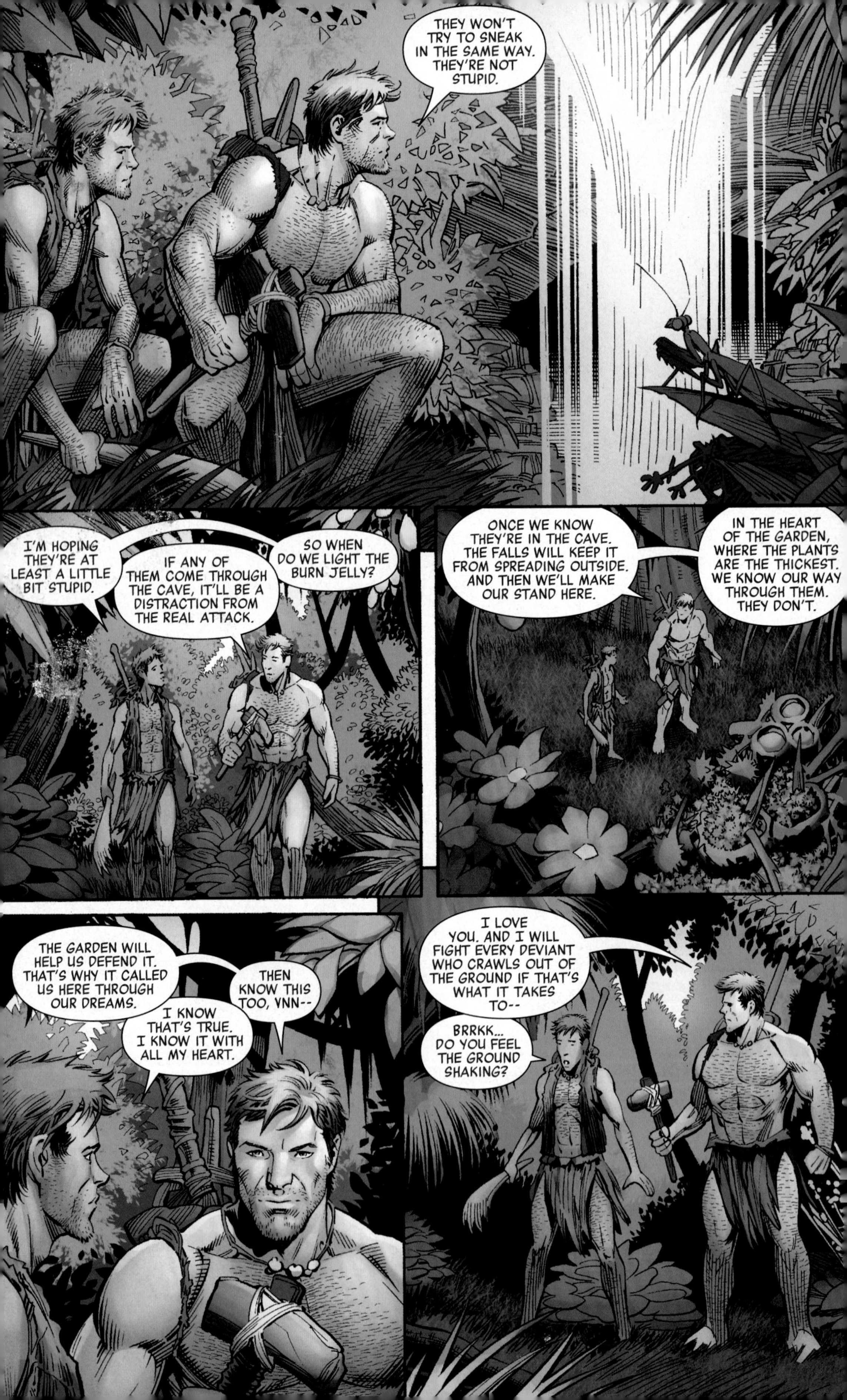
THEY WON'T TRY TO SNEAK IN THE SAME WAY. THEY'RE NOT STUPID.
I'M HOPING THEY'RE AT LEAST A LITTLE BIT STUPID.
IF ANY OF THEM COME THROUGH THE CAVE, IT'LL BE A DISTRACTION FROM THE REAL ATTACK.
SO WHEN DO WE LIGHT THE BURN JELLY?
ONCE WE KNOW THEY'RE IN THE CAVE. THE FALLS WILL KEEP IT FROM SPREADING OUTSIDE. AND THEN WE'LL MAKE OUR STAND HERE.
IN THE HEART OF THE GARDEN, WHERE THE PLANTS ARE THE THICKEST. WE KNOW OUR WAY THROUGH THEM. THEY DON'T.
THE GARDEN WILL HELP US DEFEND IT. THAT'S WHY IT CALLED US HERE THROUGH OUR DREAMS.
I KNOW THAT'S TRUE. I KNOW IT WITH ALL MY HEART.
THEN KNOW THIS TOO, VNN--
I LOVE YOU. AND I WILL FIGHT EVERY DEVIANT WHO CRAWLS OUT OF THE GROUND IF THAT'S WHAT IT TAKES TO--
BRRKK... DO YOU FEEL THE GROUND SHAKING?

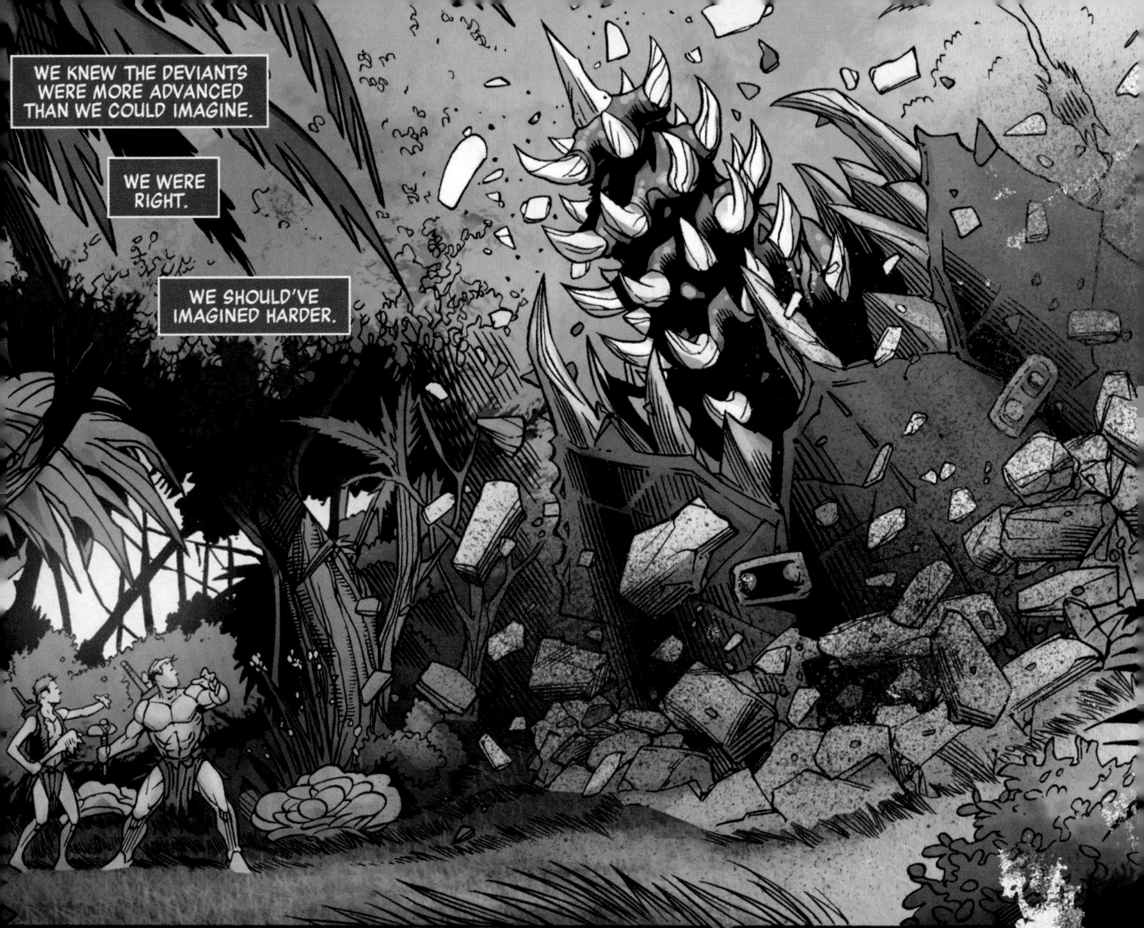
WE KNEW THE DEVIANTS WERE MORE ADVANCED THAN WE COULD IMAGINE.
WE WERE RIGHT.
WE SHOULD'VE IMAGINED HARDER.

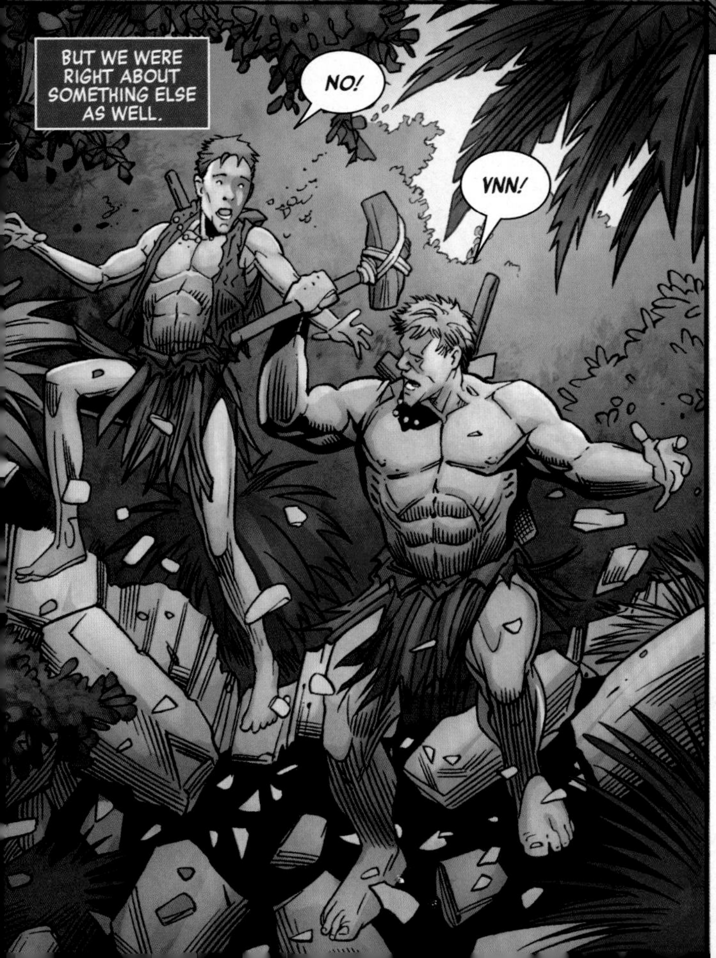
BUT WE WERE RIGHT ABOUT SOMETHING ELSE AS WELL.
NO!
VNN!

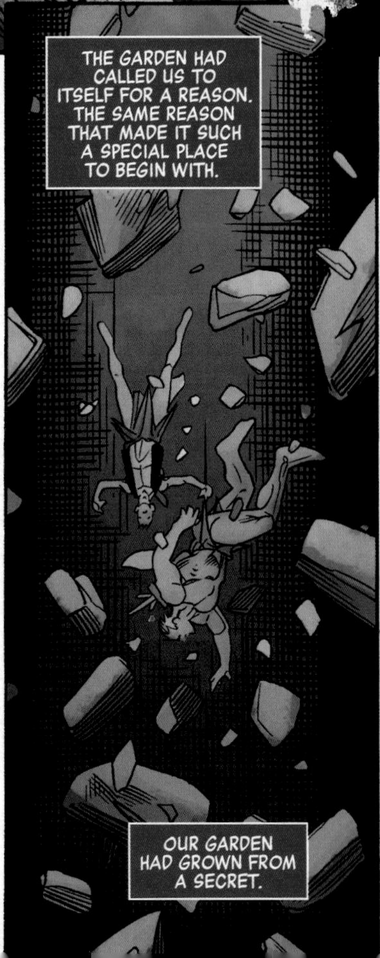
THE GARDEN HAD CALLED US TO ITSELF FOR A REASON. THE SAME REASON THAT MADE IT SUCH A SPECIAL PLACE TO BEGIN WITH.
OUR GARDEN HAD GROWN FROM A SECRET.

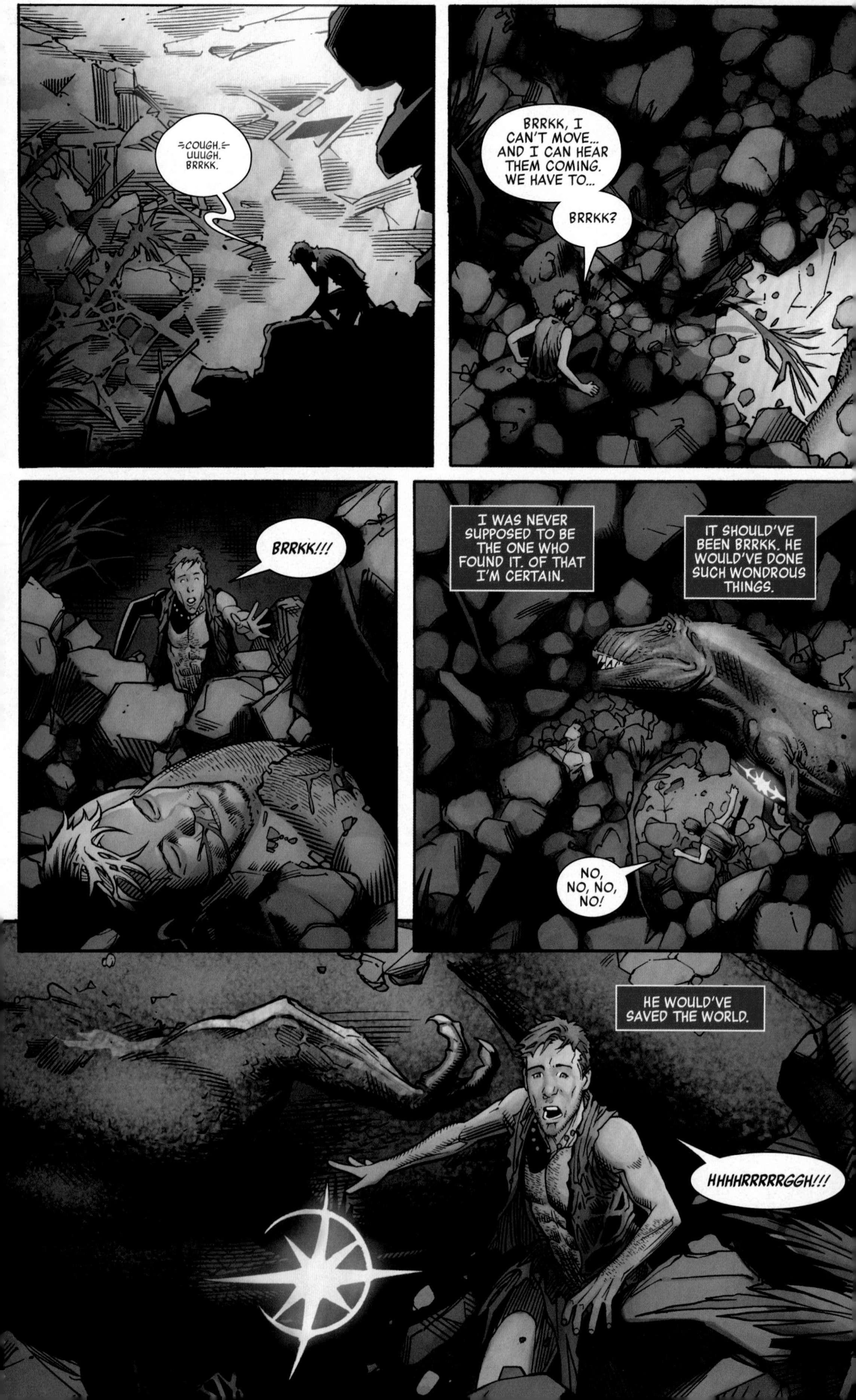

=COUGH.= UUUGH. BRRKK.
BRRKK, I CAN'T MOVE... AND I CAN HEAR THEM COMING. WE HAVE TO...
BRRKK?
BRRKK!!!
I WAS NEVER SUPPOSED TO BE THE ONE WHO FOUND IT. OF THAT I'M CERTAIN.
IT SHOULD'VE BEEN BRRKK. HE WOULD'VE DONE SUCH WONDROUS THINGS.
NO, NO, NO, NO!
HE WOULD'VE SAVED THE WORLD.
HHHHRRRRRGGH!!!

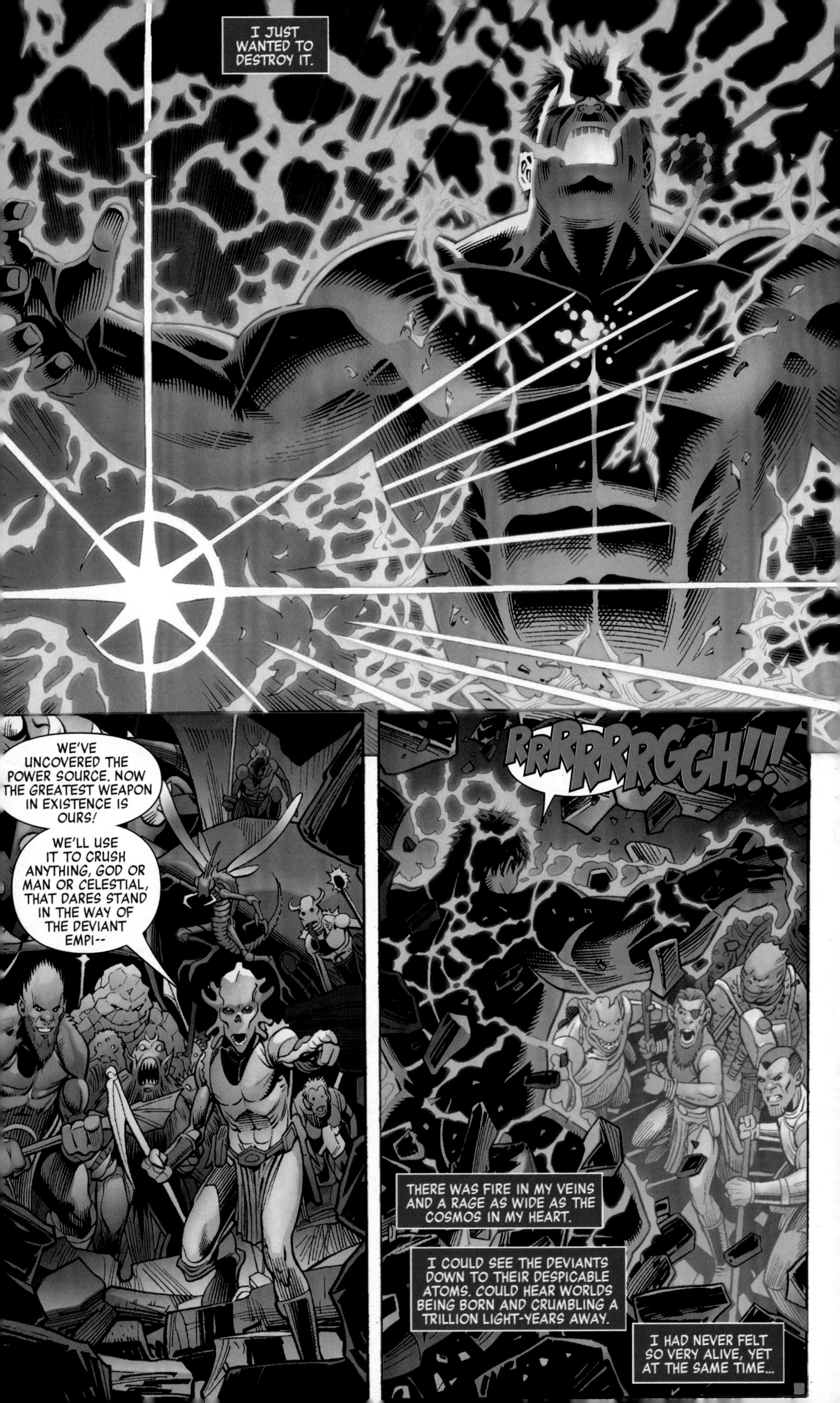
I JUST WANTED TO DESTROY IT.
WE'VE UNCOVERED THE POWER SOURCE. NOW THE GREATEST WEAPON IN EXISTENCE IS OURS!
WE'LL USE IT TO CRUSH ANYTHING, GOD OR MAN OR CELESTIAL, THAT DARES STAND IN THE WAY OF THE DEVIANT EMPI--
RRRRRRRGGH!!!
THERE WAS FIRE IN MY VEINS AND A RAGE AS WIDE AS THE COSMOS IN MY HEART.
I COULD SEE THE DEVIANTS DOWN TO THEIR DESPICABLE ATOMS. COULD HEAR WORLDS BEING BORN AND CRUMBLING A TRILLION LIGHT-YEARS AWAY.
I HAD NEVER FELT SO VERY ALIVE, YET AT THE SAME TIME...

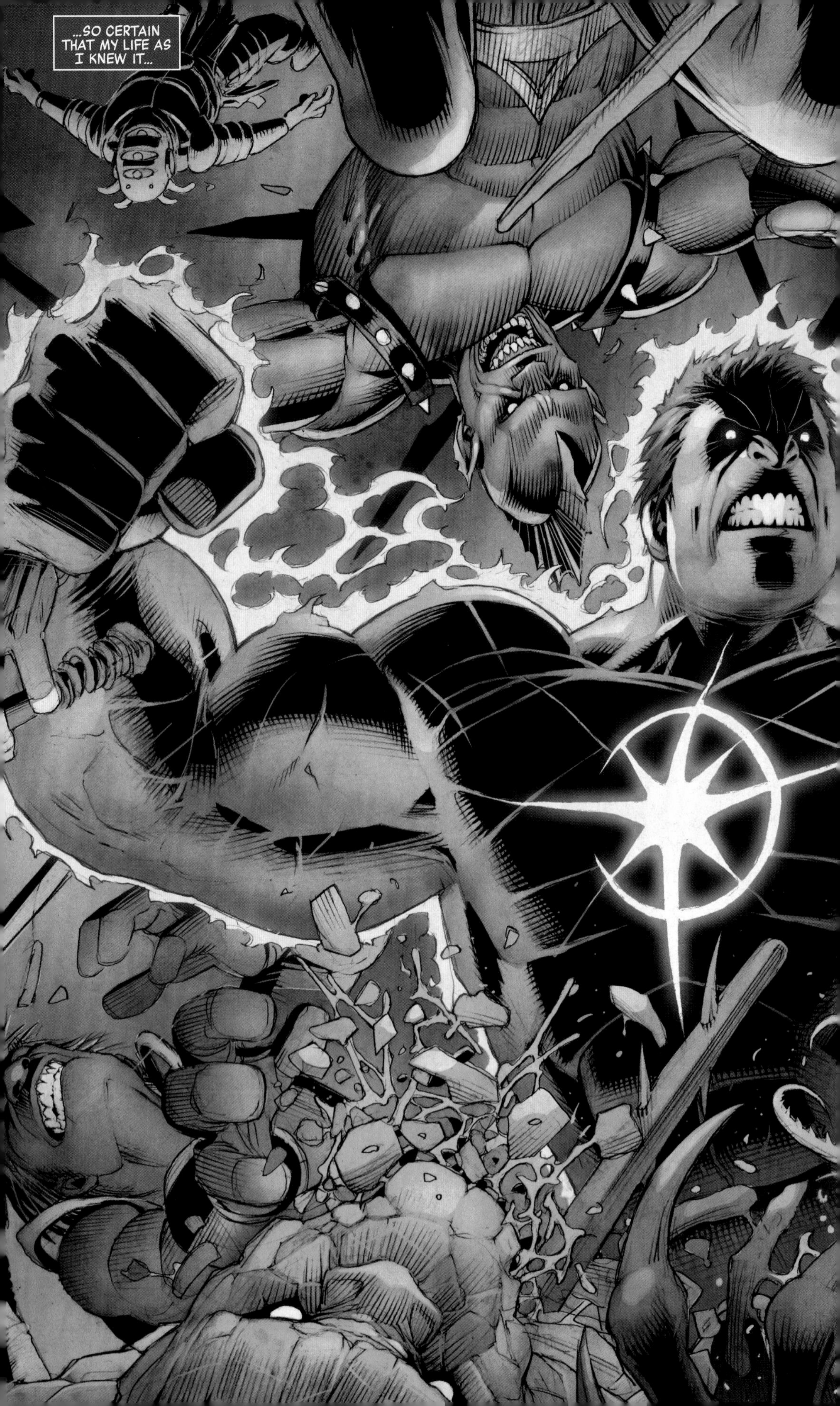
...SO CERTAIN THAT MY LIFE AS I KNEW IT...

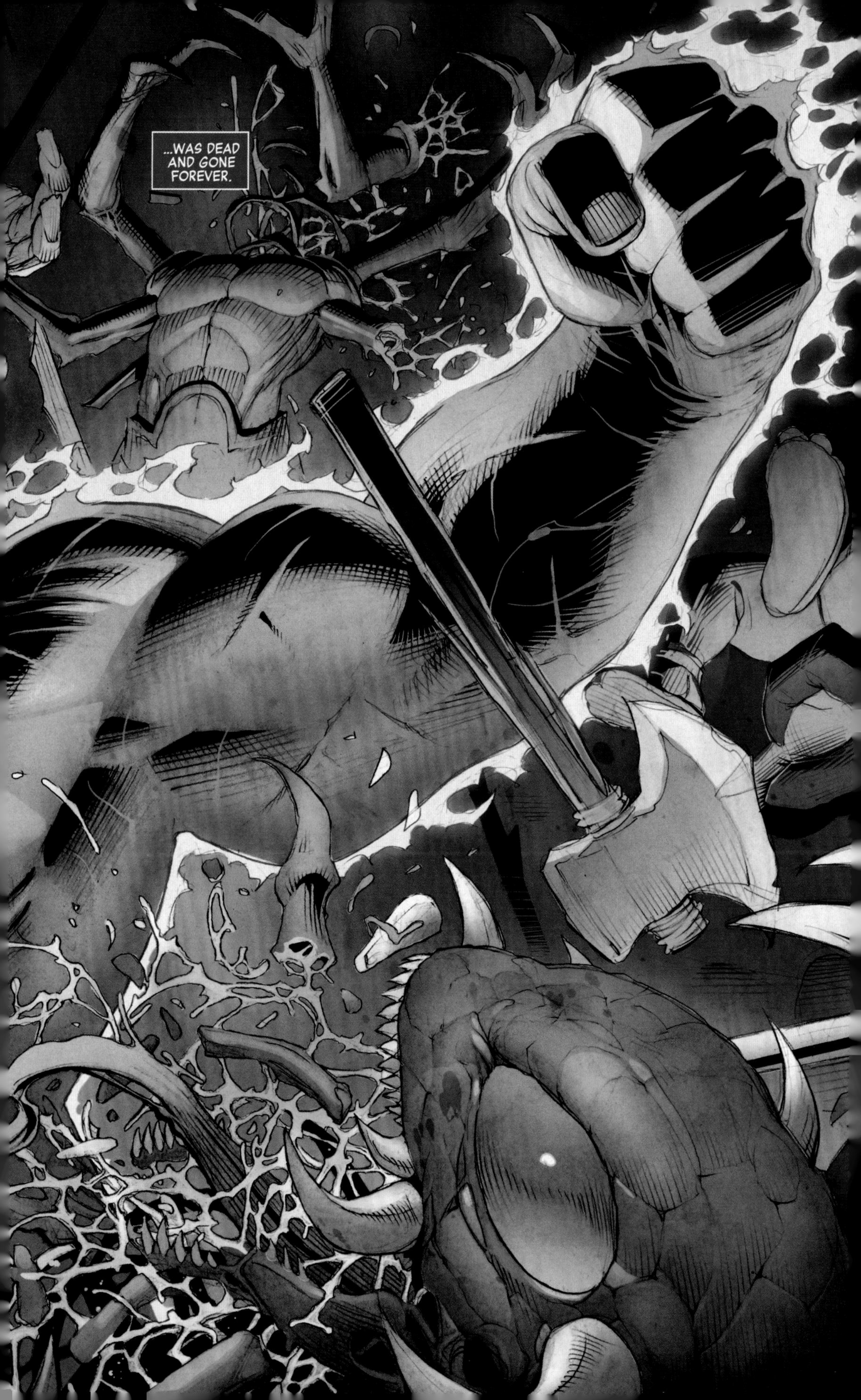
...WAS DEAD
AND GONE
FOREVER.

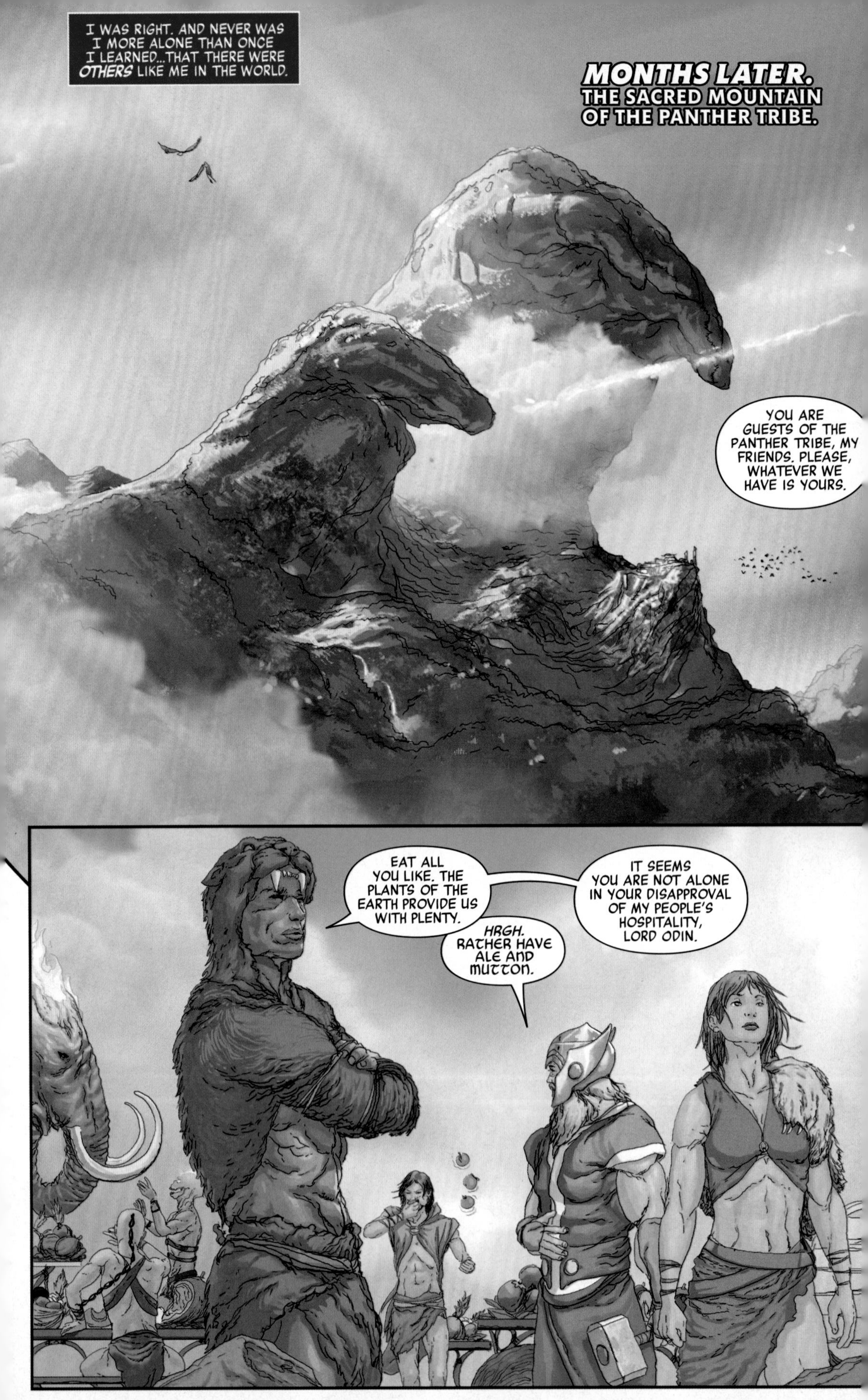
I WAS RIGHT. AND NEVER WAS I MORE ALONE THAN ONCE I LEARNED...THAT THERE WERE *OTHERS* LIKE ME IN THE WORLD.
MONTHS LATER. THE SACRED MOUNTAIN OF THE PANTHER TRIBE.
YOU ARE GUESTS OF THE PANTHER TRIBE, MY FRIENDS. PLEASE, WHATEVER WE HAVE IS YOURS.
EAT ALL YOU LIKE. THE PLANTS OF THE EARTH PROVIDE US WITH PLENTY.
HRGH. RATHER HAVE ALE AND MUTTON.
IT SEEMS YOU ARE NOT ALONE IN YOUR DISAPPROVAL OF MY PEOPLE'S HOSPITALITY, LORD ODIN.

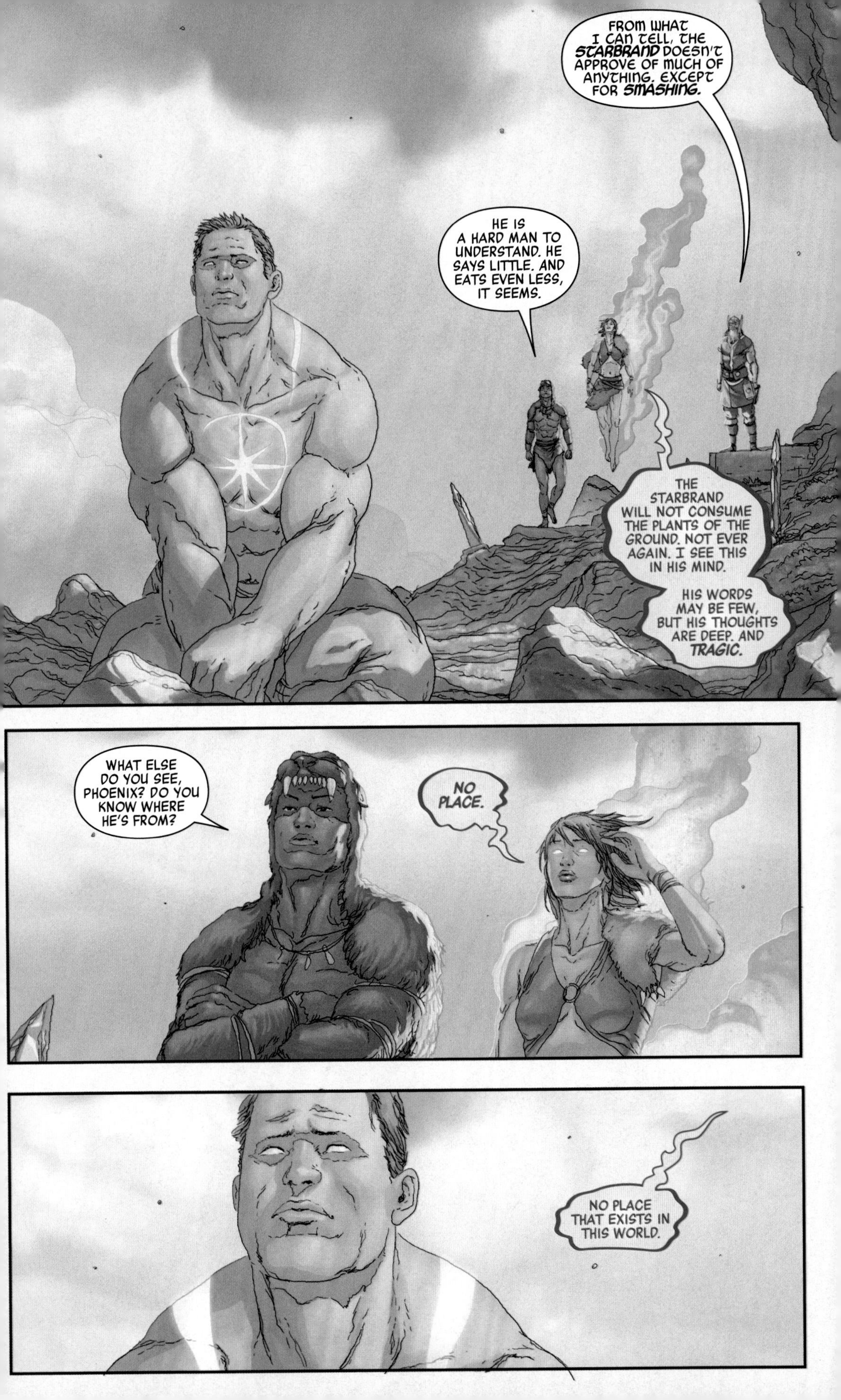
FROM WHAT I CAN TELL, THE STARBRAND DOESN'T APPROVE OF MUCH OF ANYTHING. EXCEPT FOR SMASHING.
HE IS A HARD MAN TO UNDERSTAND. HE SAYS LITTLE. AND EATS EVEN LESS, IT SEEMS.
THE STARBRAND WILL NOT CONSUME THE PLANTS OF THE GROUND. NOT EVER AGAIN. I SEE THIS IN HIS MIND.
HIS WORDS MAY BE FEW, BUT HIS THOUGHTS ARE DEEP. AND TRAGIC.
WHAT ELSE DO YOU SEE, PHOENIX? DO YOU KNOW WHERE HE'S FROM?
NO PLACE.
NO PLACE THAT EXISTS IN THIS WORLD.

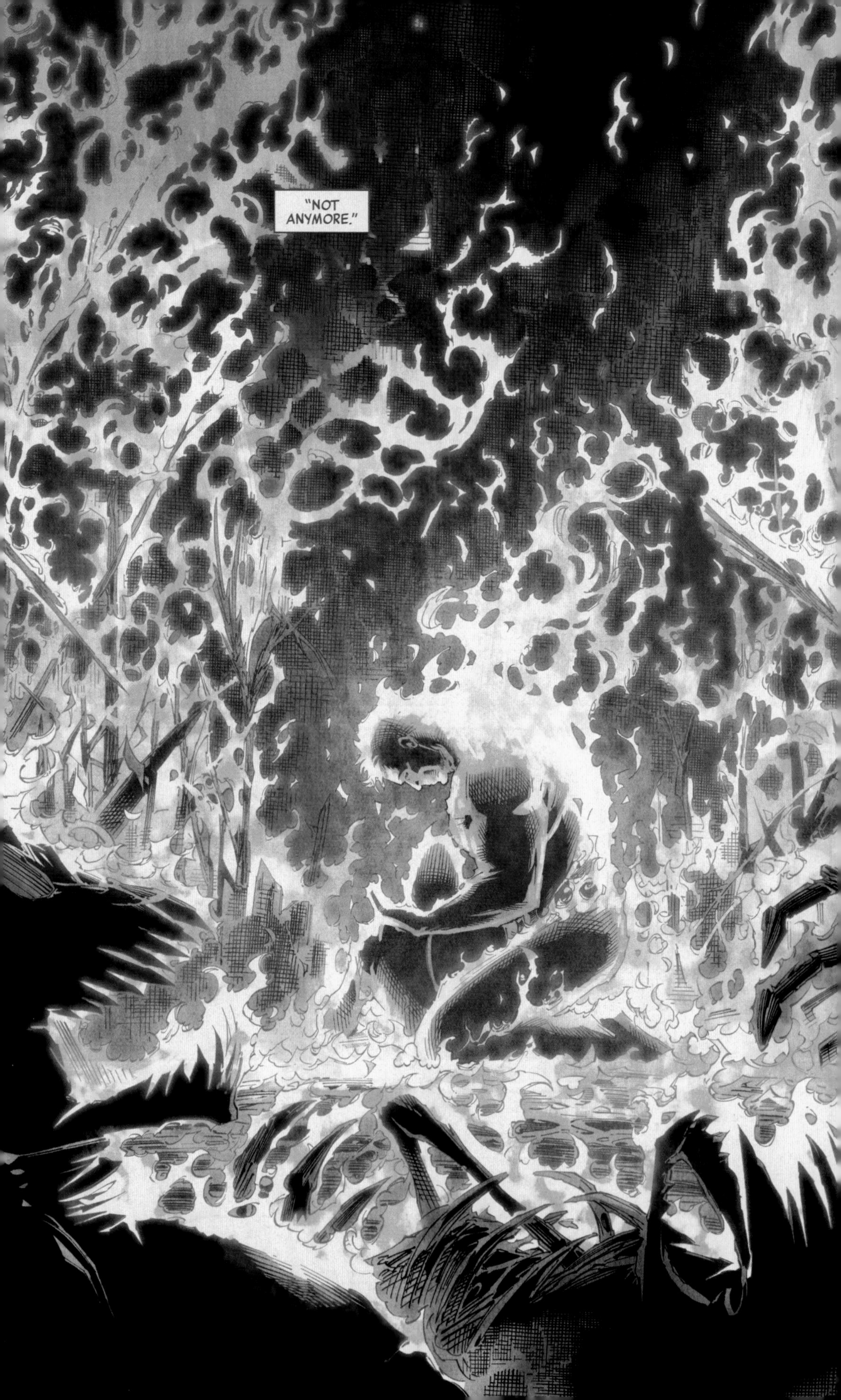
"NOT ANYMORE."

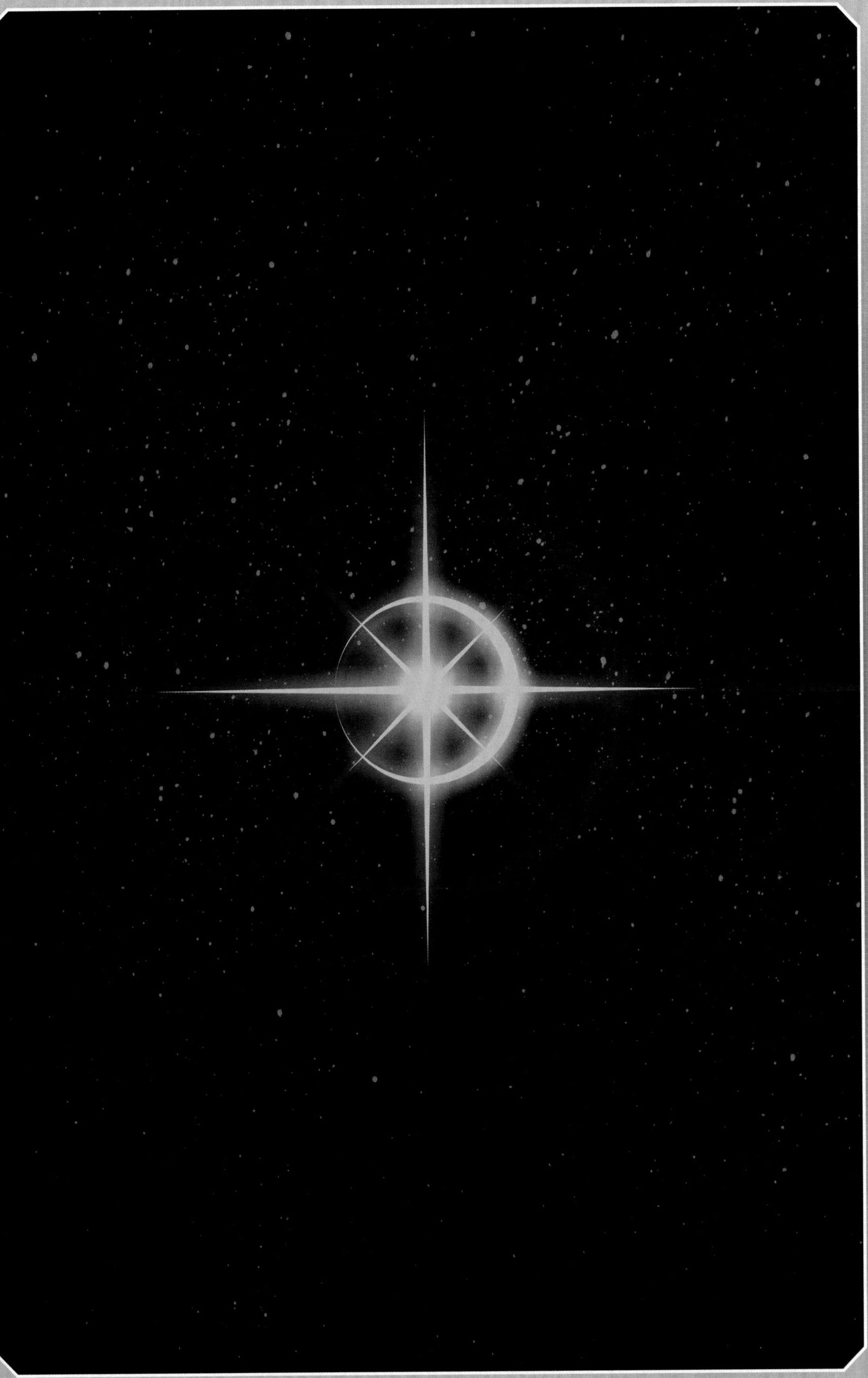

27 STARBRAND VARIANT

27 STARBRAND REBORN PART 1
RIOT IN THE PRISON GALAXY

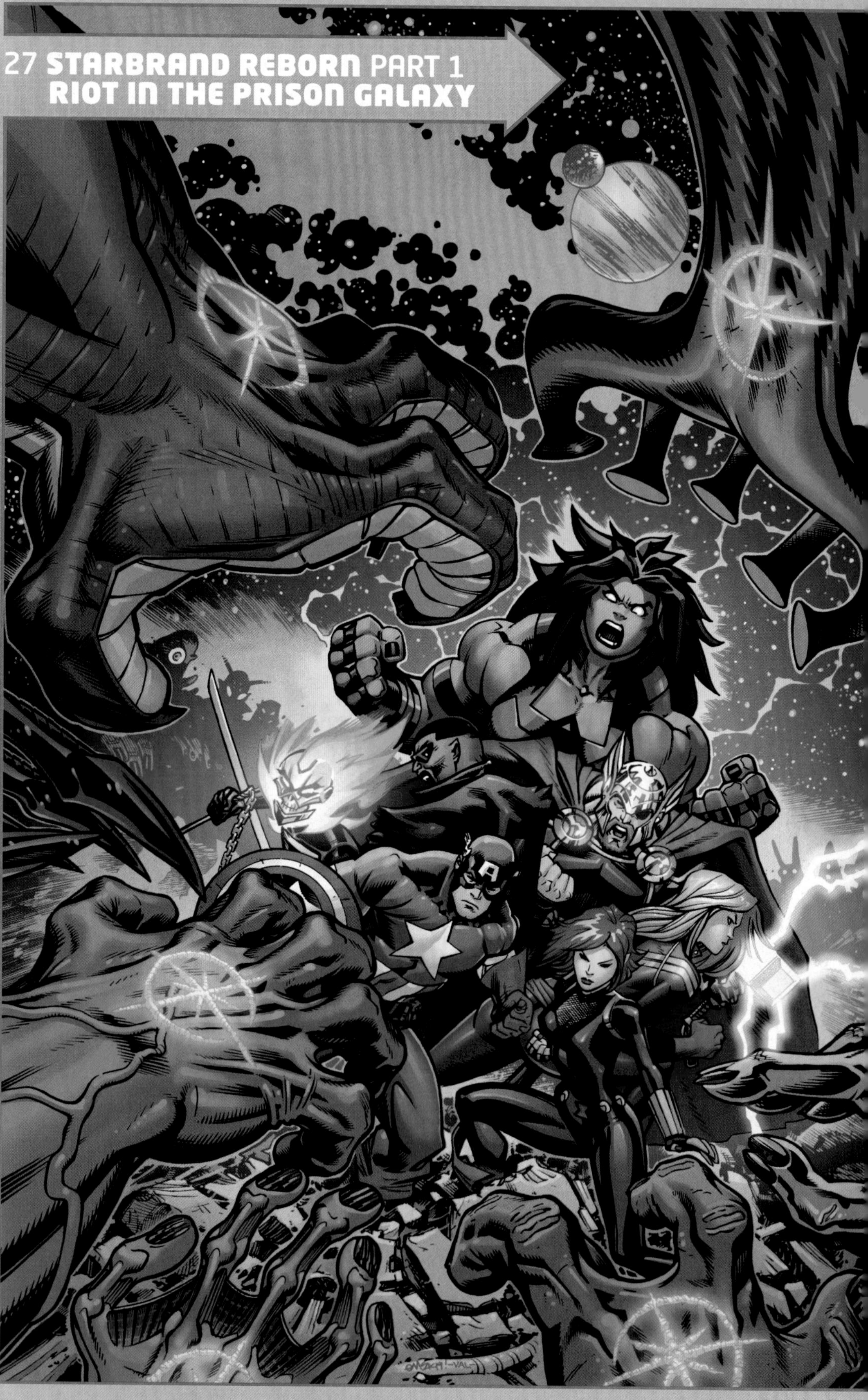

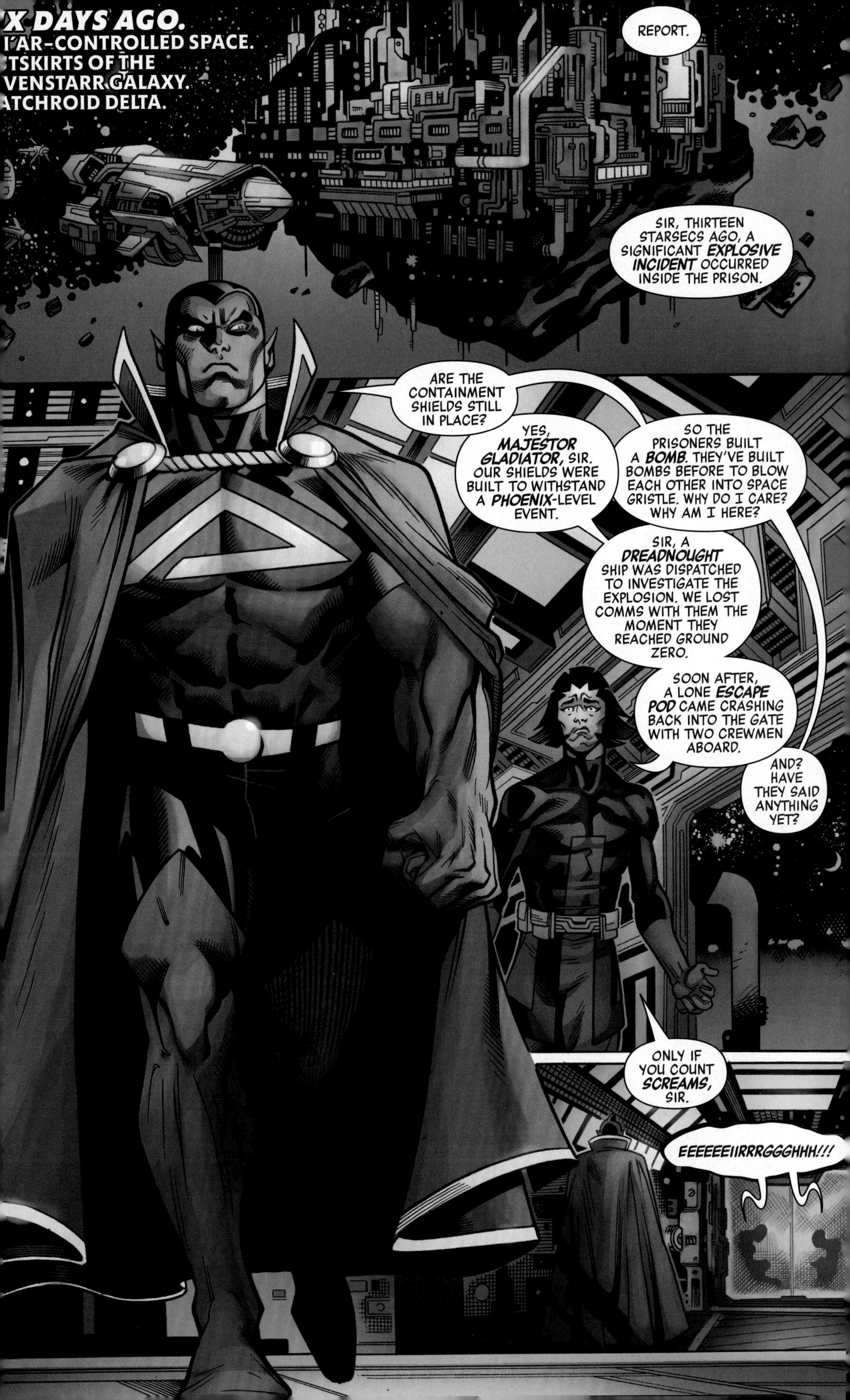
X DAYS AGO.
I'AR-CONTROLLED SPACE.
TSKIRTS OF THE
VENSTARR GALAXY.
ATCHROID DELTA.
REPORT.
SIR, THIRTEEN STARSECS AGO, A SIGNIFICANT EXPLOSIVE INCIDENT OCCURRED INSIDE THE PRISON.
ARE THE CONTAINMENT SHIELDS STILL IN PLACE?
YES, MAJESTOR GLADIATOR, SIR. OUR SHIELDS WERE BUILT TO WITHSTAND A PHOENIX-LEVEL EVENT.
SO THE PRISONERS BUILT A BOMB. THEY'VE BUILT BOMBS BEFORE TO BLOW EACH OTHER INTO SPACE GRISTLE. WHY DO I CARE? WHY AM I HERE?
SIR, A DREADNOUGHT SHIP WAS DISPATCHED TO INVESTIGATE THE EXPLOSION. WE LOST COMMS WITH THEM THE MOMENT THEY REACHED GROUND ZERO.
SOON AFTER, A LONE ESCAPE POD CAME CRASHING BACK INTO THE GATE WITH TWO CREWMEN ABOARD.
AND? HAVE THEY SAID ANYTHING YET?
ONLY IF YOU COUNT SCREAMS, SIR.
EEEEEEIIRRRGGGHHH!!!

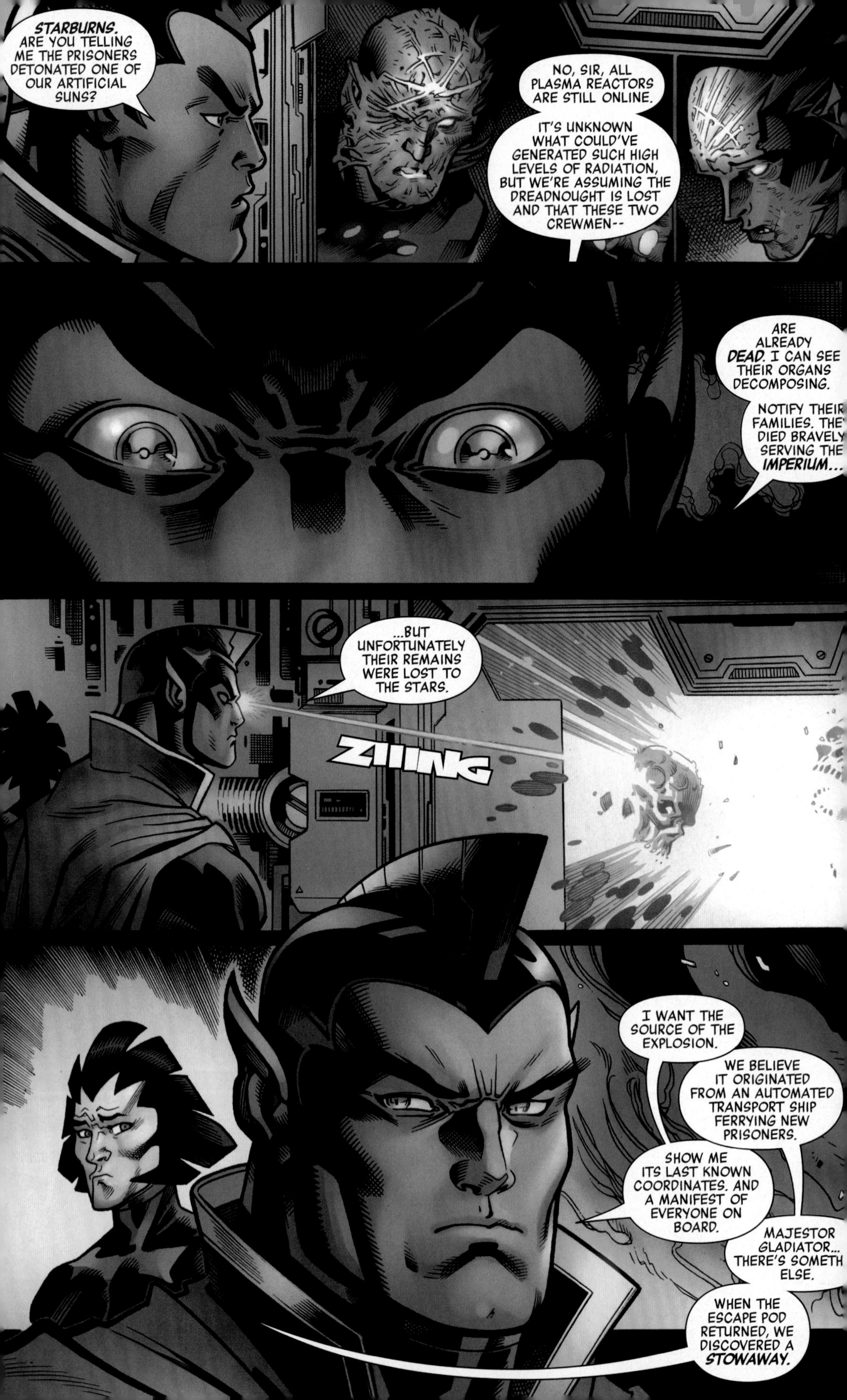
STARBURNS. ARE YOU TELLING ME THE PRISONERS DETONATED ONE OF OUR ARTIFICIAL SUNS?
NO, SIR, ALL PLASMA REACTORS ARE STILL ONLINE.
IT'S UNKNOWN WHAT COULD'VE GENERATED SUCH HIGH LEVELS OF RADIATION, BUT WE'RE ASSUMING THE DREADNOUGHT IS LOST AND THAT THESE TWO CREWMEN--
ARE ALREADY DEAD. I CAN SEE THEIR ORGANS DECOMPOSING.
NOTIFY THEIR FAMILIES. THE DIED BRAVELY SERVING THE IMPERIUM...
...BUT UNFORTUNATELY THEIR REMAINS WERE LOST TO THE STARS.
ZIIING
I WANT THE SOURCE OF THE EXPLOSION.
WE BELIEVE IT ORIGINATED FROM AN AUTOMATED TRANSPORT SHIP FERRYING NEW PRISONERS.
SHOW ME ITS LAST KNOWN COORDINATES. AND A MANIFEST OF EVERYONE ON BOARD.
MAJESTOR GLADIATOR... THERE'S SOMETH ELSE.
WHEN THE ESCAPE POD RETURNED, WE DISCOVERED A STOWAWAY.

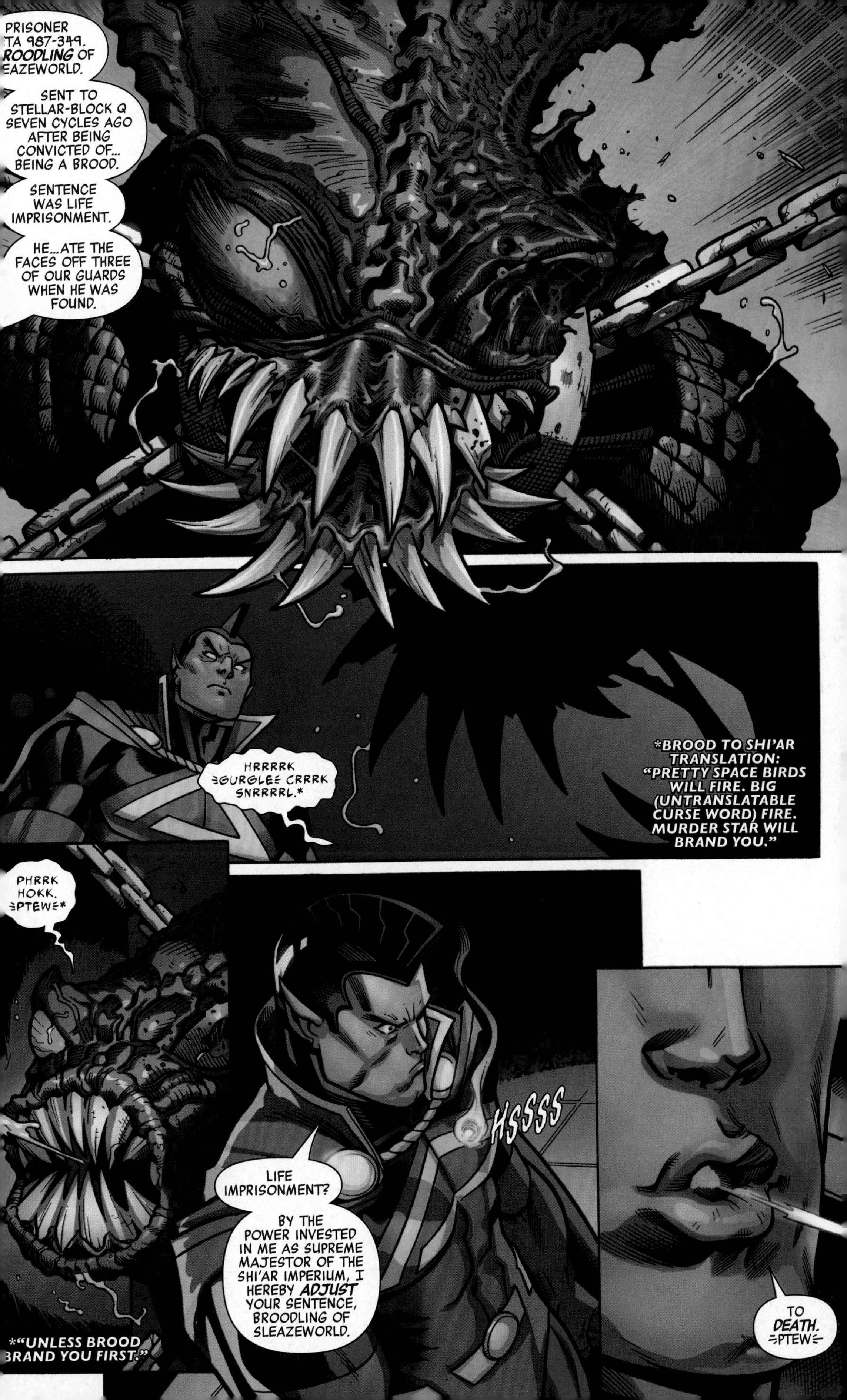
PRISONER
TA 987-349.
ROODLING OF
EAZEWORLD.
SENT TO
STELLAR-BLOCK Q
SEVEN CYCLES AGO
AFTER BEING
CONVICTED OF...
BEING A BROOD.
SENTENCE
WAS LIFE
IMPRISONMENT.
HE...ATE THE
FACES OFF THREE
OF OUR GUARDS
WHEN HE WAS
FOUND.
HRRRRK =GURGLE= CRRRK SNRRRRL.*
*BROOD TO SHI'AR TRANSLATION: "PRETTY SPACE BIRDS WILL FIRE. BIG (UNTRANSLATABLE CURSE WORD) FIRE. MURDER STAR WILL BRAND YOU."
PHRRK HOKK. =PTEW=*
*"UNLESS BROOD BRAND YOU FIRST."
HSSSS
LIFE IMPRISONMENT?
BY THE POWER INVESTED IN ME AS SUPREME MAJESTOR OF THE SHI'AR IMPERIUM, I HEREBY ADJUST YOUR SENTENCE, BROODLING OF SLEAZEWORLD.
TO DEATH.
=PTEW=

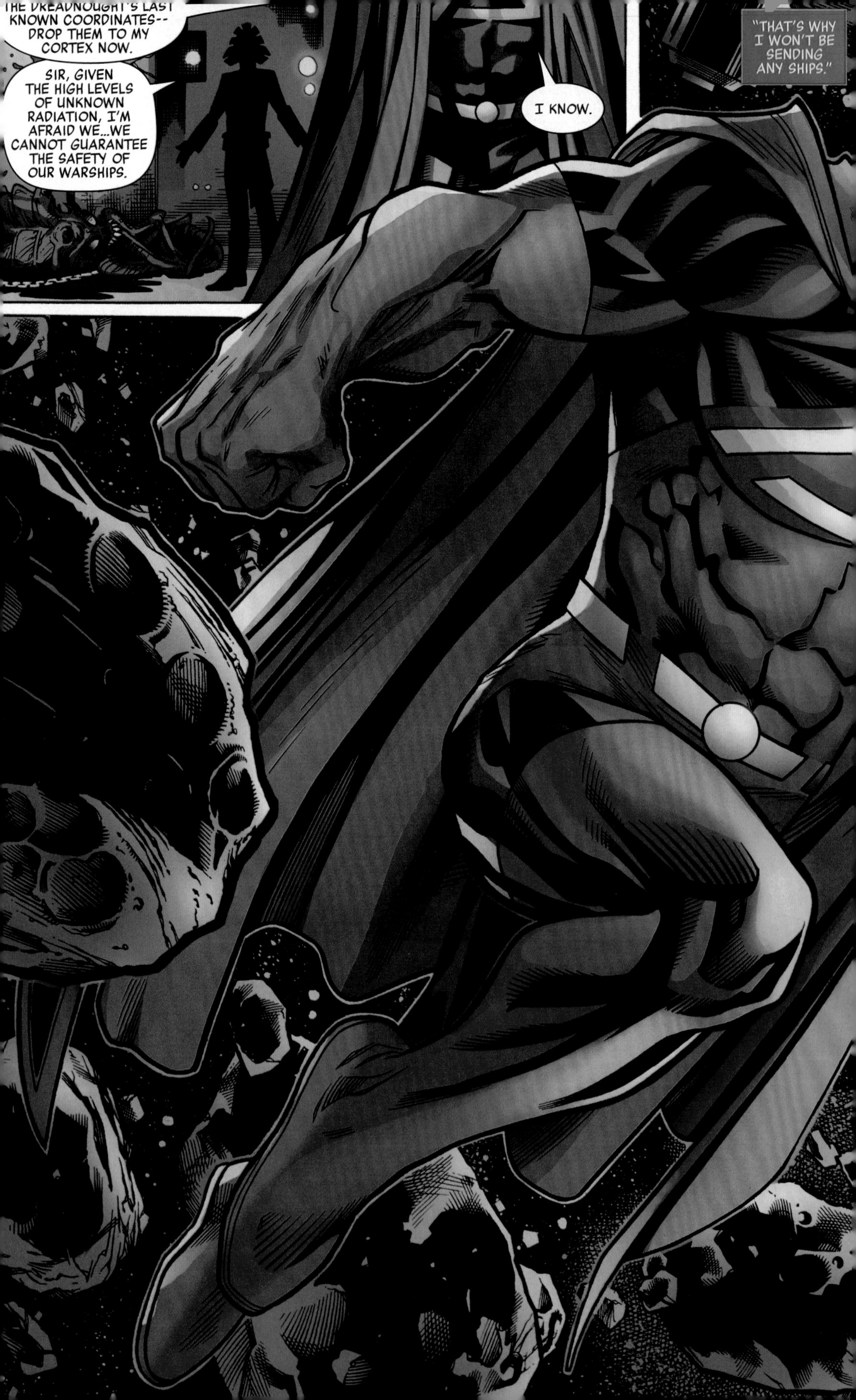
THE DREADNOUGHT'S LAST KNOWN COORDINATES-- DROP THEM TO MY CORTEX NOW.
SIR, GIVEN THE HIGH LEVELS OF UNKNOWN RADIATION, I'M AFRAID WE...WE CANNOT GUARANTEE THE SAFETY OF OUR WARSHIPS.
I KNOW.
"THAT'S WHY I WON'T BE SENDING ANY SHIPS."

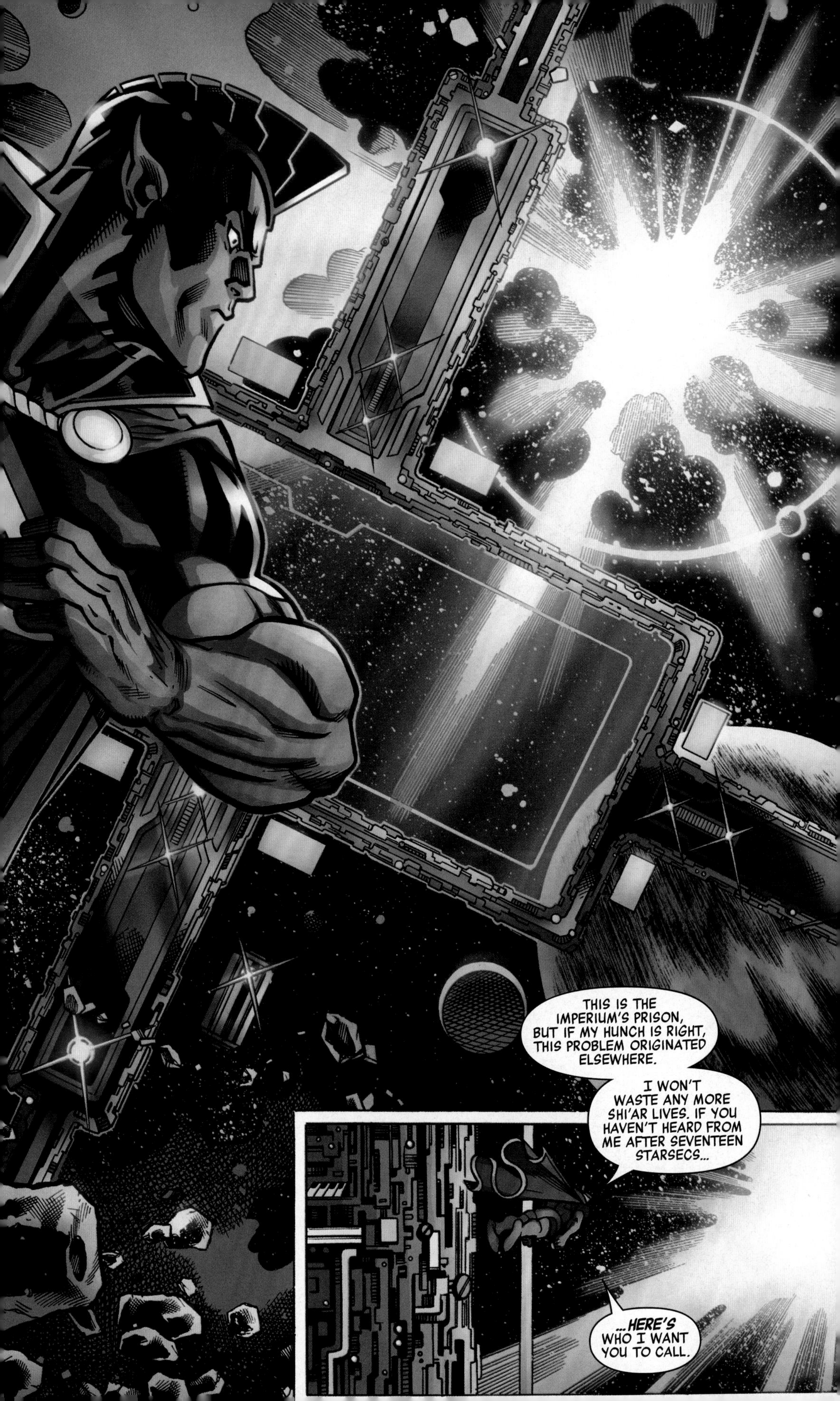
THIS IS THE IMPERIUM'S PRISON, BUT IF MY HUNCH IS RIGHT, THIS PROBLEM ORIGINATED ELSEWHERE.
I WON'T WASTE ANY MORE SHI'AR LIVES. IF YOU HAVEN'T HEARD FROM ME AFTER SEVENTEEN STARSECS...
...HERE'S WHO I WANT YOU TO CALL.

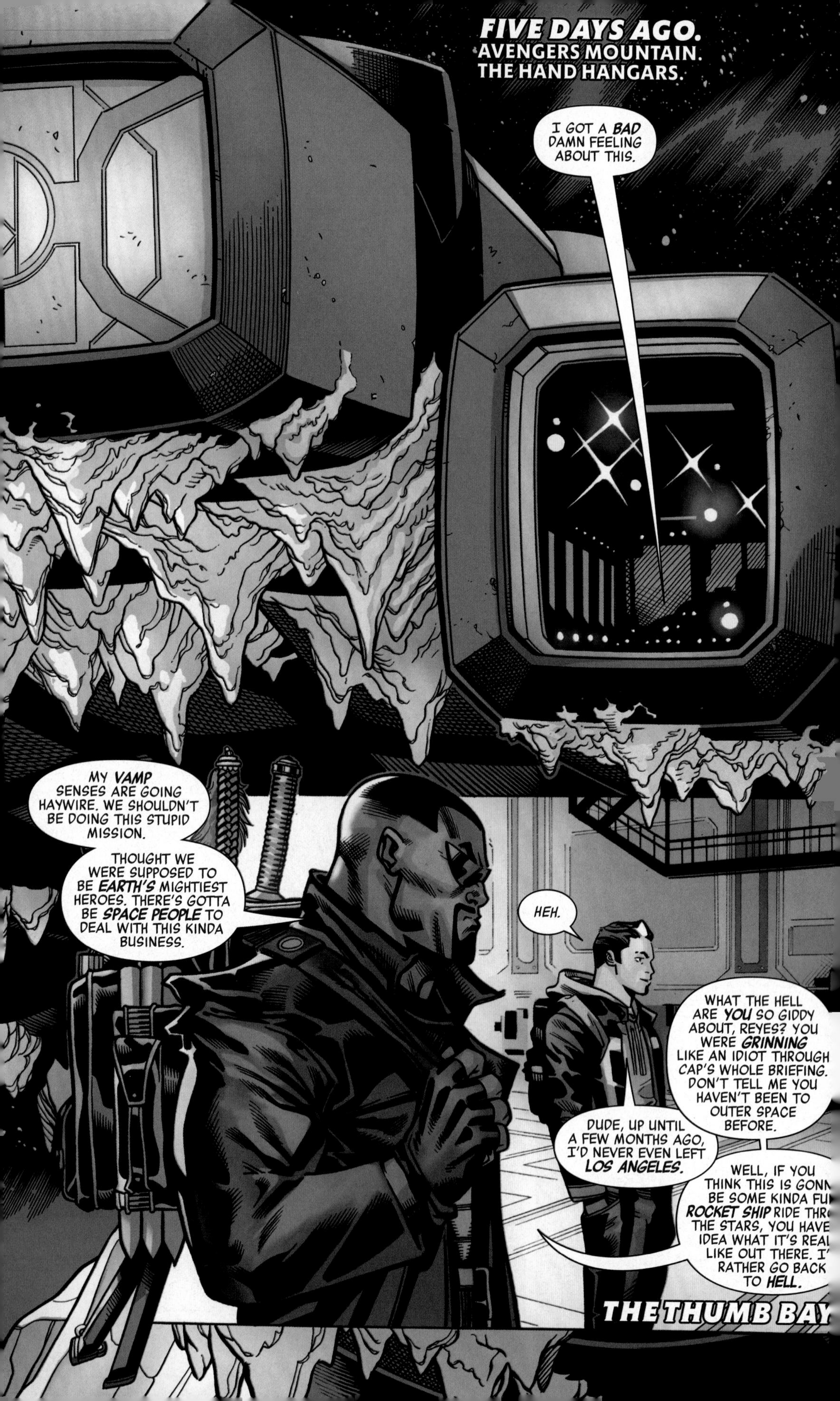
FIVE DAYS AGO.
AVENGERS MOUNTAIN.
THE HAND HANGARS.
I GOT A BAD DAMN FEELING ABOUT THIS.
MY VAMP SENSES ARE GOING HAYWIRE. WE SHOULDN'T BE DOING THIS STUPID MISSION.
THOUGHT WE WERE SUPPOSED TO BE EARTH'S MIGHTIEST HEROES. THERE'S GOTTA BE SPACE PEOPLE TO DEAL WITH THIS KINDA BUSINESS.
HEH.
WHAT THE HELL ARE YOU SO GIDDY ABOUT, REYES? YOU WERE GRINNING LIKE AN IDIOT THROUGH CAP'S WHOLE BRIEFING. DON'T TELL ME YOU HAVEN'T BEEN TO OUTER SPACE BEFORE.
DUDE, UP UNTIL A FEW MONTHS AGO, I'D NEVER EVEN LEFT LOS ANGELES.
WELL, IF YOU THINK THIS IS GONN BE SOME KINDA FU ROCKET SHIP RIDE THR THE STARS, YOU HAVE IDEA WHAT IT'S REA LIKE OUT THERE. I' RATHER GO BACK TO HELL.
THE THUMB BAY

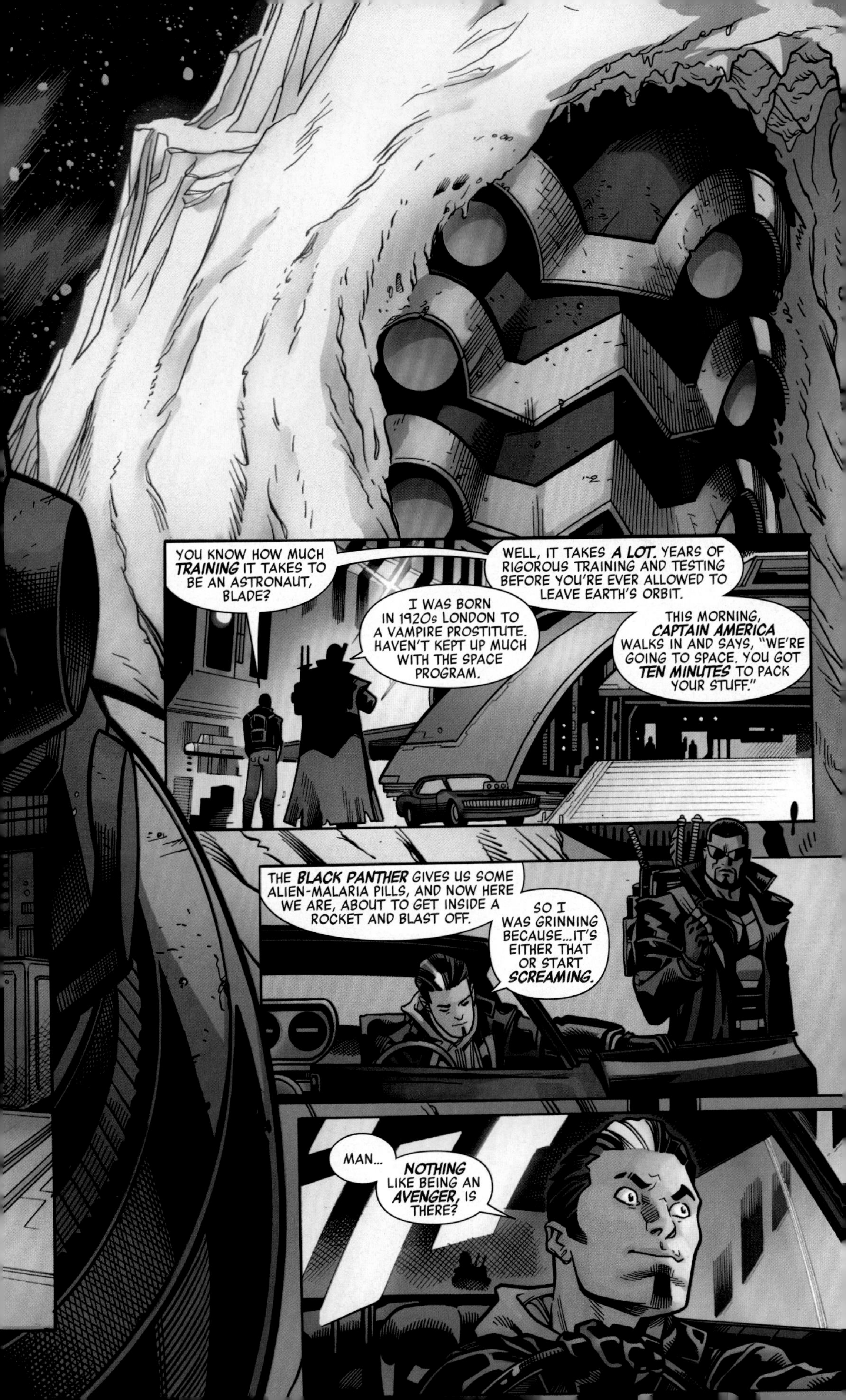

YOU KNOW HOW MUCH TRAINING IT TAKES TO BE AN ASTRONAUT, BLADE?
I WAS BORN IN 1920s LONDON TO A VAMPIRE PROSTITUTE. HAVEN'T KEPT UP MUCH WITH THE SPACE PROGRAM.
WELL, IT TAKES A LOT. YEARS OF RIGOROUS TRAINING AND TESTING BEFORE YOU'RE EVER ALLOWED TO LEAVE EARTH'S ORBIT.
THIS MORNING, CAPTAIN AMERICA WALKS IN AND SAYS, "WE'RE GOING TO SPACE. YOU GOT TEN MINUTES TO PACK YOUR STUFF."
THE BLACK PANTHER GIVES US SOME ALIEN-MALARIA PILLS, AND NOW HERE WE ARE, ABOUT TO GET INSIDE A ROCKET AND BLAST OFF.
SO I WAS GRINNING BECAUSE...IT'S EITHER THAT OR START SCREAMING.
MAN...
NOTHING LIKE BEING AN AVENGER, IS THERE?

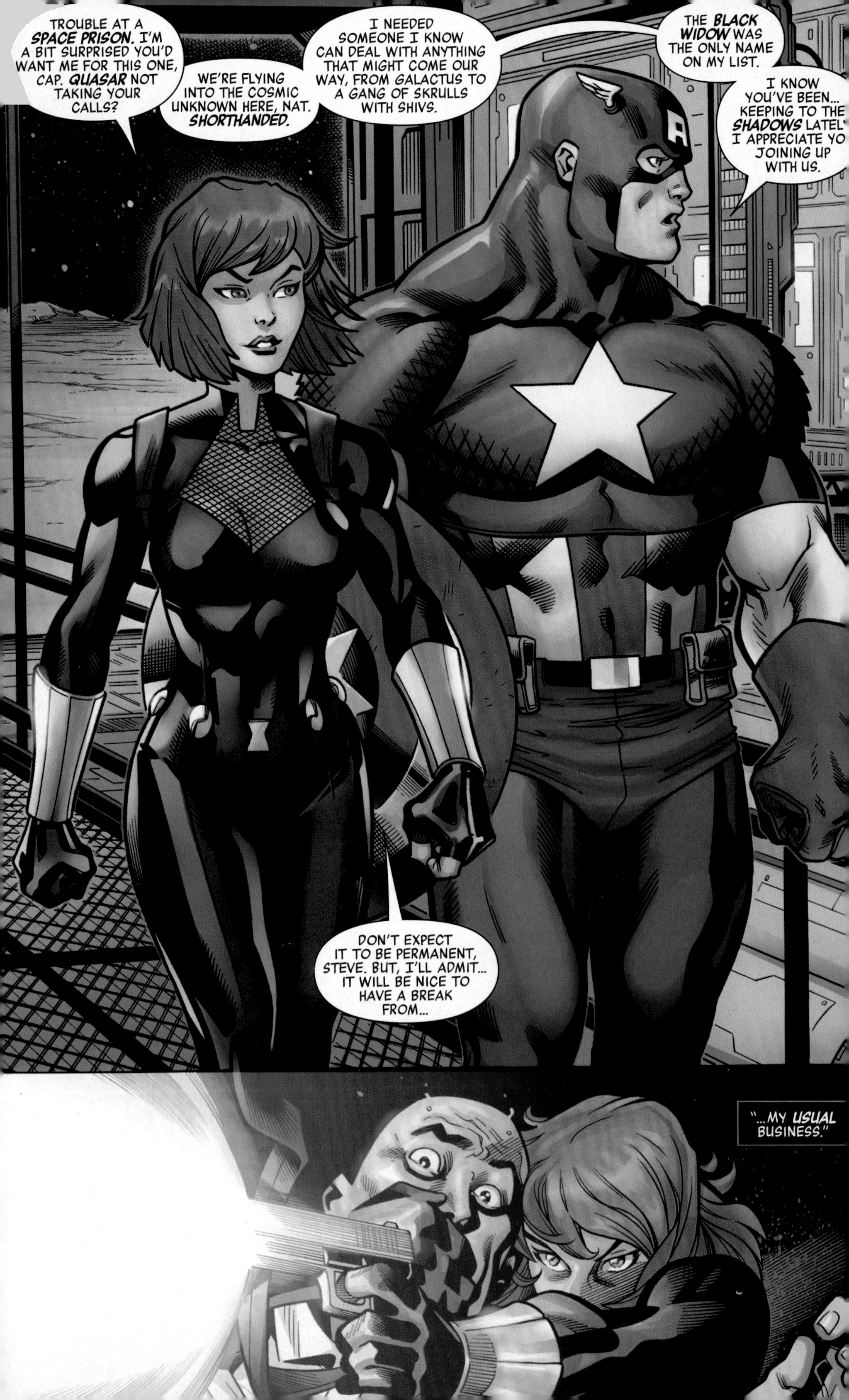
TROUBLE AT A SPACE PRISON. I'M A BIT SURPRISED YOU'D WANT ME FOR THIS ONE, CAP. QUASAR NOT TAKING YOUR CALLS?
WE'RE FLYING INTO THE COSMIC UNKNOWN HERE, NAT. SHORTHANDED.
I NEEDED SOMEONE I KNOW CAN DEAL WITH ANYTHING THAT MIGHT COME OUR WAY, FROM GALACTUS TO A GANG OF SKRULLS WITH SHIVS.
THE BLACK WIDOW WAS THE ONLY NAME ON MY LIST.
I KNOW YOU'VE BEEN... KEEPING TO THE SHADOWS LATEL I APPRECIATE YO JOINING UP WITH US.
DON'T EXPECT IT TO BE PERMANENT, STEVE. BUT, I'LL ADMIT... IT WILL BE NICE TO HAVE A BREAK FROM...
"...MY USUAL BUSINESS."

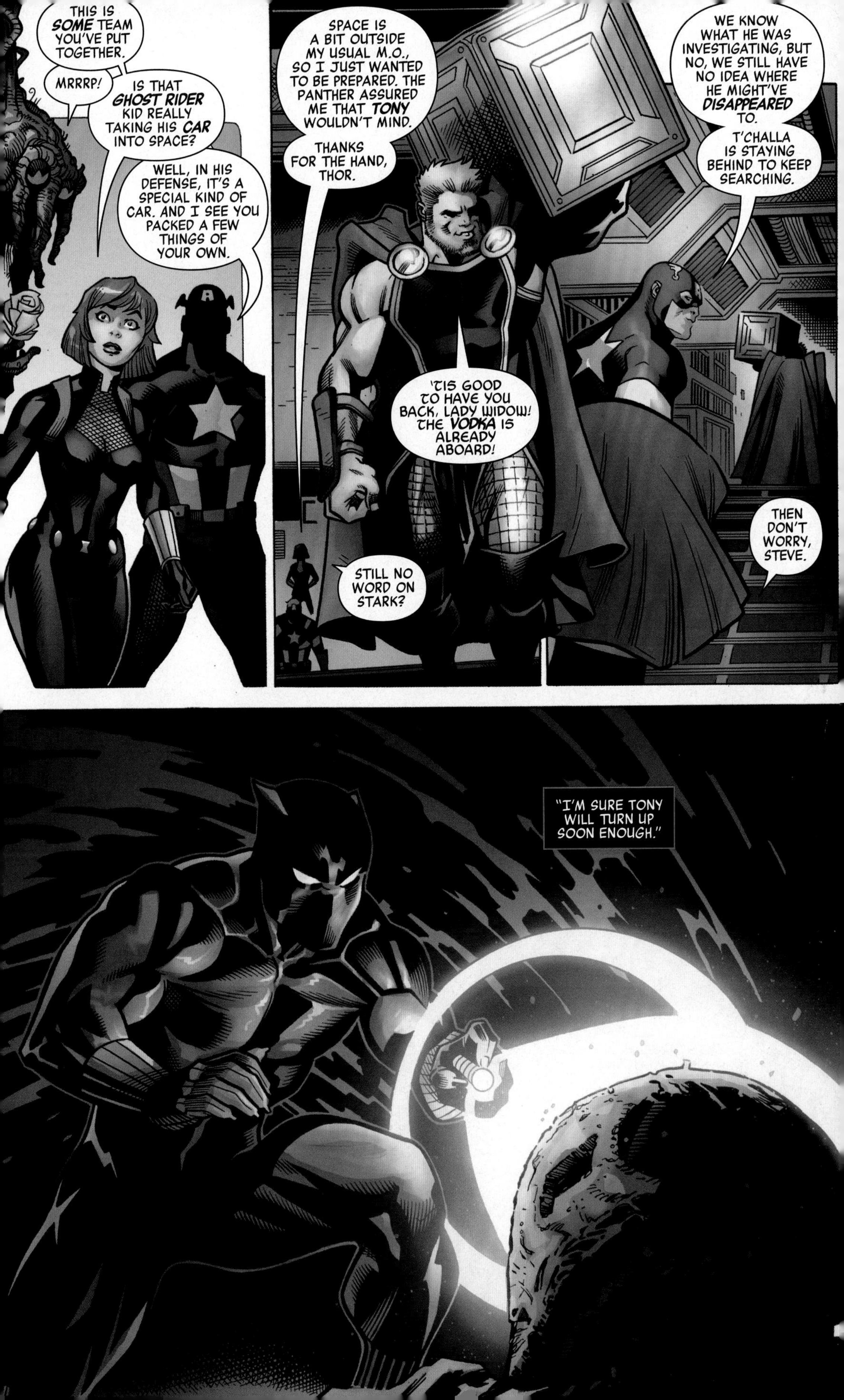

THIS IS SOME TEAM YOU'VE PUT TOGETHER.
MRRRP!
IS THAT GHOST RIDER KID REALLY TAKING HIS CAR INTO SPACE?
WELL, IN HIS DEFENSE, IT'S A SPECIAL KIND OF CAR. AND I SEE YOU PACKED A FEW THINGS OF YOUR OWN.
SPACE IS A BIT OUTSIDE MY USUAL M.O., SO I JUST WANTED TO BE PREPARED. THE PANTHER ASSURED ME THAT TONY WOULDN'T MIND.
THANKS FOR THE HAND, THOR.
'TIS GOOD TO HAVE YOU BACK, LADY WIDOW! THE VODKA IS ALREADY ABOARD!
STILL NO WORD ON STARK?
WE KNOW WHAT HE WAS INVESTIGATING, BUT NO, WE STILL HAVE NO IDEA WHERE HE MIGHT'VE DISAPPEARED TO.
T'CHALLA IS STAYING BEHIND TO KEEP SEARCHING.
THEN DON'T WORRY, STEVE.
"I'M SURE TONY WILL TURN UP SOON ENOUGH."

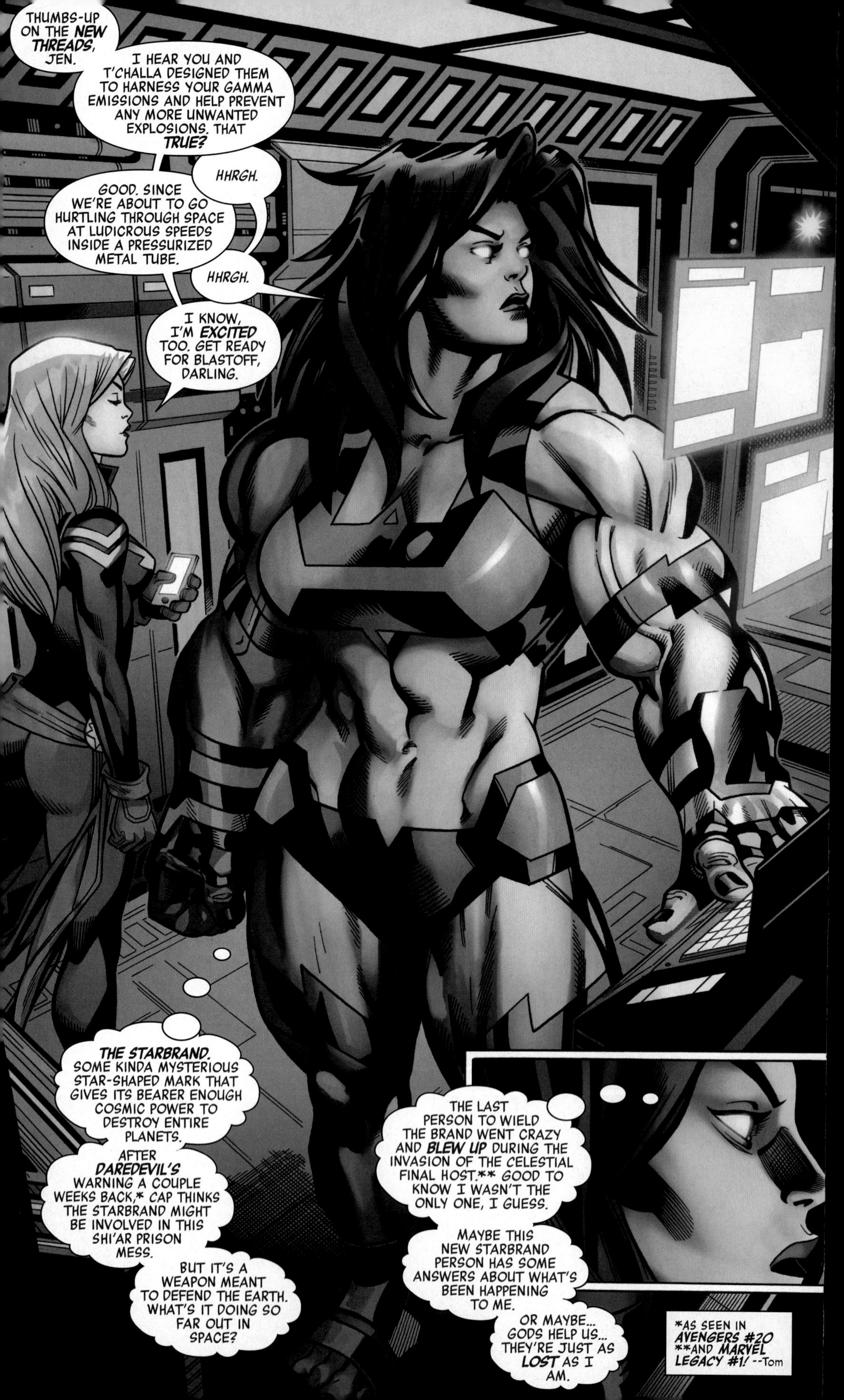

THUMBS-UP ON THE NEW THREADS, JEN.
I HEAR YOU AND T'CHALLA DESIGNED THEM TO HARNESS YOUR GAMMA EMISSIONS AND HELP PREVENT ANY MORE UNWANTED EXPLOSIONS. THAT TRUE?
HHRGH.
GOOD. SINCE WE'RE ABOUT TO GO HURTLING THROUGH SPACE AT LUDICROUS SPEEDS INSIDE A PRESSURIZED METAL TUBE.
HHRGH.
I KNOW, I'M EXCITED TOO. GET READY FOR BLASTOFF, DARLING.
THE STARBRAND. SOME KINDA MYSTERIOUS STAR-SHAPED MARK THAT GIVES ITS BEARER ENOUGH COSMIC POWER TO DESTROY ENTIRE PLANETS.
AFTER DAREDEVIL'S WARNING A COUPLE WEEKS BACK,* CAP THINKS THE STARBRAND MIGHT BE INVOLVED IN THIS SHI'AR PRISON MESS.
BUT IT'S A WEAPON MEANT TO DEFEND THE EARTH. WHAT'S IT DOING SO FAR OUT IN SPACE?
THE LAST PERSON TO WIELD THE BRAND WENT CRAZY AND BLEW UP DURING THE INVASION OF THE CELESTIAL FINAL HOST.** GOOD TO KNOW I WASN'T THE ONLY ONE, I GUESS.
MAYBE THIS NEW STARBRAND PERSON HAS SOME ANSWERS ABOUT WHAT'S BEEN HAPPENING TO ME.
OR MAYBE... GODS HELP US... THEY'RE JUST AS LOST AS I AM.
*AS SEEN IN AVENGERS #20 **AND MARVEL LEGACY #1! --Tom

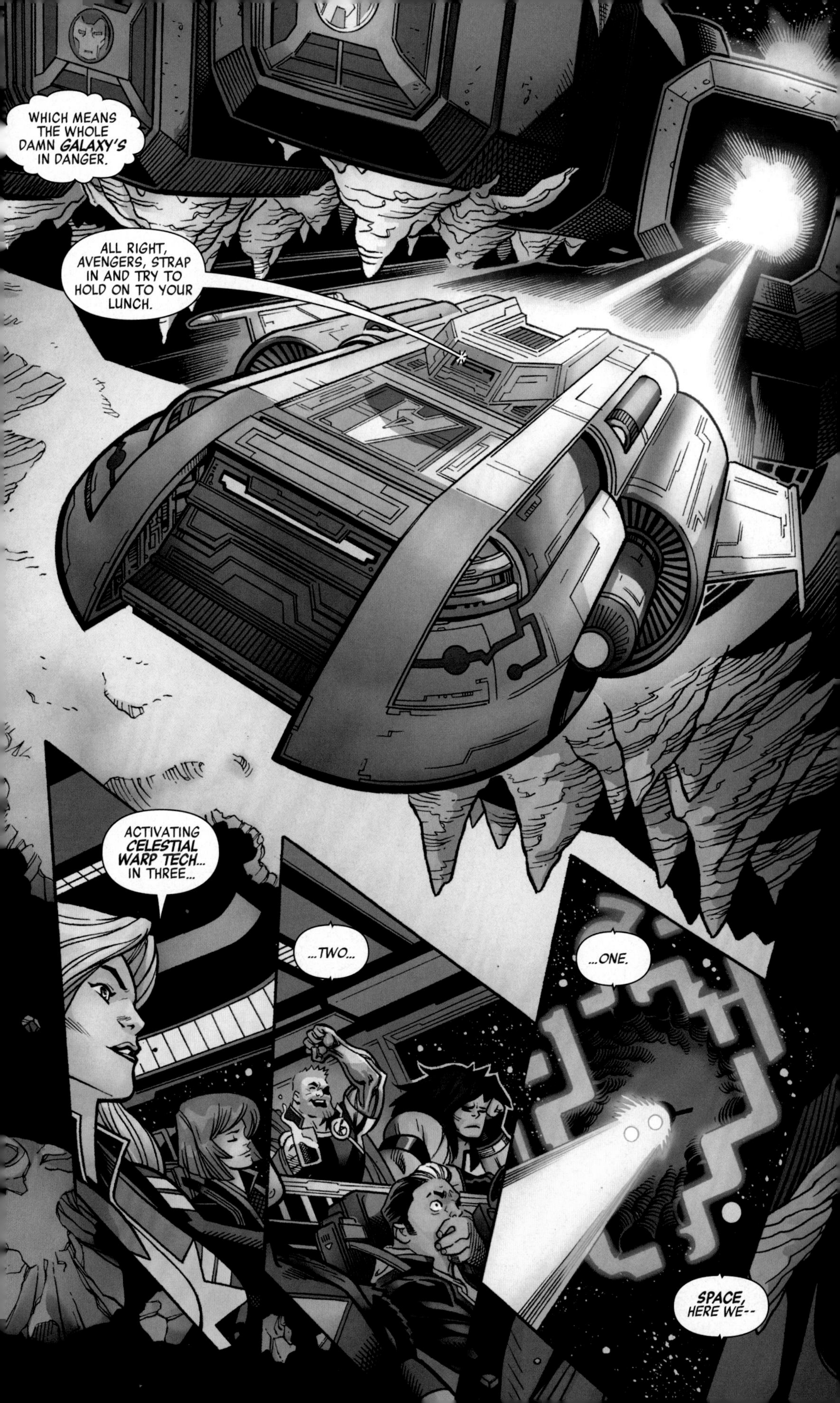
WHICH MEANS THE WHOLE DAMN GALAXY'S IN DANGER.
ALL RIGHT, AVENGERS, STRAP IN AND TRY TO HOLD ON TO YOUR LUNCH.
ACTIVATING CELESTIAL WARP TECH... IN THREE...
...TWO...
...ONE.
SPACE, HERE WE--

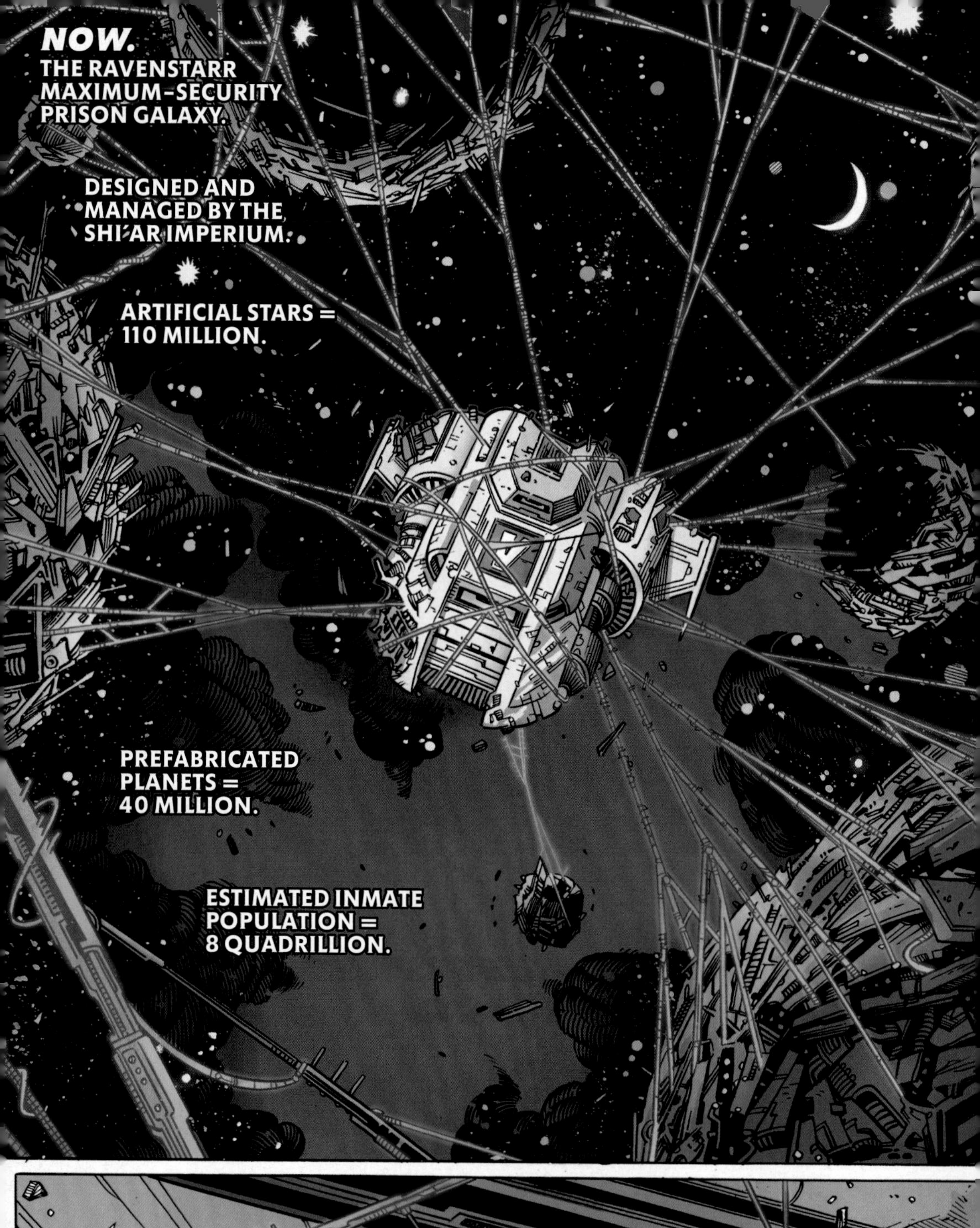
NOW.
THE RAVENSTARR MAXIMUM-SECURITY PRISON GALAXY.
DESIGNED AND MANAGED BY THE SHI'AR IMPERIUM.
ARTIFICIAL STARS = 110 MILLION.
PREFABRICATED PLANETS = 40 MILLION.
ESTIMATED INMATE POPULATION = 8 QUADRILLION.

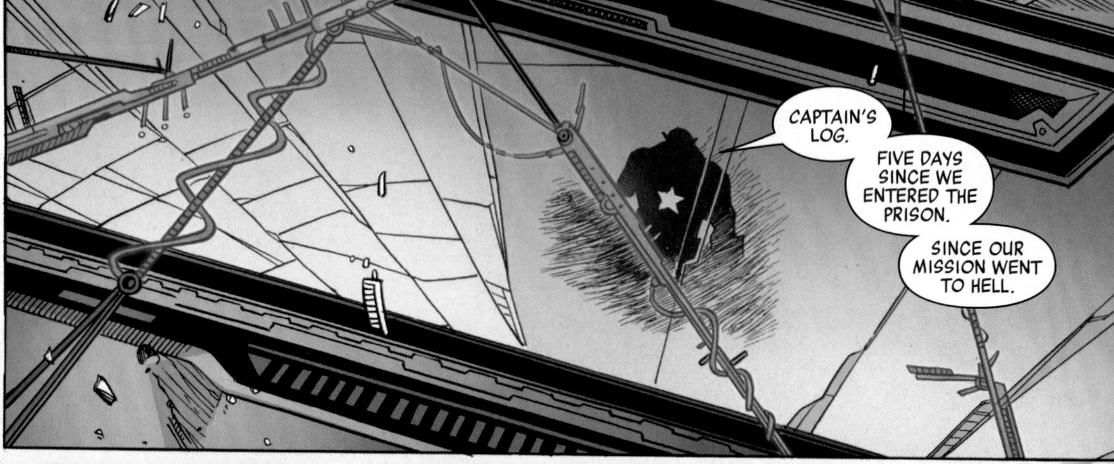
CAPTAIN'S LOG.
FIVE DAYS SINCE WE ENTERED THE PRISON.
SINCE OUR MISSION WENT TO HELL.

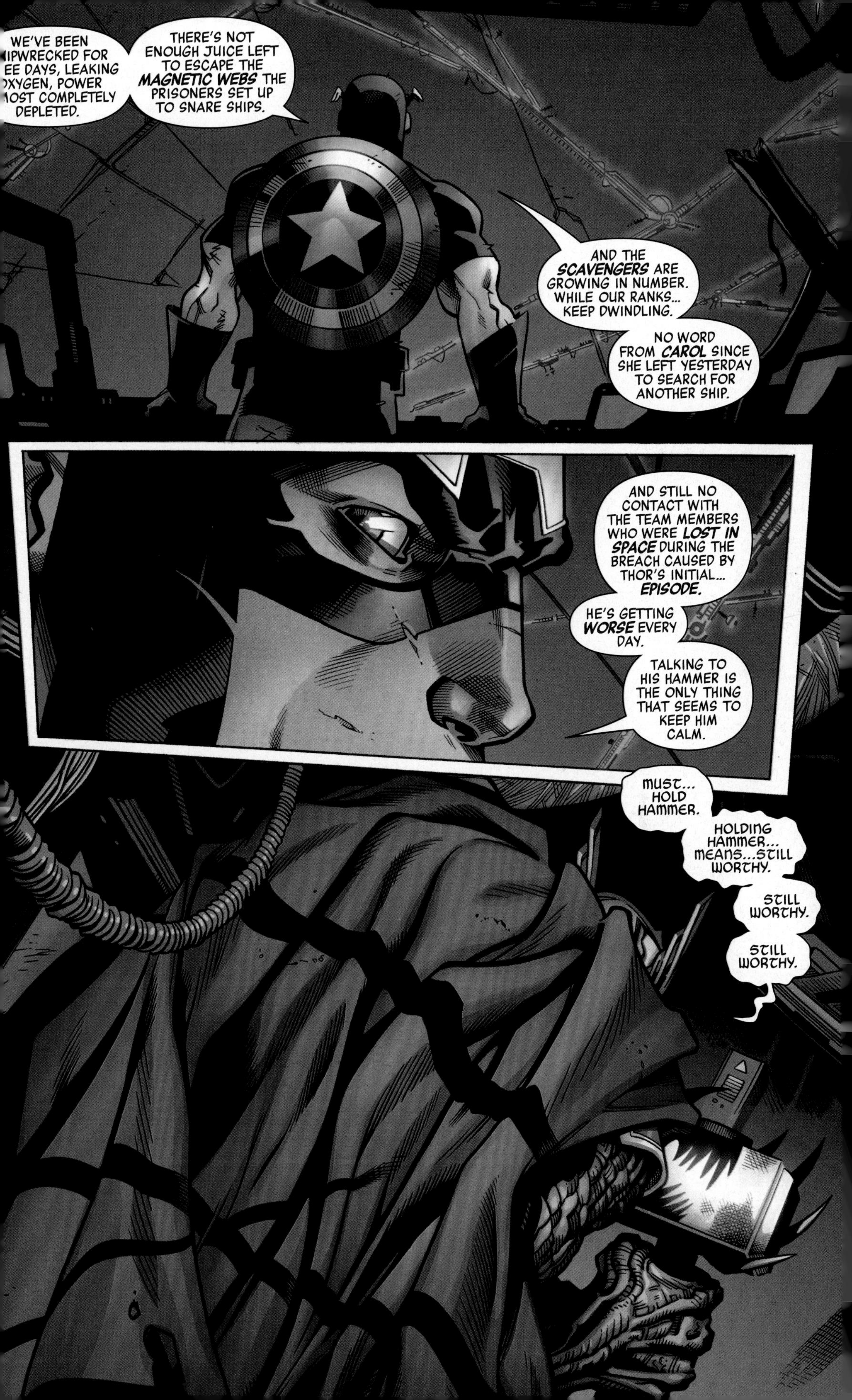
WE'VE BEEN IPWRECKED FOR EE DAYS, LEAKING OXYGEN, POWER OST COMPLETELY DEPLETED.
THERE'S NOT ENOUGH JUICE LEFT TO ESCAPE THE MAGNETIC WEBS THE PRISONERS SET UP TO SNARE SHIPS.
AND THE SCAVENGERS ARE GROWING IN NUMBER. WHILE OUR RANKS... KEEP DWINDLING.
NO WORD FROM CAROL SINCE SHE LEFT YESTERDAY TO SEARCH FOR ANOTHER SHIP.
AND STILL NO CONTACT WITH THE TEAM MEMBERS WHO WERE LOST IN SPACE DURING THE BREACH CAUSED BY THOR'S INITIAL... EPISODE.
HE'S GETTING WORSE EVERY DAY.
TALKING TO HIS HAMMER IS THE ONLY THING THAT SEEMS TO KEEP HIM CALM.
MUST... HOLD HAMMER.
HOLDING HAMMER... MEANS...STILL WORTHY.
STILL WORTHY.
STILL WORTHY.

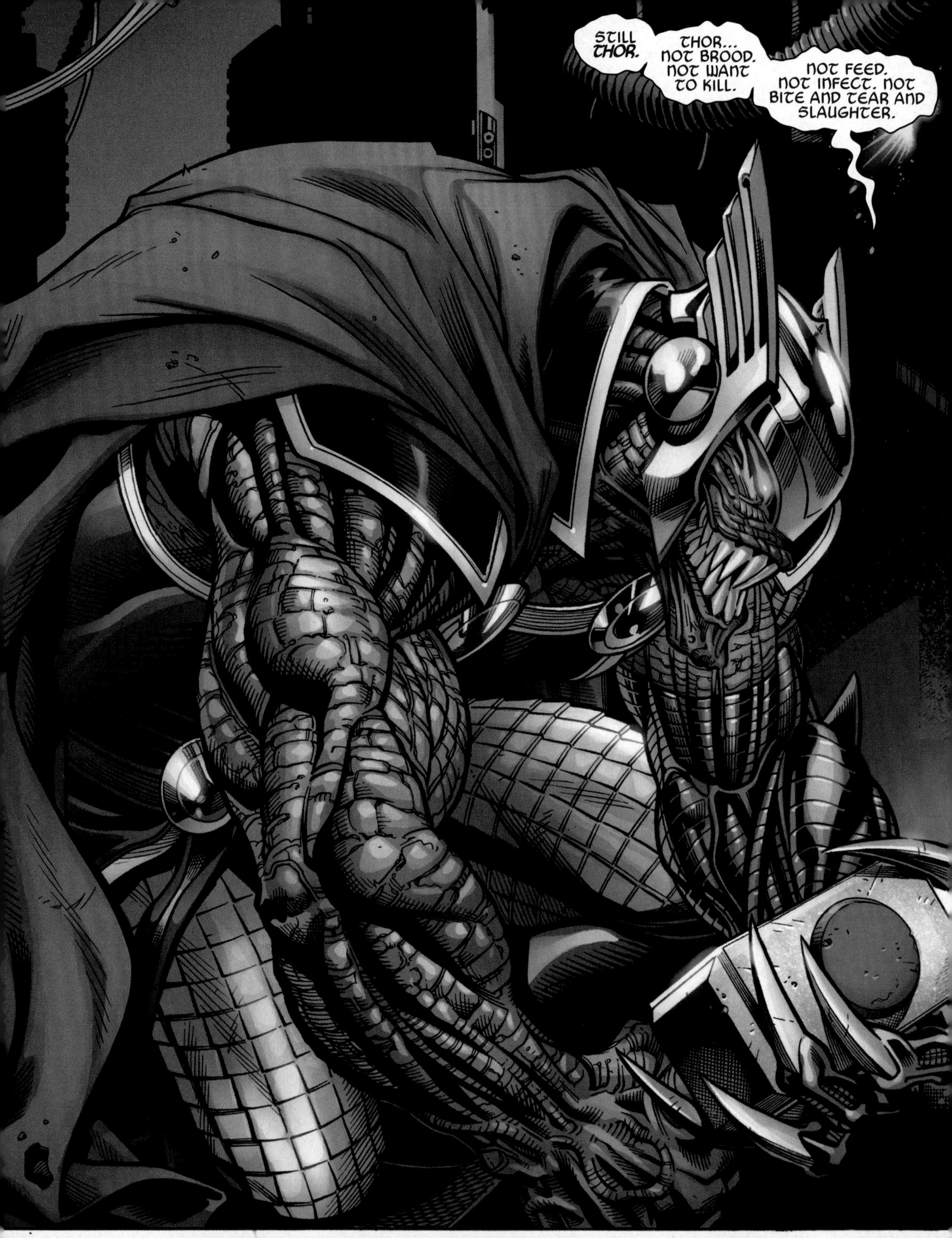
STILL THOR.
THOR... NOT BROOD. NOT WANT TO KILL.
NOT FEED. NOT INFECT. NOT BITE AND TEAR AND SLAUGHTER.

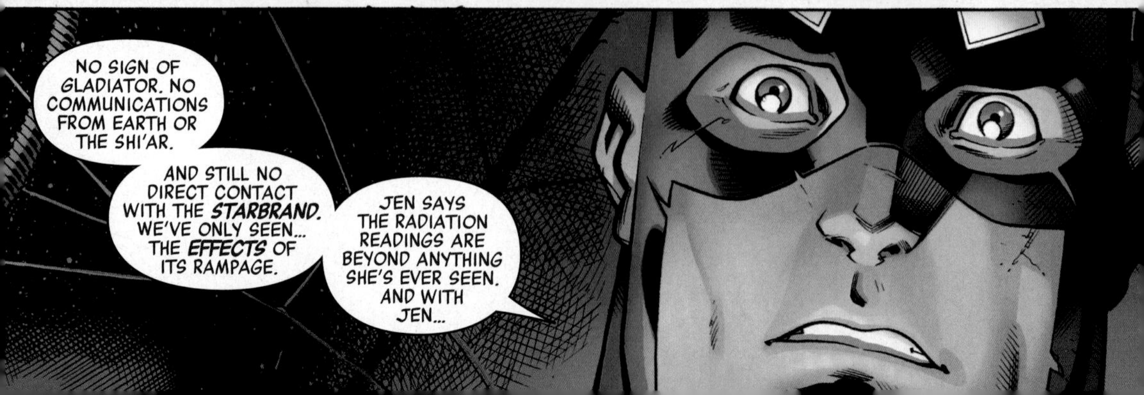
NO SIGN OF GLADIATOR. NO COMMUNICATIONS FROM EARTH OR THE SHI'AR.
AND STILL NO DIRECT CONTACT WITH THE STARBRAND. WE'VE ONLY SEEN... THE EFFECTS OF ITS RAMPAGE.
JEN SAYS THE RADIATION READINGS ARE BEYOND ANYTHING SHE'S EVER SEEN. AND WITH JEN...

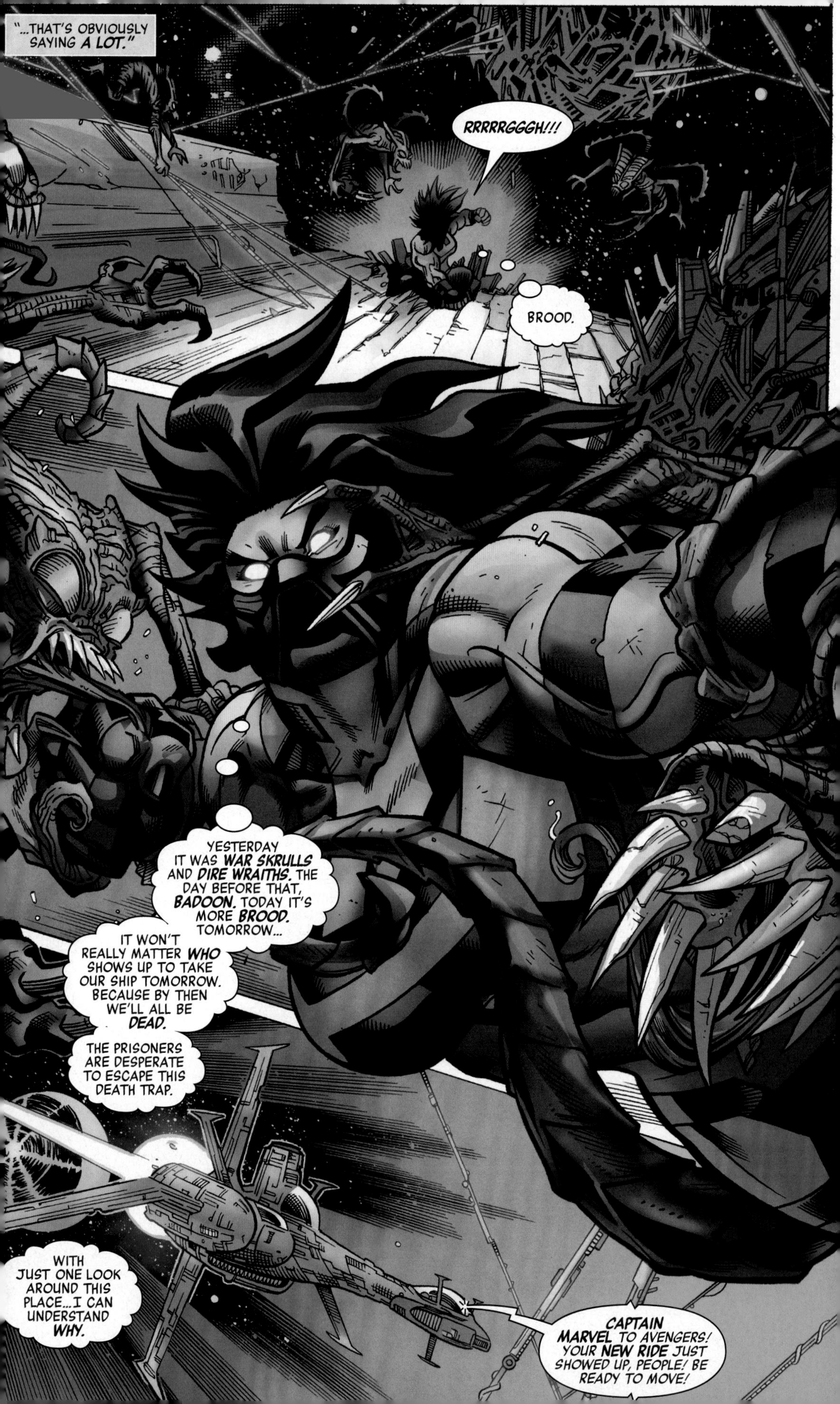
"...THAT'S OBVIOUSLY SAYING A LOT."
RRRRRGGGH!!!
BROOD.
YESTERDAY IT WAS WAR SKRULLS AND DIRE WRAITHS. THE DAY BEFORE THAT, BADOON. TODAY IT'S MORE BROOD. TOMORROW...
IT WON'T REALLY MATTER WHO SHOWS UP TO TAKE OUR SHIP TOMORROW. BECAUSE BY THEN WE'LL ALL BE DEAD.
THE PRISONERS ARE DESPERATE TO ESCAPE THIS DEATH TRAP.
WITH JUST ONE LOOK AROUND THIS PLACE...I CAN UNDERSTAND WHY.
CAPTAIN MARVEL TO AVENGERS! YOUR NEW RIDE JUST SHOWED UP, PEOPLE! BE READY TO MOVE!

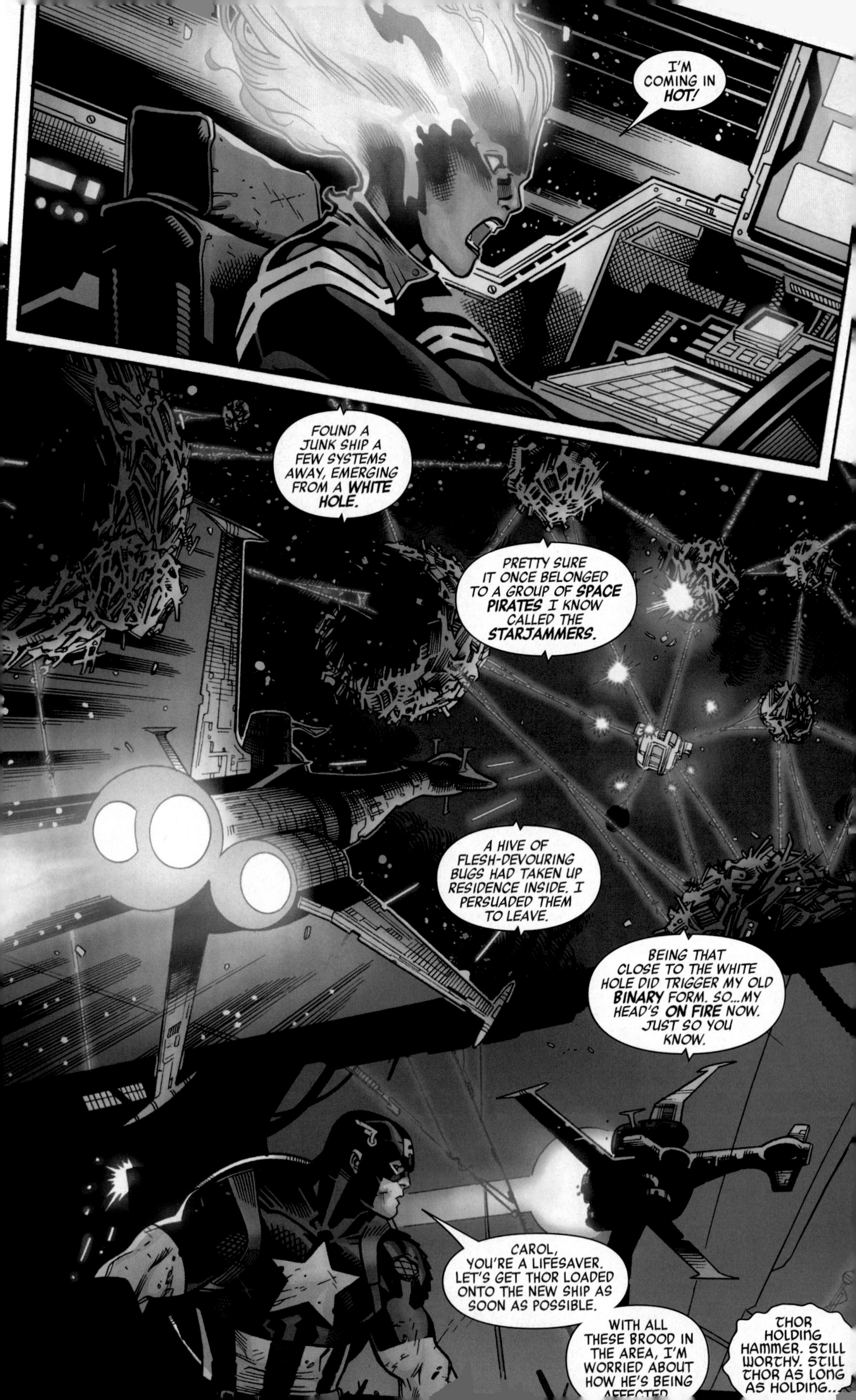
I'M COMING IN HOT!
FOUND A JUNK SHIP A FEW SYSTEMS AWAY, EMERGING FROM A WHITE HOLE.
PRETTY SURE IT ONCE BELONGED TO A GROUP OF SPACE PIRATES I KNOW CALLED THE STARJAMMERS.
A HIVE OF FLESH-DEVOURING BUGS HAD TAKEN UP RESIDENCE INSIDE. I PERSUADED THEM TO LEAVE.
BEING THAT CLOSE TO THE WHITE HOLE DID TRIGGER MY OLD BINARY FORM. SO...MY HEAD'S ON FIRE NOW. JUST SO YOU KNOW.
CAROL, YOU'RE A LIFESAVER. LET'S GET THOR LOADED ONTO THE NEW SHIP AS SOON AS POSSIBLE.
WITH ALL THESE BROOD IN THE AREA, I'M WORRIED ABOUT HOW HE'S BEING
THOR HOLDING HAMMER. STILL WORTHY. STILL THOR AS LONG AS HOLDING...

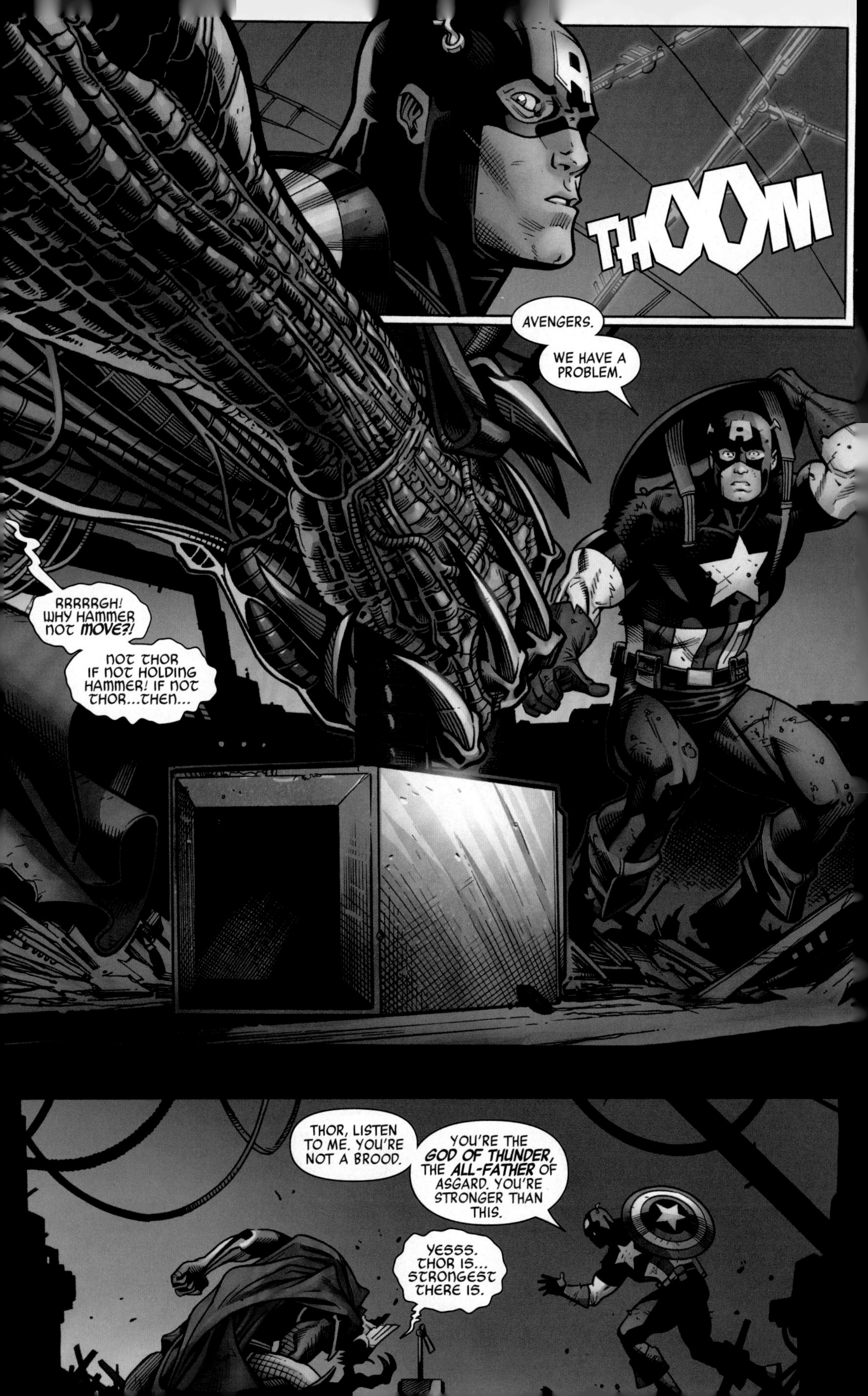
THOOM
AVENGERS.
WE HAVE A PROBLEM.
RRRRRGH! WHY HAMMER NOT MOVE?!
NOT THOR IF NOT HOLDING HAMMER! IF NOT THOR...THEN...
THOR, LISTEN TO ME. YOU'RE NOT A BROOD.
YOU'RE THE GOD OF THUNDER, THE ALL-FATHER OF ASGARD. YOU'RE STRONGER THAN THIS.
YESSS. THOR IS... STRONGEST THERE IS.

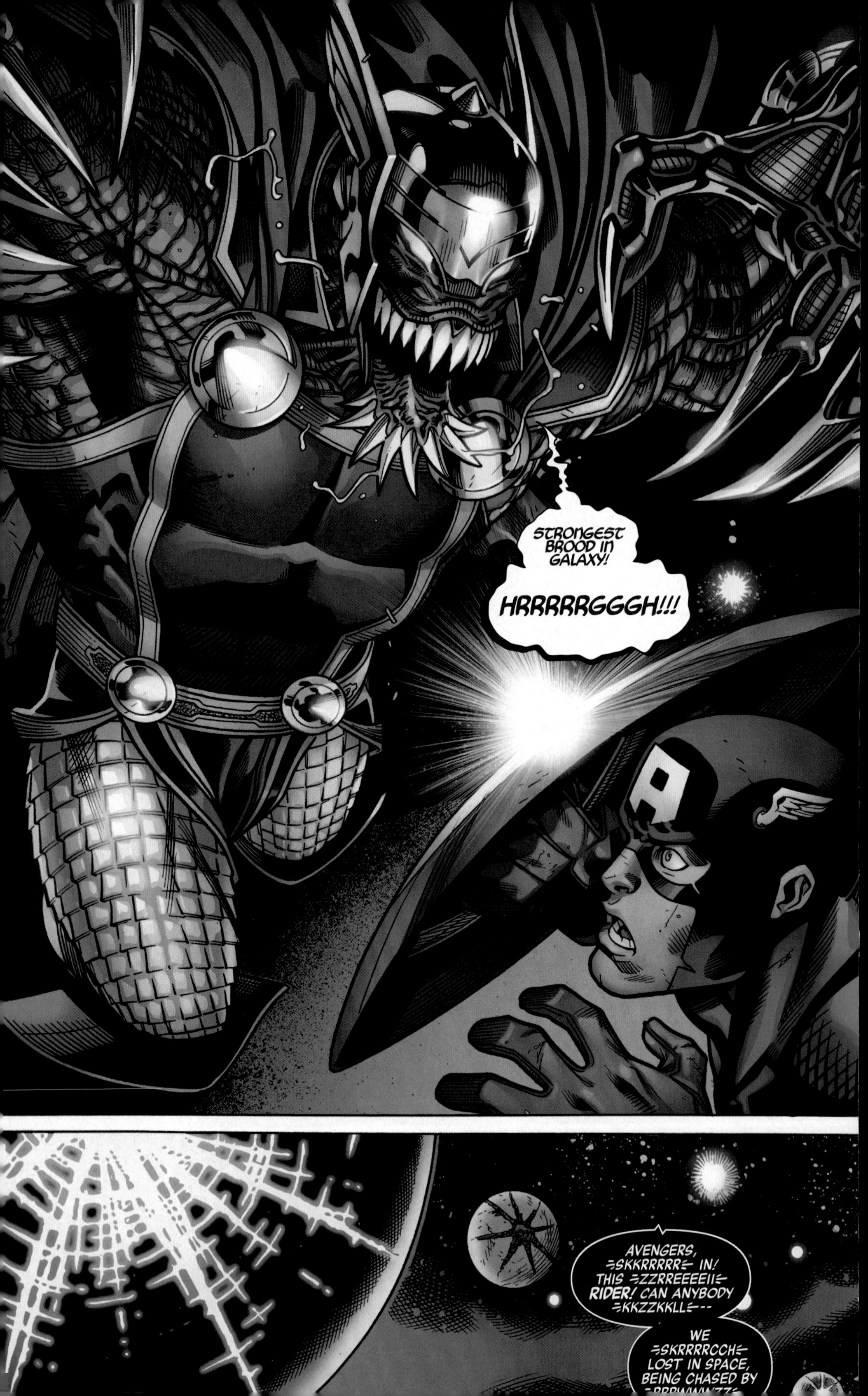
STRONGEST BROOD IN GALAXY!
HRRRRRGGGH!!!
AVENGERS, =SKKRRRRR= IN! THIS =ZZRREEEEII= RIDER! CAN ANYBODY =KKZZKKLL=--
WE =SKRRRRCCH= LOST IN SPACE, BEING CHASED BY

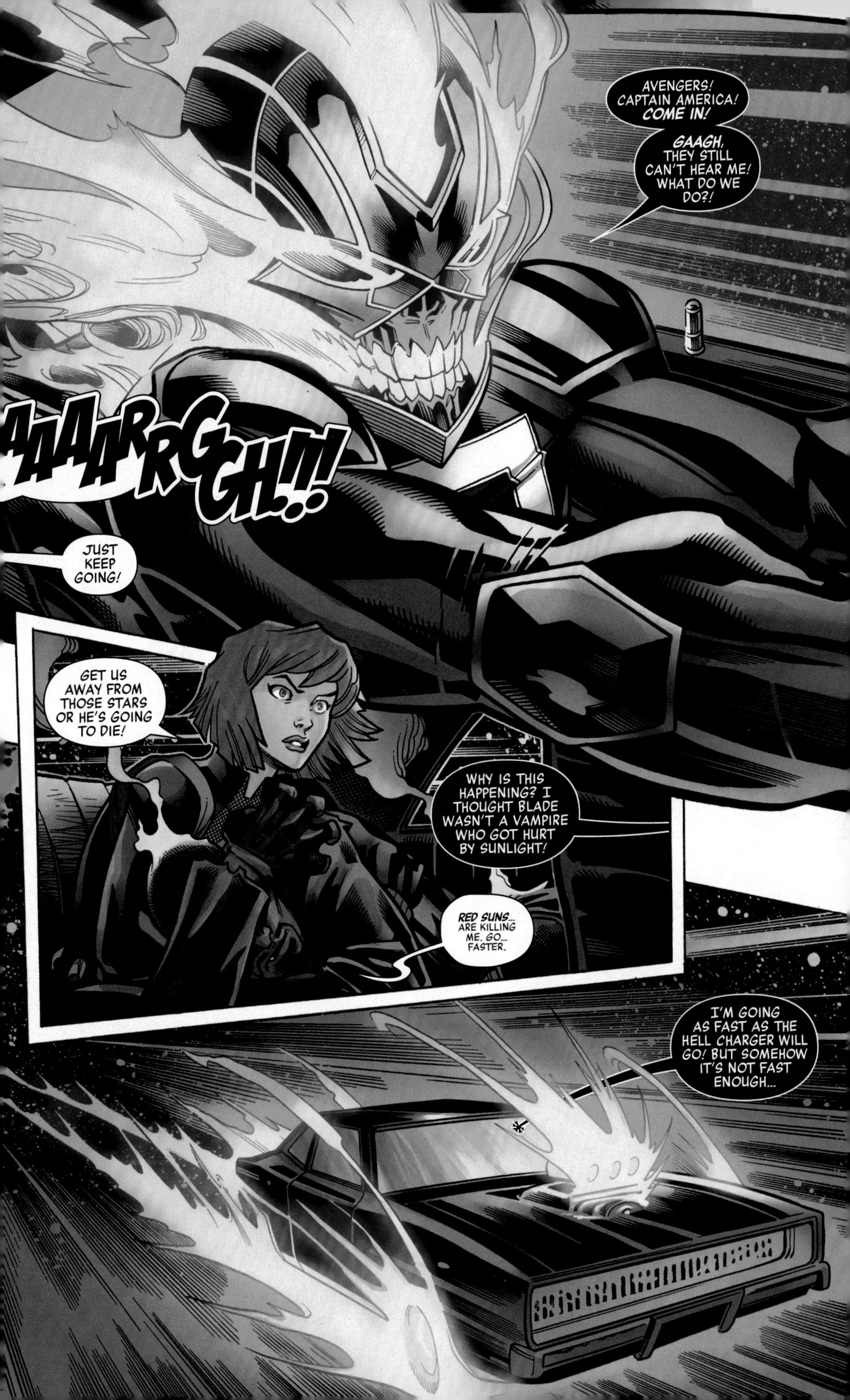
AVENGERS! CAPTAIN AMERICA! COME IN!
GAAGH, THEY STILL CAN'T HEAR ME! WHAT DO WE DO?!
AAAARRGGH!!!
JUST KEEP GOING!
GET US AWAY FROM THOSE STARS OR HE'S GOING TO DIE!
WHY IS THIS HAPPENING? I THOUGHT BLADE WASN'T A VAMPIRE WHO GOT HURT BY SUNLIGHT!
RED SUNS... ARE KILLING ME. GO... FASTER.
I'M GOING AS FAST AS THE HELL CHARGER WILL GO! BUT SOMEHOW IT'S NOT FAST ENOUGH...

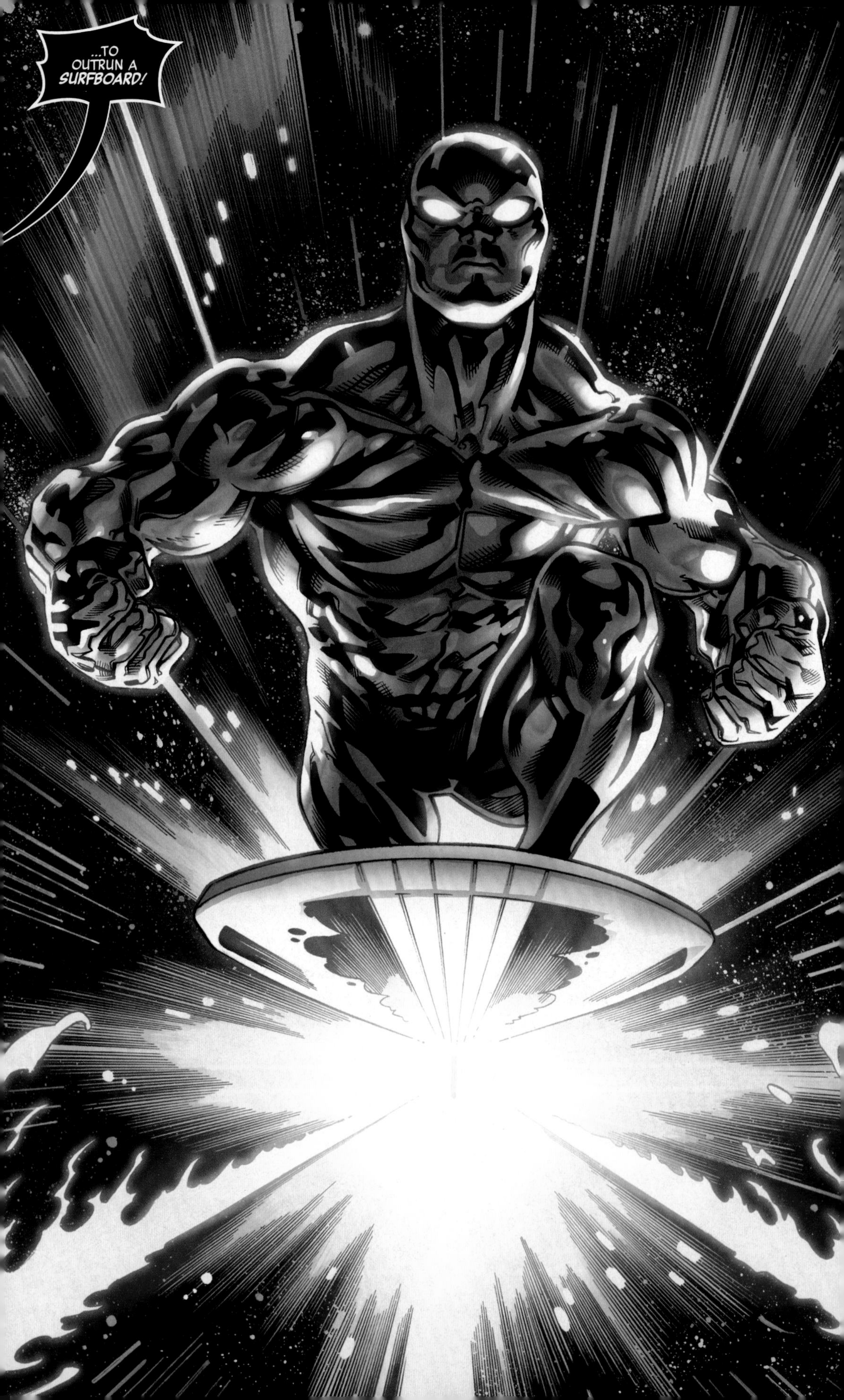
...TO OUTRUN A SURFBOARD!

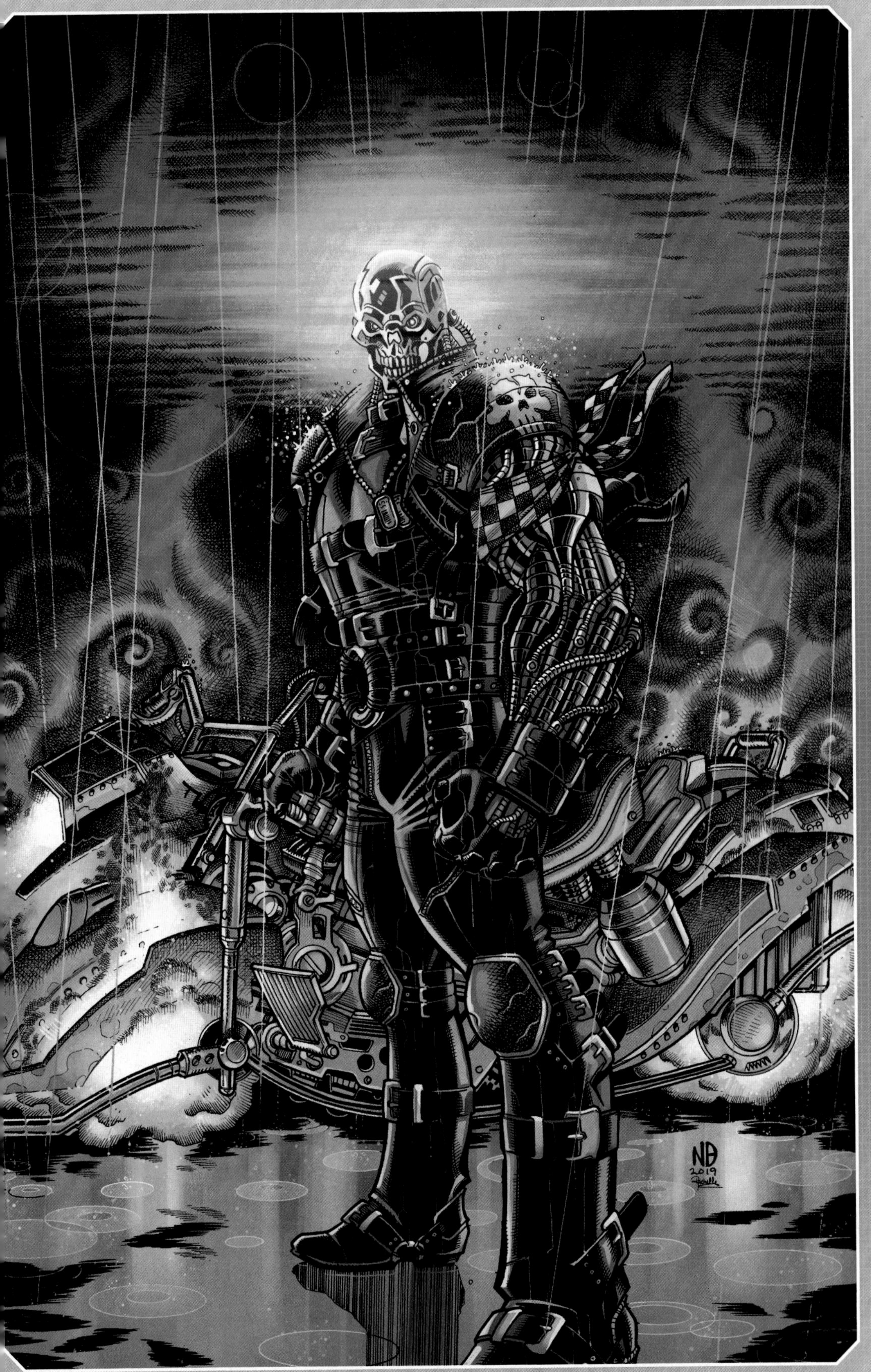
NB
2019
Rachelle

NICK BRADSHAW & RACHELLE ROSENBERG
27 2099 VARIANT

28 STARBRAND REBORN PART 2
THE THREE HERALDS

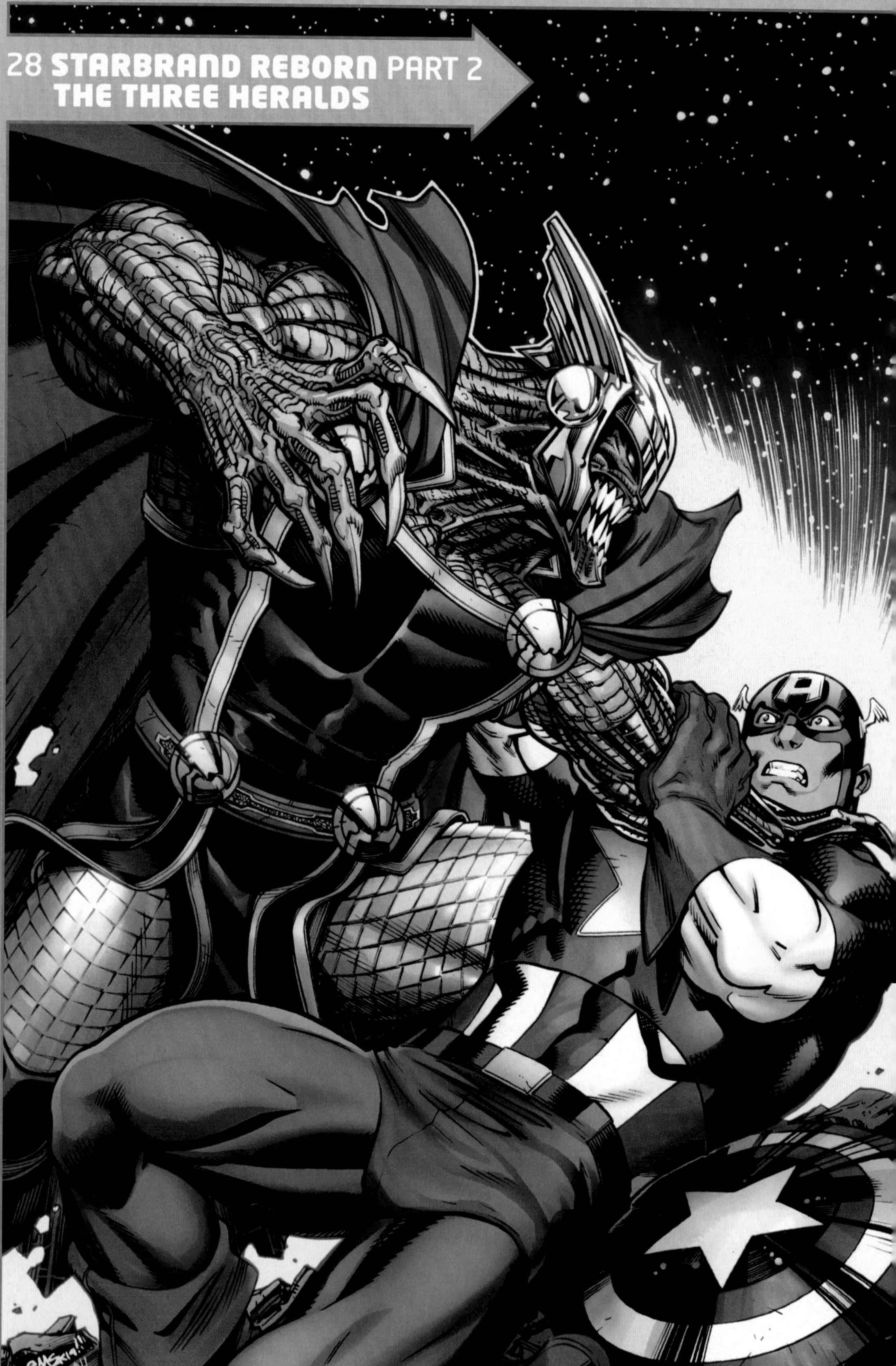

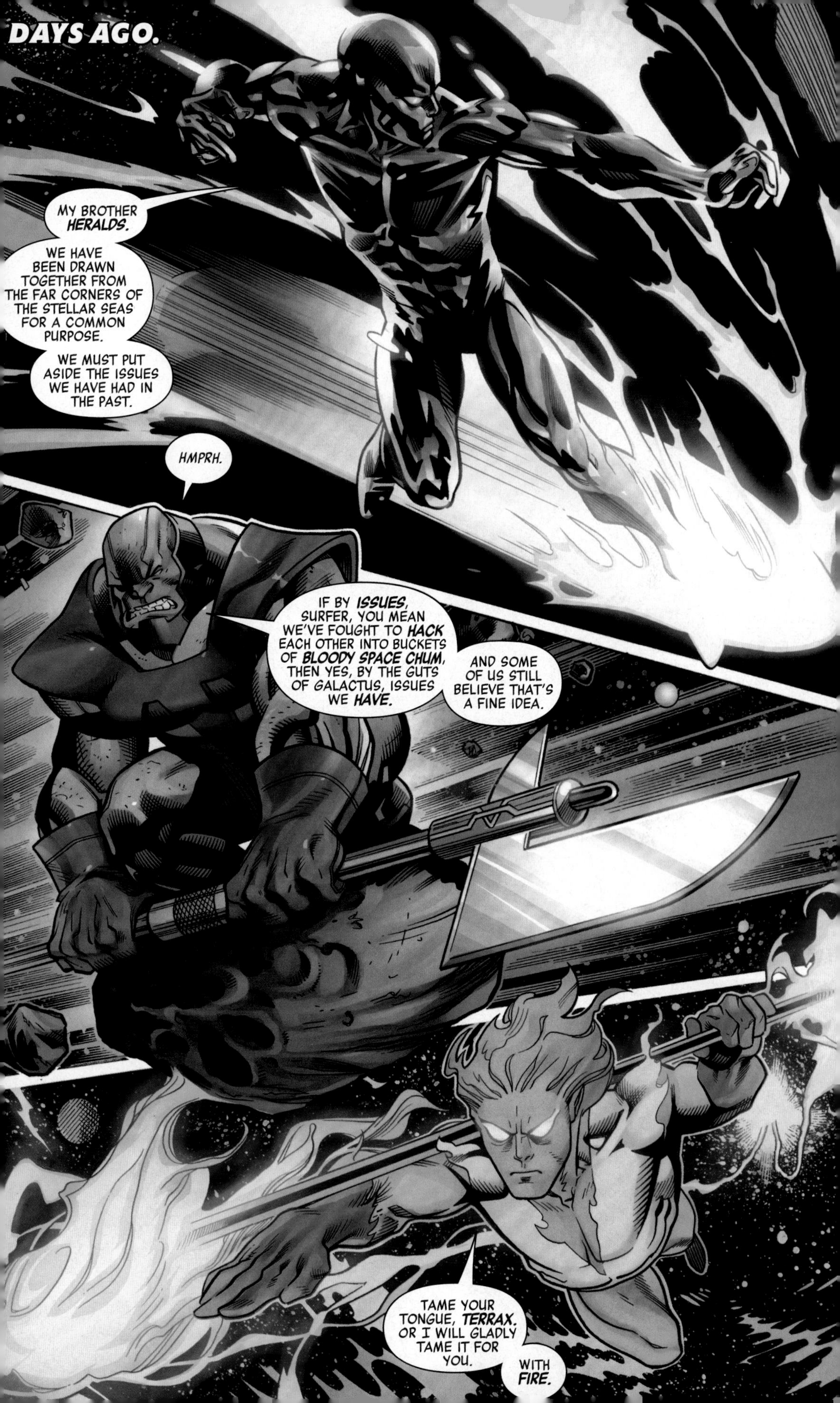
DAYS AGO.
MY BROTHER HERALDS.
WE HAVE BEEN DRAWN TOGETHER FROM THE FAR CORNERS OF THE STELLAR SEAS FOR A COMMON PURPOSE.
WE MUST PUT ASIDE THE ISSUES WE HAVE HAD IN THE PAST.
HMPRH.
IF BY ISSUES, SURFER, YOU MEAN WE'VE FOUGHT TO HACK EACH OTHER INTO BUCKETS OF BLOODY SPACE CHUM, THEN YES, BY THE GUTS OF GALACTUS, ISSUES WE HAVE.
AND SOME OF US STILL BELIEVE THAT'S A FINE IDEA.
TAME YOUR TONGUE, TERRAX, OR I WILL GLADLY TAME IT FOR YOU.
WITH FIRE.

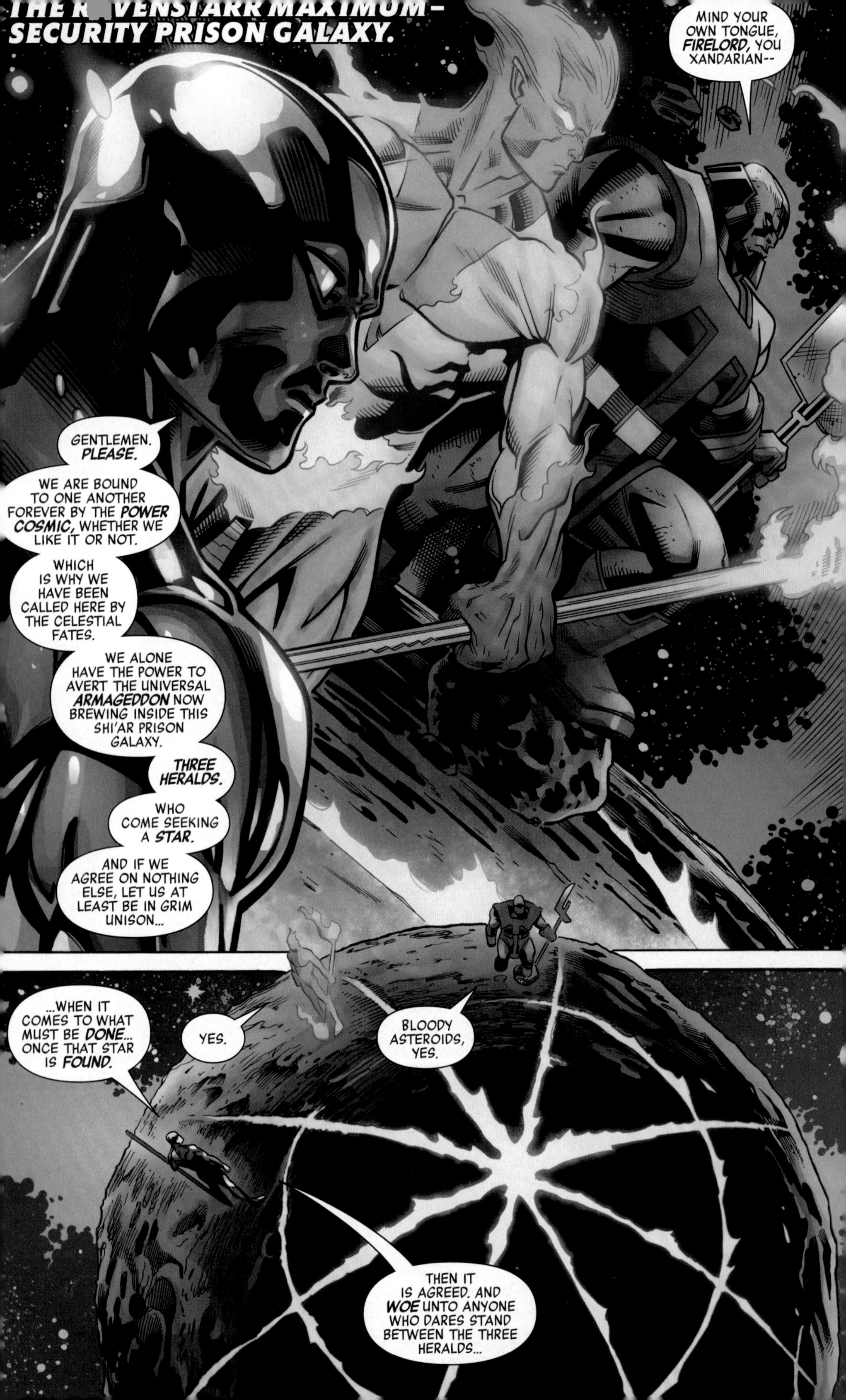

THE R VENSTARR MAXIMUM–SECURITY PRISON GALAXY.
MIND YOUR OWN TONGUE, FIRELORD, YOU XANDARIAN--
GENTLEMEN. PLEASE.
WE ARE BOUND TO ONE ANOTHER FOREVER BY THE POWER COSMIC, WHETHER WE LIKE IT OR NOT.
WHICH IS WHY WE HAVE BEEN CALLED HERE BY THE CELESTIAL FATES.
WE ALONE HAVE THE POWER TO AVERT THE UNIVERSAL ARMAGEDDON NOW BREWING INSIDE THIS SHI'AR PRISON GALAXY.
THREE HERALDS.
WHO COME SEEKING A STAR.
AND IF WE AGREE ON NOTHING ELSE, LET US AT LEAST BE IN GRIM UNISON...
...WHEN IT COMES TO WHAT MUST BE DONE... ONCE THAT STAR IS FOUND.
YES.
BLOODY ASTEROIDS, YES.
THEN IT IS AGREED. AND WOE UNTO ANYONE WHO DARES STAND BETWEEN THE THREE HERALDS...

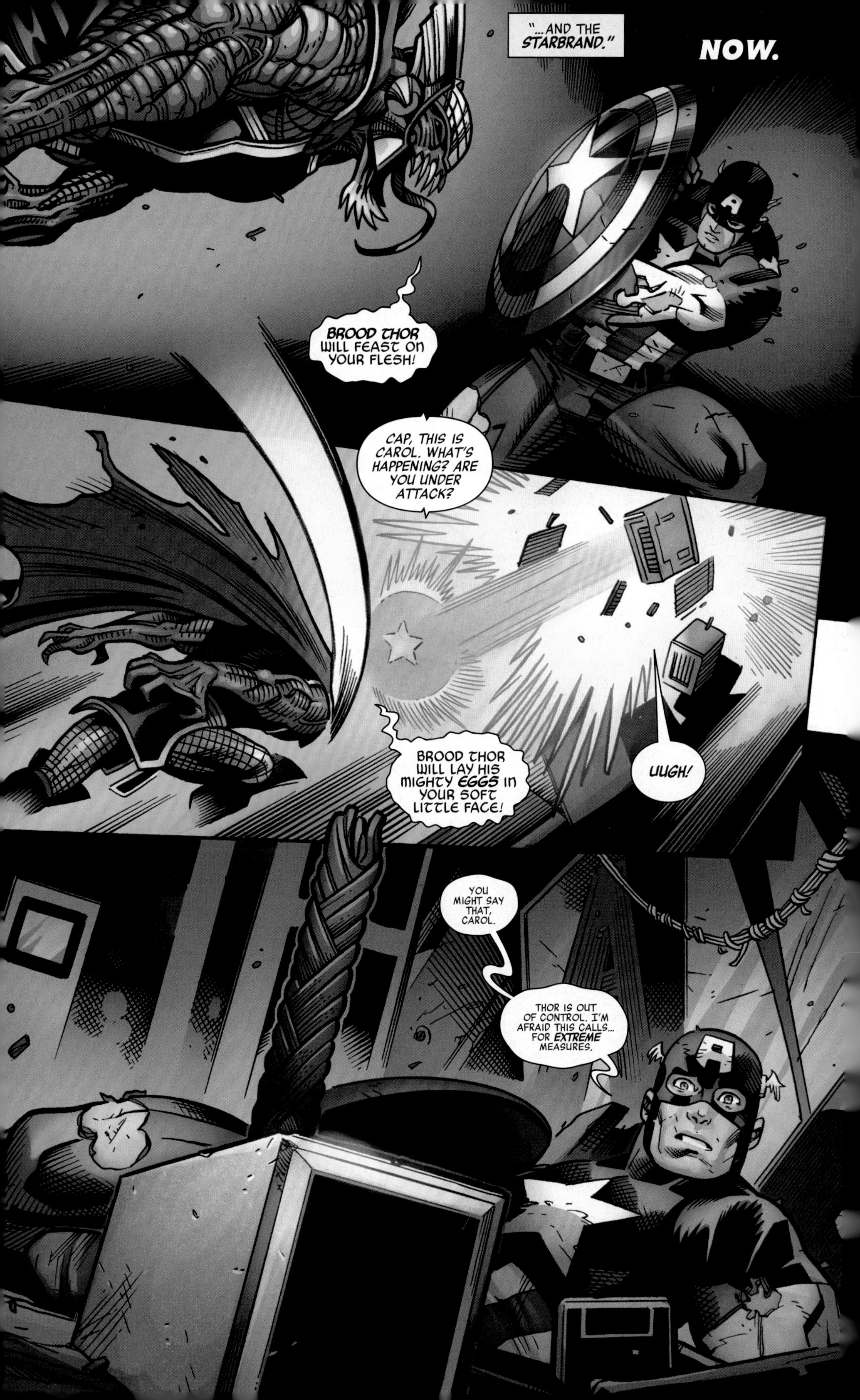
"...AND THE STARBRAND."
NOW.
BROOD THOR WILL FEAST ON YOUR FLESH!
CAP, THIS IS CAROL. WHAT'S HAPPENING? ARE YOU UNDER ATTACK?
BROOD THOR WILL LAY HIS MIGHTY EGGS IN YOUR SOFT LITTLE FACE!
UUGH!
YOU MIGHT SAY THAT, CAROL.
THOR IS OUT OF CONTROL. I'M AFRAID THIS CALLS... FOR EXTREME MEASURES.

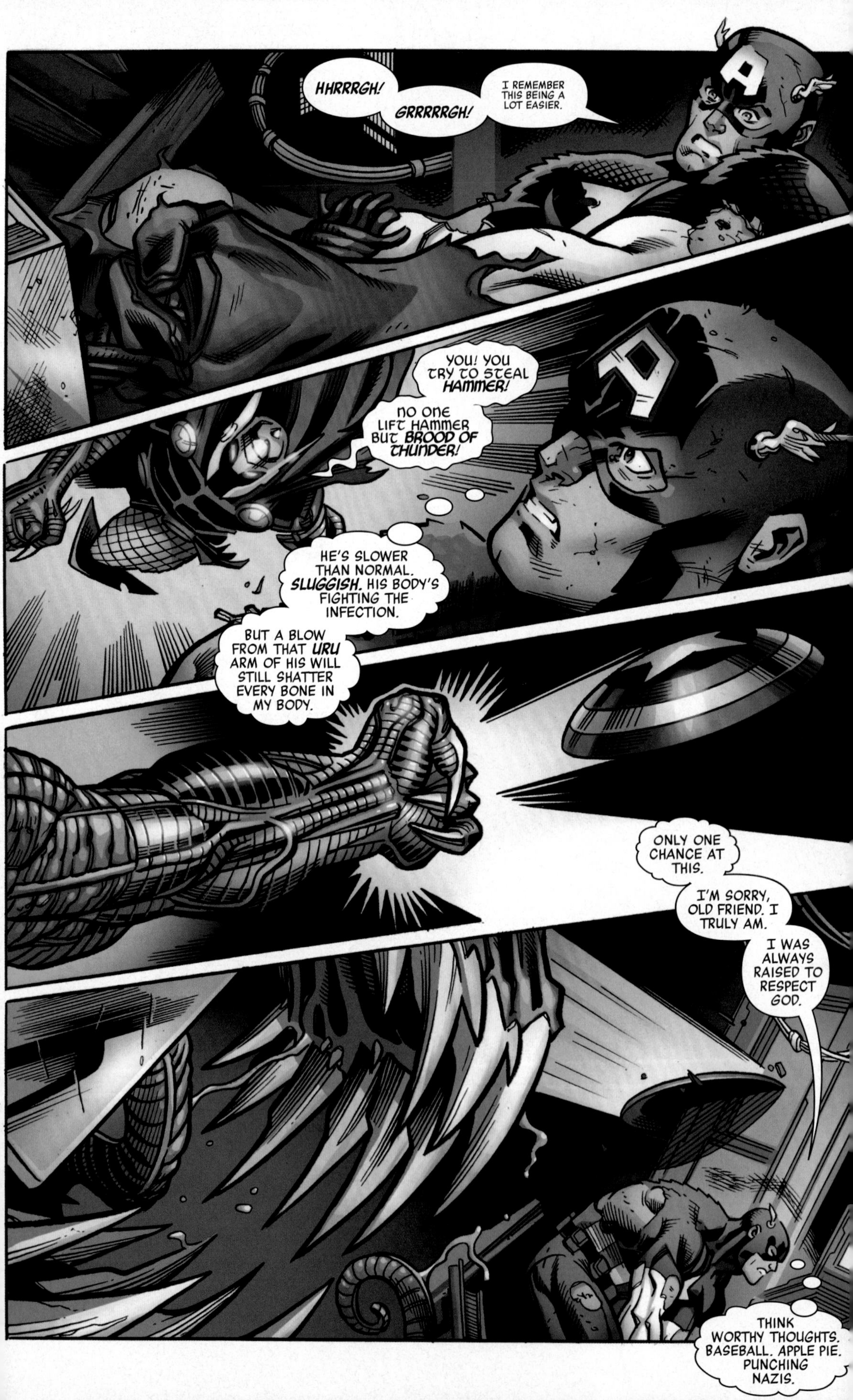
HHRRRGH!
GRRRRRGH!
I REMEMBER THIS BEING A LOT EASIER.
YOU! YOU TRY TO STEAL HAMMER!
NO ONE LIFT HAMMER BUT BROOD OF THUNDER!
HE'S SLOWER THAN NORMAL. SLUGGISH. HIS BODY'S FIGHTING THE INFECTION.
BUT A BLOW FROM THAT URU ARM OF HIS WILL STILL SHATTER EVERY BONE IN MY BODY.
ONLY ONE CHANCE AT THIS.
I'M SORRY, OLD FRIEND. I TRULY AM.
I WAS ALWAYS RAISED TO RESPECT GOD.
THINK WORTHY THOUGHTS. BASEBALL. APPLE PIE. PUNCHING NAZIS.

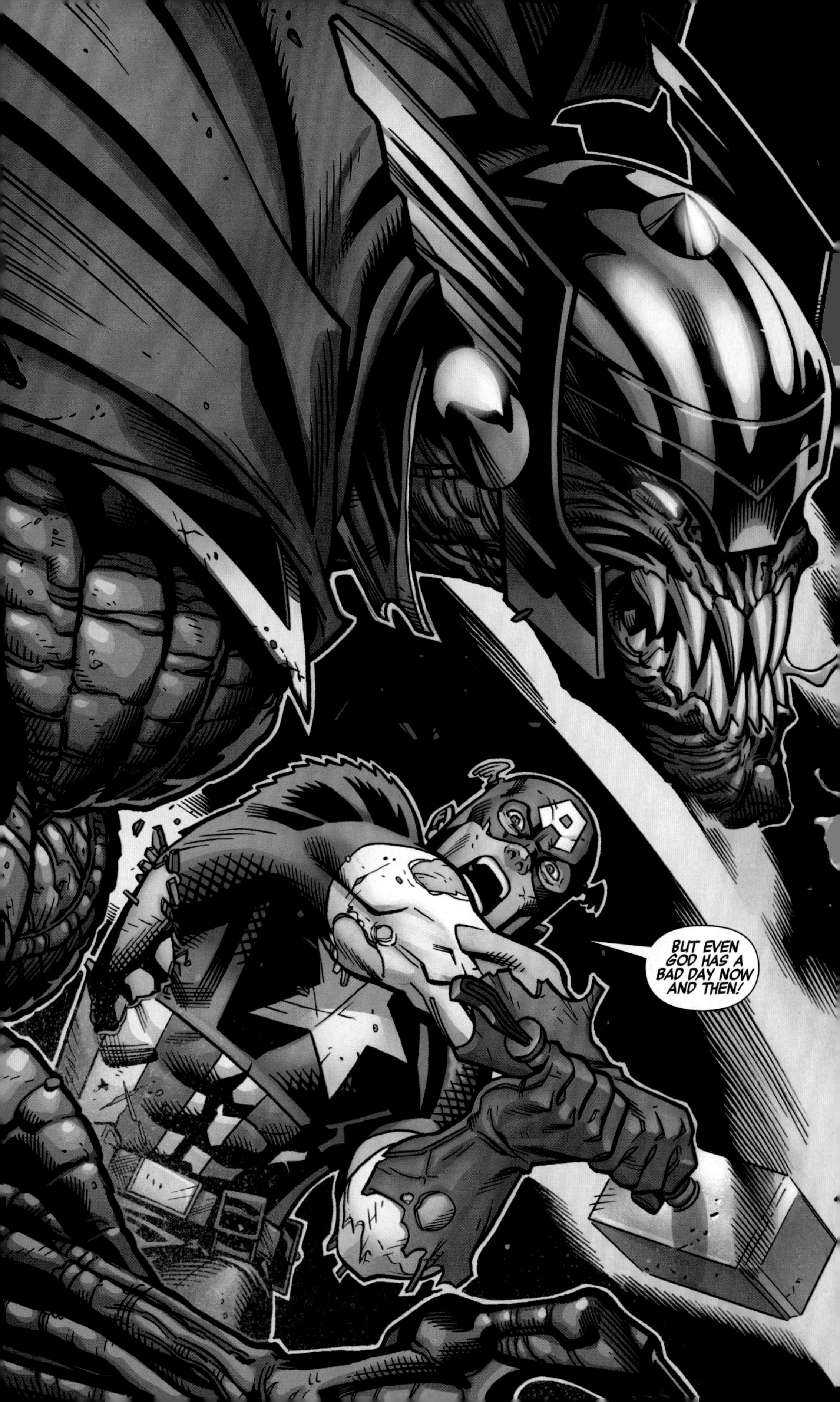
BUT EVEN GOD HAS A BAD DAY NOW AND THEN!

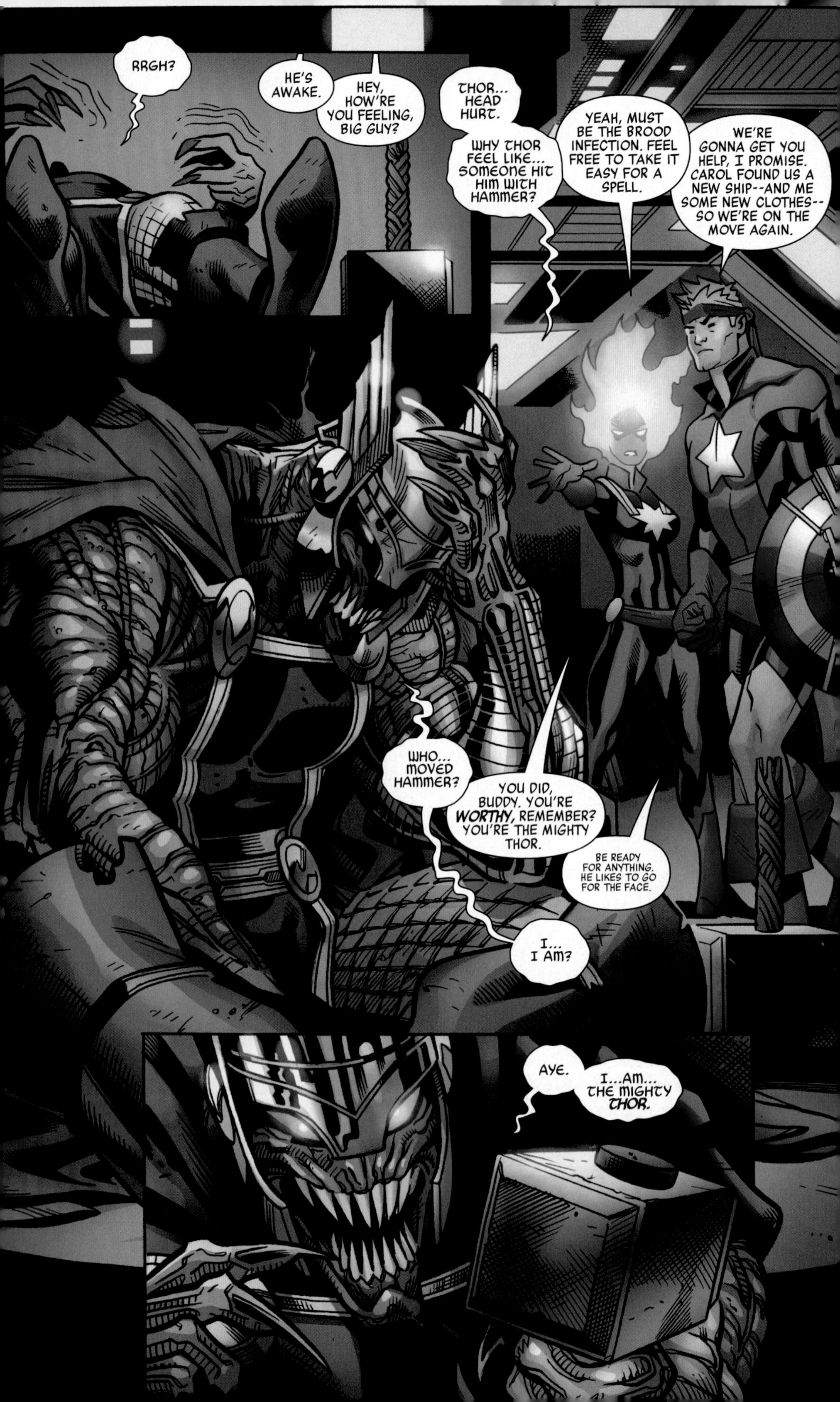
RRGH?
HE'S AWAKE.
HEY, HOW'RE YOU FEELING, BIG GUY?
THOR... HEAD HURT.
WHY THOR FEEL LIKE... SOMEONE HIT HIM WITH HAMMER?
YEAH, MUST BE THE BROOD INFECTION. FEEL FREE TO TAKE IT EASY FOR A SPELL.
WE'RE GONNA GET YOU HELP, I PROMISE. CAROL FOUND US A NEW SHIP--AND ME SOME NEW CLOTHES--SO WE'RE ON THE MOVE AGAIN.
WHO... MOVED HAMMER?
YOU DID, BUDDY. YOU'RE WORTHY, REMEMBER? YOU'RE THE MIGHTY THOR.
BE READY FOR ANYTHING. HE LIKES TO GO FOR THE FACE.
I... I AM?
AYE.
I...AM... THE MIGHTY THOR.

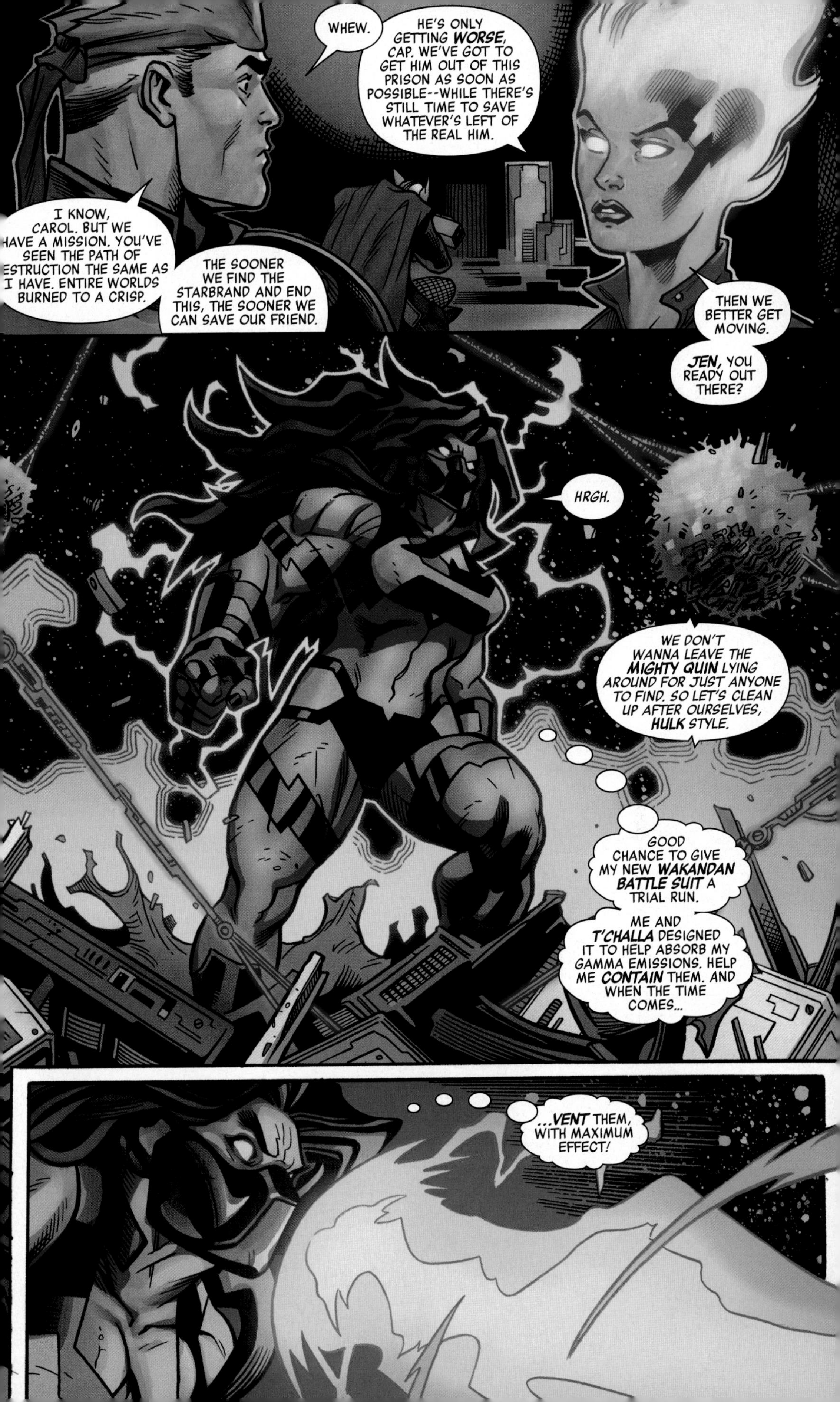
WHEW.
HE'S ONLY GETTING WORSE, CAP. WE'VE GOT TO GET HIM OUT OF THIS PRISON AS SOON AS POSSIBLE--WHILE THERE'S STILL TIME TO SAVE WHATEVER'S LEFT OF THE REAL HIM.
I KNOW, CAROL. BUT WE HAVE A MISSION. YOU'VE SEEN THE PATH OF ESTRUCTION THE SAME AS I HAVE. ENTIRE WORLDS BURNED TO A CRISP.
THE SOONER WE FIND THE STARBRAND AND END THIS, THE SOONER WE CAN SAVE OUR FRIEND.
THEN WE BETTER GET MOVING.
JEN, YOU READY OUT THERE?
HRGH.
WE DON'T WANNA LEAVE THE MIGHTY QUIN LYING AROUND FOR JUST ANYONE TO FIND. SO LET'S CLEAN UP AFTER OURSELVES, HULK STYLE.
GOOD CHANCE TO GIVE MY NEW WAKANDAN BATTLE SUIT A TRIAL RUN.
ME AND T'CHALLA DESIGNED IT TO HELP ABSORB MY GAMMA EMISSIONS. HELP ME CONTAIN THEM. AND WHEN THE TIME COMES...
...VENT THEM, WITH MAXIMUM EFFECT!

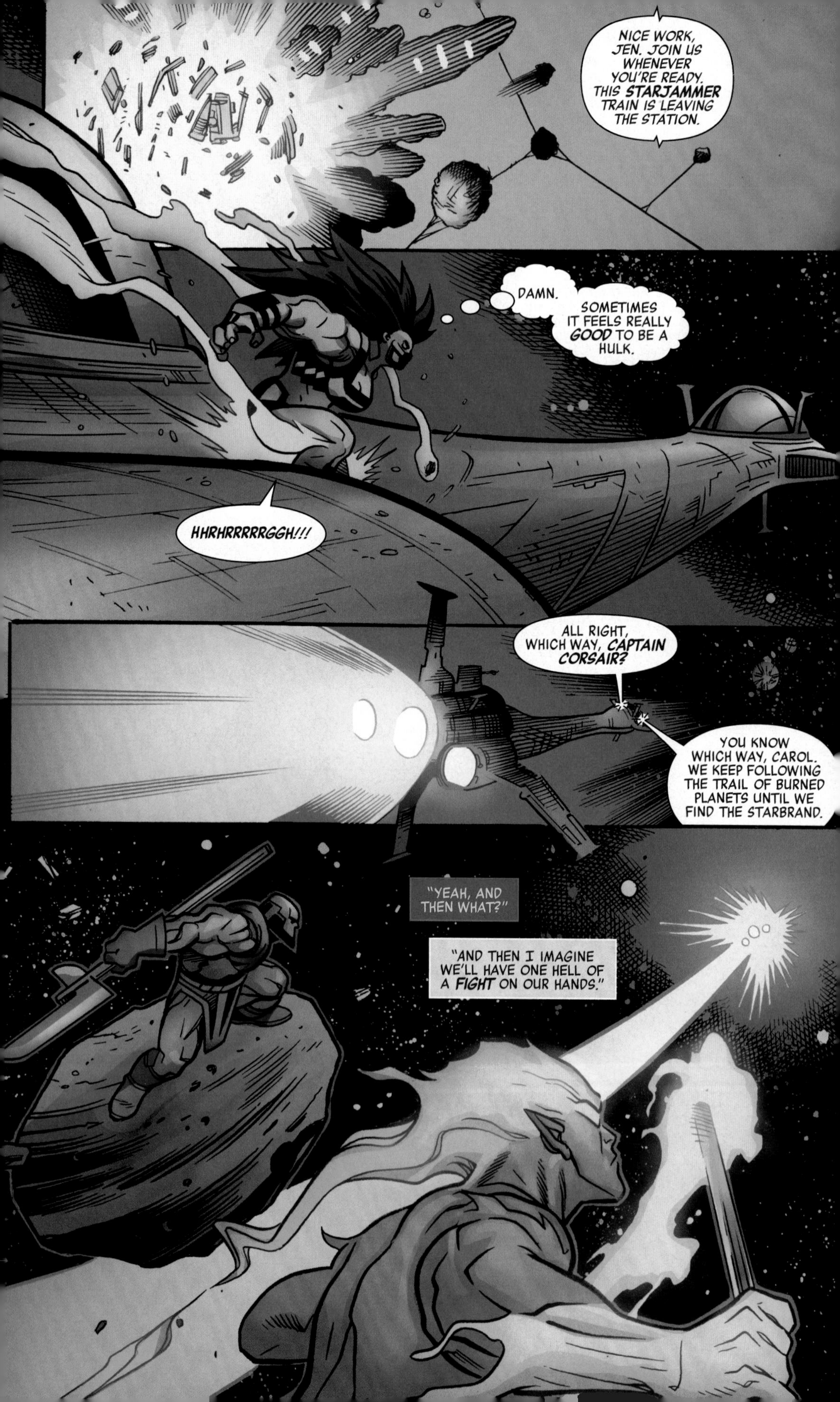
NICE WORK, JEN. JOIN US WHENEVER YOU'RE READY. THIS STARJAMMER TRAIN IS LEAVING THE STATION.
DAMN.
SOMETIMES IT FEELS REALLY GOOD TO BE A HULK.
HHRHRRRRRGGH!!!
ALL RIGHT, WHICH WAY, CAPTAIN CORSAIR?
YOU KNOW WHICH WAY, CAROL. WE KEEP FOLLOWING THE TRAIL OF BURNED PLANETS UNTIL WE FIND THE STARBRAND.
"YEAH, AND THEN WHAT?"
"AND THEN I IMAGINE WE'LL HAVE ONE HELL OF A FIGHT ON OUR HANDS."

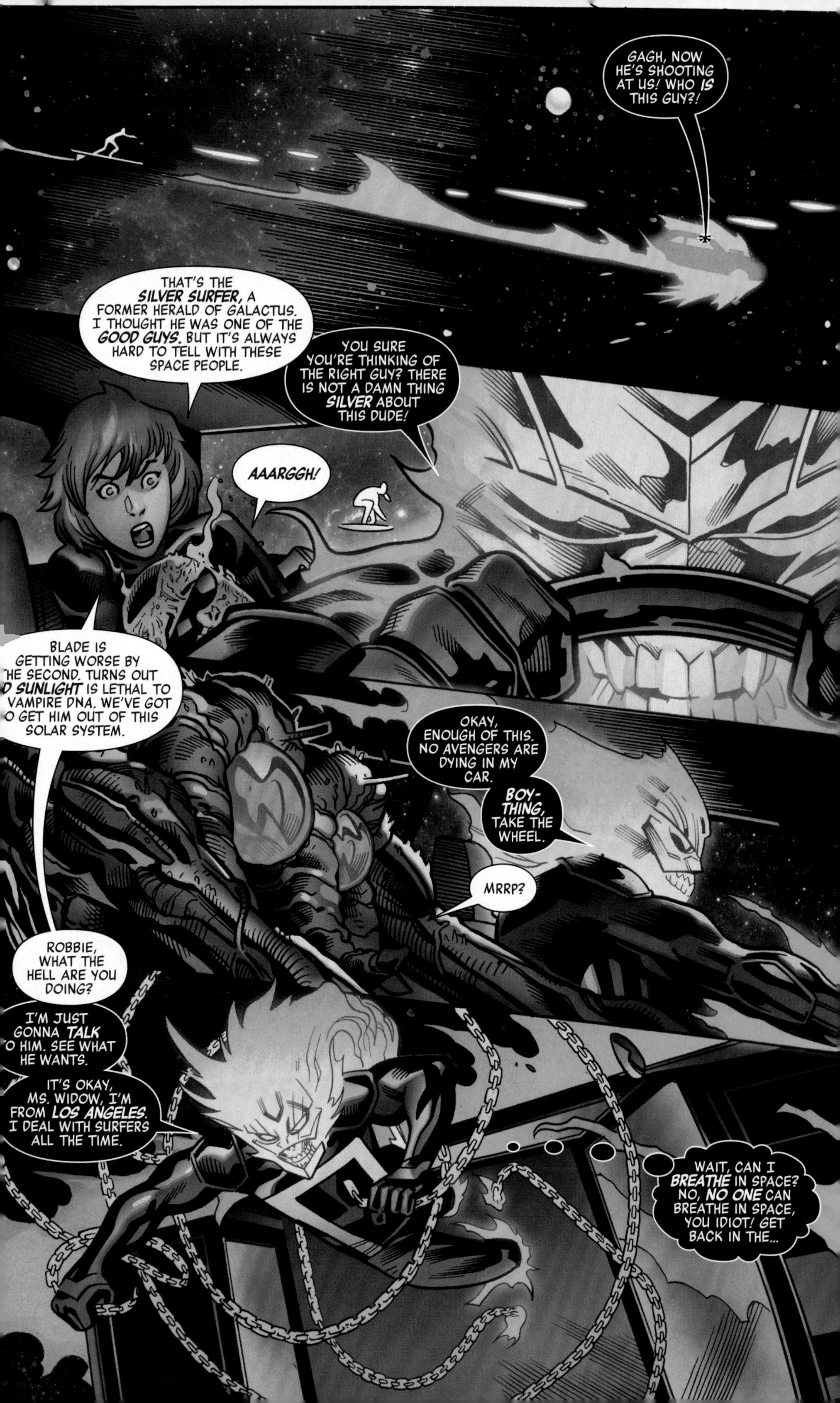

GAGH, NOW HE'S SHOOTING AT US! WHO IS THIS GUY?!
THAT'S THE SILVER SURFER, A FORMER HERALD OF GALACTUS. I THOUGHT HE WAS ONE OF THE GOOD GUYS. BUT IT'S ALWAYS HARD TO TELL WITH THESE SPACE PEOPLE.
YOU SURE YOU'RE THINKING OF THE RIGHT GUY? THERE IS NOT A DAMN THING SILVER ABOUT THIS DUDE!
AAARGGH!
BLADE IS GETTING WORSE BY HE SECOND. TURNS OUT D SUNLIGHT IS LETHAL TO VAMPIRE DNA. WE'VE GOT O GET HIM OUT OF THIS SOLAR SYSTEM.
OKAY, ENOUGH OF THIS. NO AVENGERS ARE DYING IN MY CAR.
BOY-THING, TAKE THE WHEEL.
MRRP?
ROBBIE, WHAT THE HELL ARE YOU DOING?
I'M JUST GONNA TALK O HIM. SEE WHAT HE WANTS.
IT'S OKAY, MS. WIDOW, I'M FROM LOS ANGELES. I DEAL WITH SURFERS ALL THE TIME.
WAIT, CAN I BREATHE IN SPACE? NO, NO ONE CAN BREATHE IN SPACE, YOU IDIOT! GET BACK IN THE...

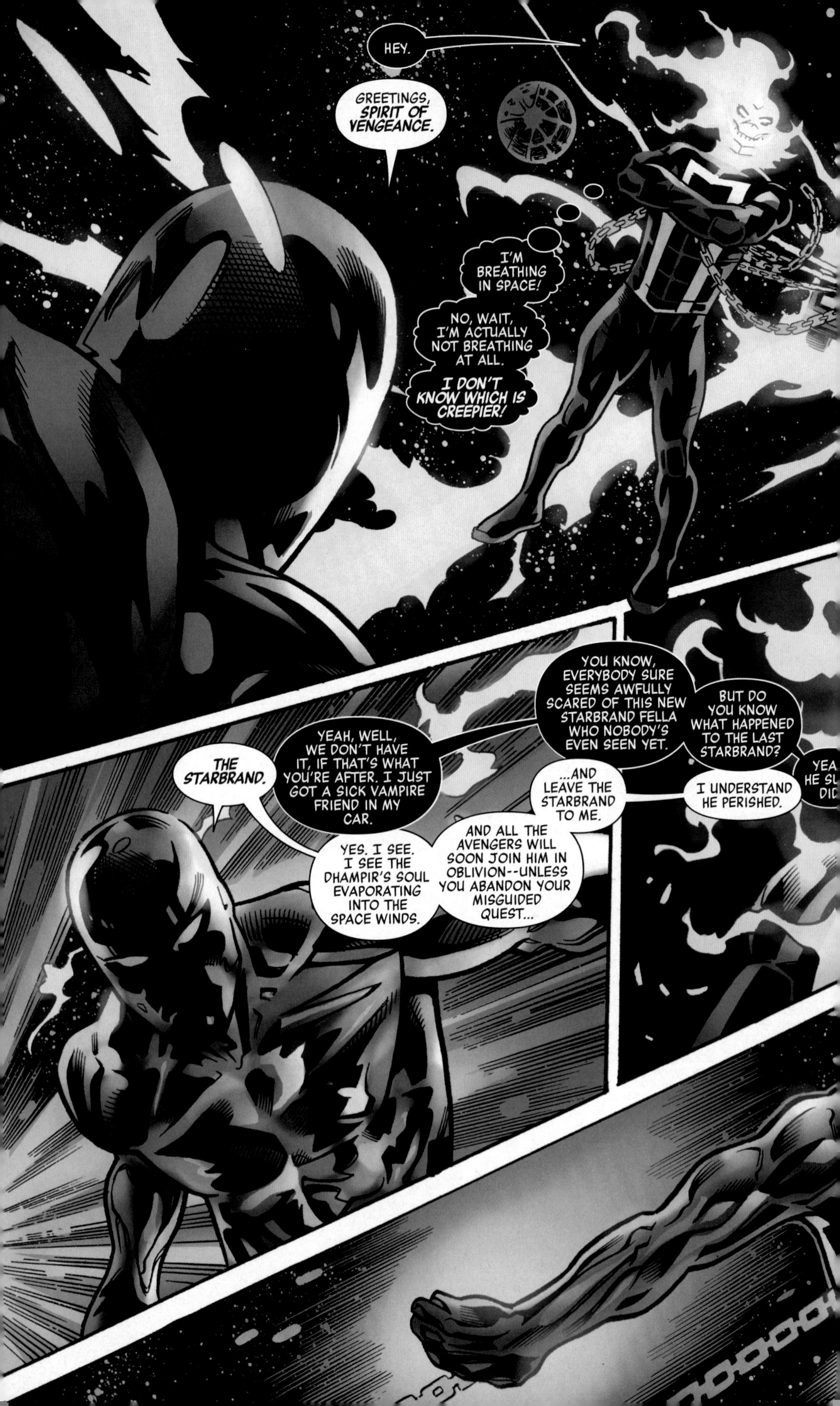
HEY.
GREETINGS, *SPIRIT OF VENGEANCE.*
I'M BREATHING IN SPACE!
NO, WAIT, I'M ACTUALLY NOT BREATHING AT ALL.
I DON'T KNOW WHICH IS CREEPIER!
THE STARBRAND.
YEAH, WELL, WE DON'T HAVE IT, IF THAT'S WHAT YOU'RE AFTER. I JUST GOT A SICK VAMPIRE FRIEND IN MY CAR.
YOU KNOW, EVERYBODY SURE SEEMS AWFULLY SCARED OF THIS NEW STARBRAND FELLA WHO NOBODY'S EVEN SEEN YET.
BUT DO YOU KNOW WHAT HAPPENED TO THE LAST STARBRAND?
YES. I SEE. I SEE THE DHAMPIR'S SOUL EVAPORATING INTO THE SPACE WINDS.
AND ALL THE AVENGERS WILL SOON JOIN HIM IN OBLIVION--UNLESS YOU ABANDON YOUR MISGUIDED QUEST...
...AND LEAVE THE STARBRAND TO ME.
I UNDERSTAND HE PERISHED.

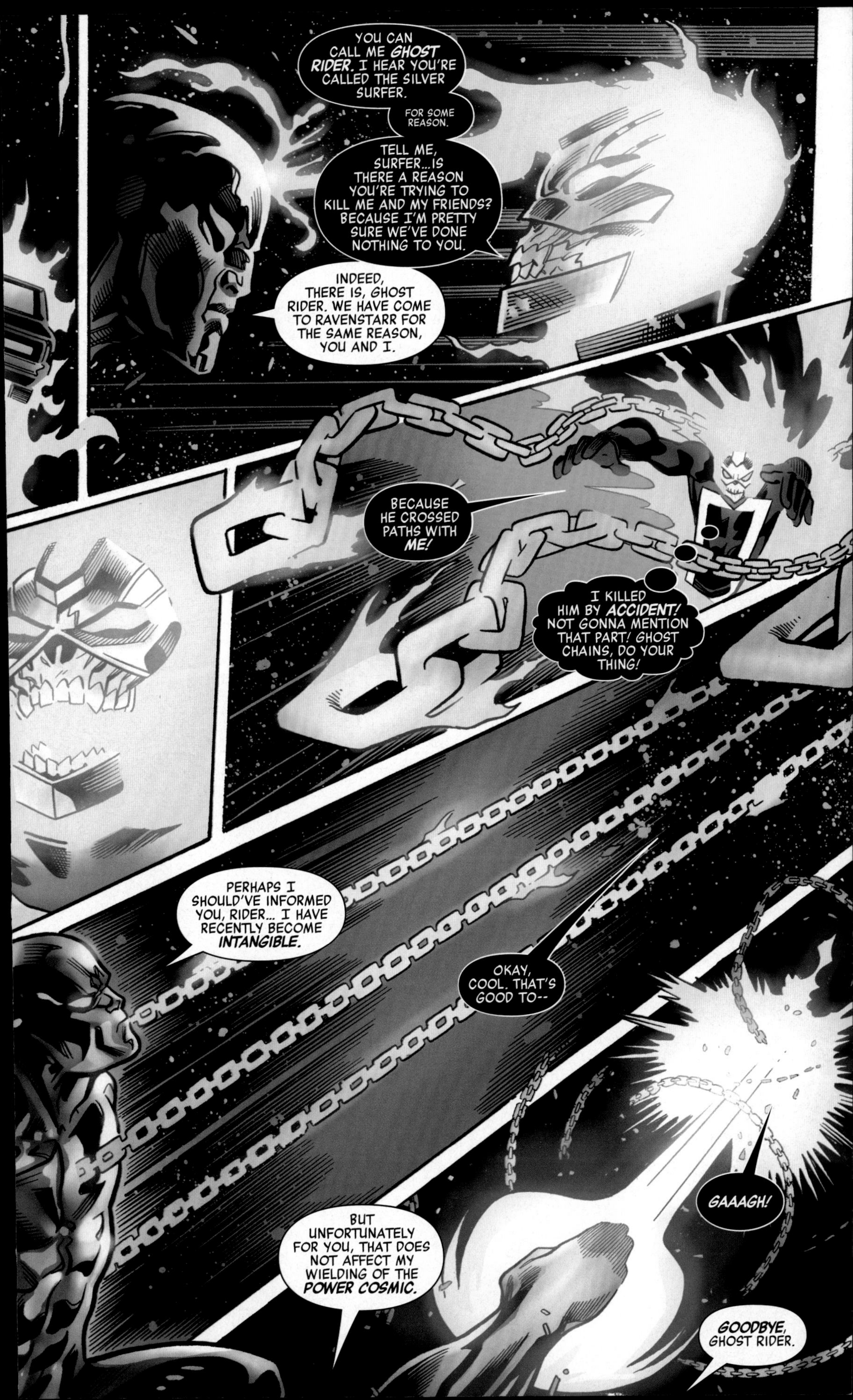
YOU CAN CALL ME GHOST RIDER. I HEAR YOU'RE CALLED THE SILVER SURFER.
FOR SOME REASON.
TELL ME, SURFER...IS THERE A REASON YOU'RE TRYING TO KILL ME AND MY FRIENDS? BECAUSE I'M PRETTY SURE WE'VE DONE NOTHING TO YOU.
INDEED, THERE IS, GHOST RIDER. WE HAVE COME TO RAVENSTARR FOR THE SAME REASON, YOU AND I.
BECAUSE HE CROSSED PATHS WITH ME!
I KILLED HIM BY ACCIDENT! NOT GONNA MENTION THAT PART! GHOST CHAINS, DO YOUR THING!
PERHAPS I SHOULD'VE INFORMED YOU, RIDER... I HAVE RECENTLY BECOME INTANGIBLE.
OKAY, COOL. THAT'S GOOD TO--
GAAAGH!
BUT UNFORTUNATELY FOR YOU, THAT DOES NOT AFFECT MY WIELDING OF THE POWER COSMIC.
GOODBYE, GHOST RIDER.

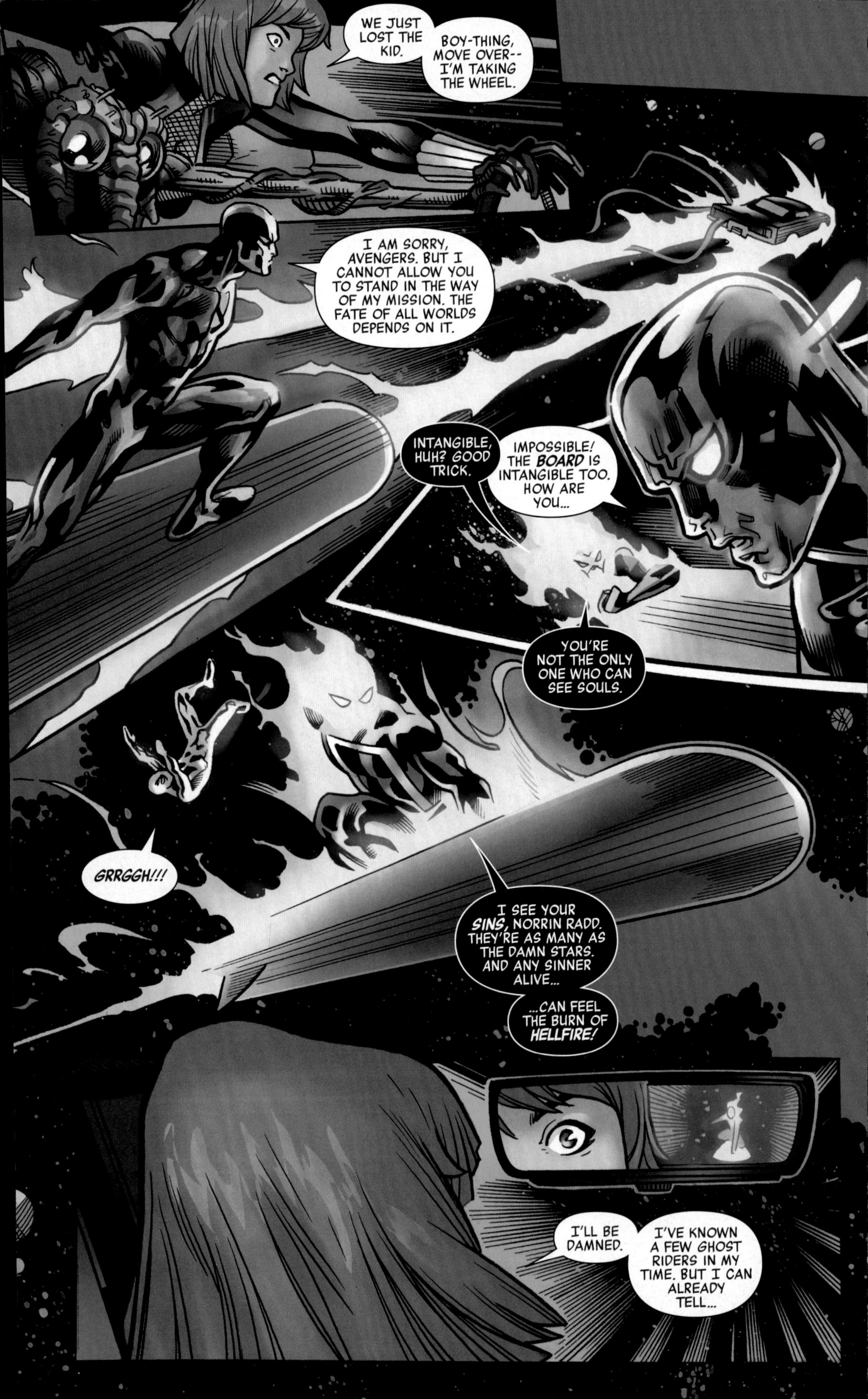
WE JUST LOST THE KID.
BOY-THING, MOVE OVER-- I'M TAKING THE WHEEL.
I AM SORRY, AVENGERS. BUT I CANNOT ALLOW YOU TO STAND IN THE WAY OF MY MISSION. THE FATE OF ALL WORLDS DEPENDS ON IT.
INTANGIBLE, HUH? GOOD TRICK.
IMPOSSIBLE! THE BOARD IS INTANGIBLE TOO. HOW ARE YOU...
YOU'RE NOT THE ONLY ONE WHO CAN SEE SOULS.
GRRGGH!!!
I SEE YOUR SINS, NORRIN RADD. THEY'RE AS MANY AS THE DAMN STARS. AND ANY SINNER ALIVE...
...CAN FEEL THE BURN OF HELLFIRE!
I'LL BE DAMNED.
I'VE KNOWN A FEW GHOST RIDERS IN MY TIME. BUT I CAN ALREADY TELL...

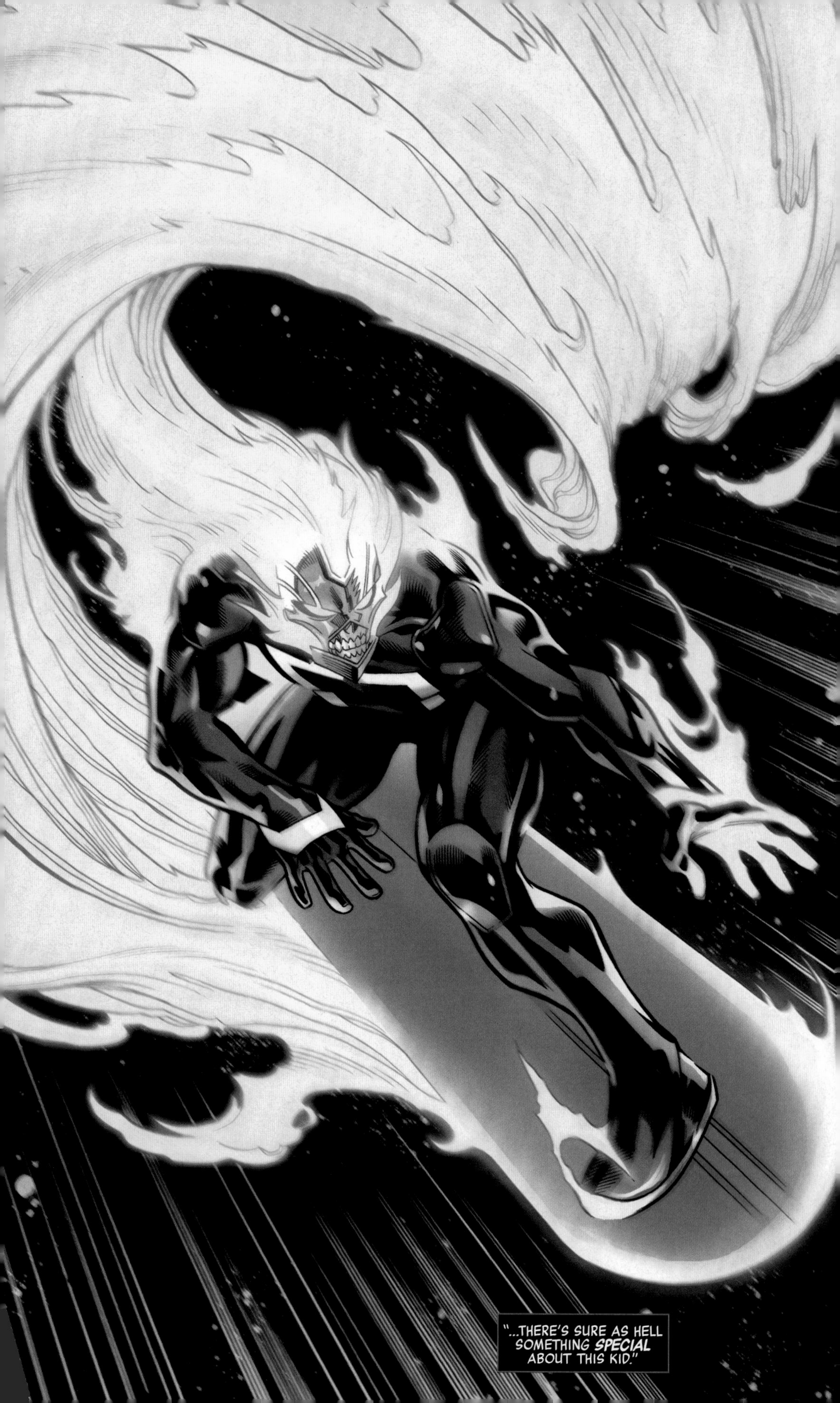
"...THERE'S SURE AS HELL SOMETHING *SPECIAL* ABOUT THIS KID."

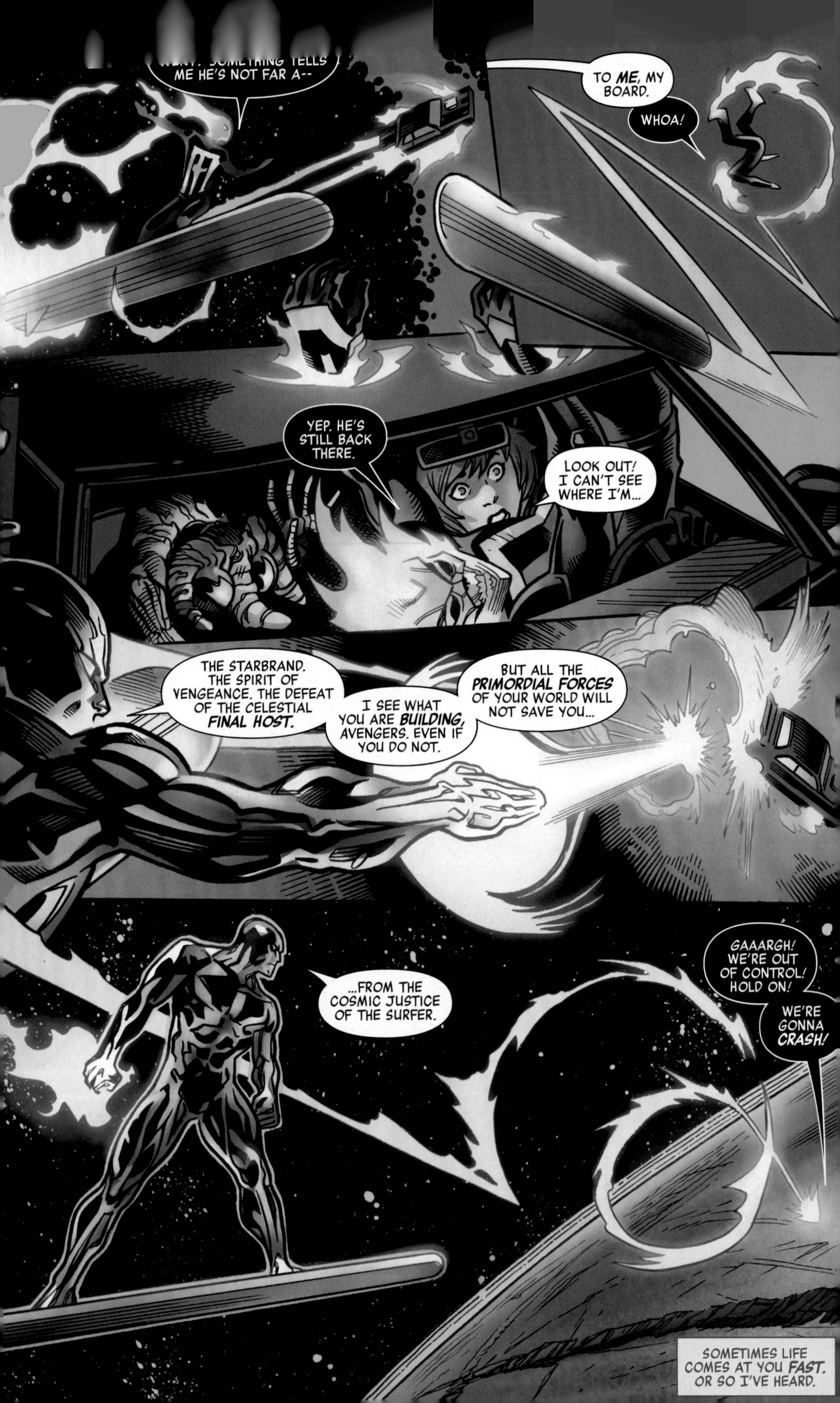
ME HE'S NOT FAR A--
TO ME, MY BOARD.
WHOA!
YEP. HE'S STILL BACK THERE.
LOOK OUT! I CAN'T SEE WHERE I'M...
THE STARBRAND. THE SPIRIT OF VENGEANCE. THE DEFEAT OF THE CELESTIAL FINAL HOST.
I SEE WHAT YOU ARE BUILDING, AVENGERS. EVEN IF YOU DO NOT.
BUT ALL THE PRIMORDIAL FORCES OF YOUR WORLD WILL NOT SAVE YOU...
...FROM THE COSMIC JUSTICE OF THE SURFER.
GAAARGH! WE'RE OUT OF CONTROL! HOLD ON!
WE'RE GONNA CRASH!
SOMETIMES LIFE COMES AT YOU FAST. OR SO I'VE HEARD.

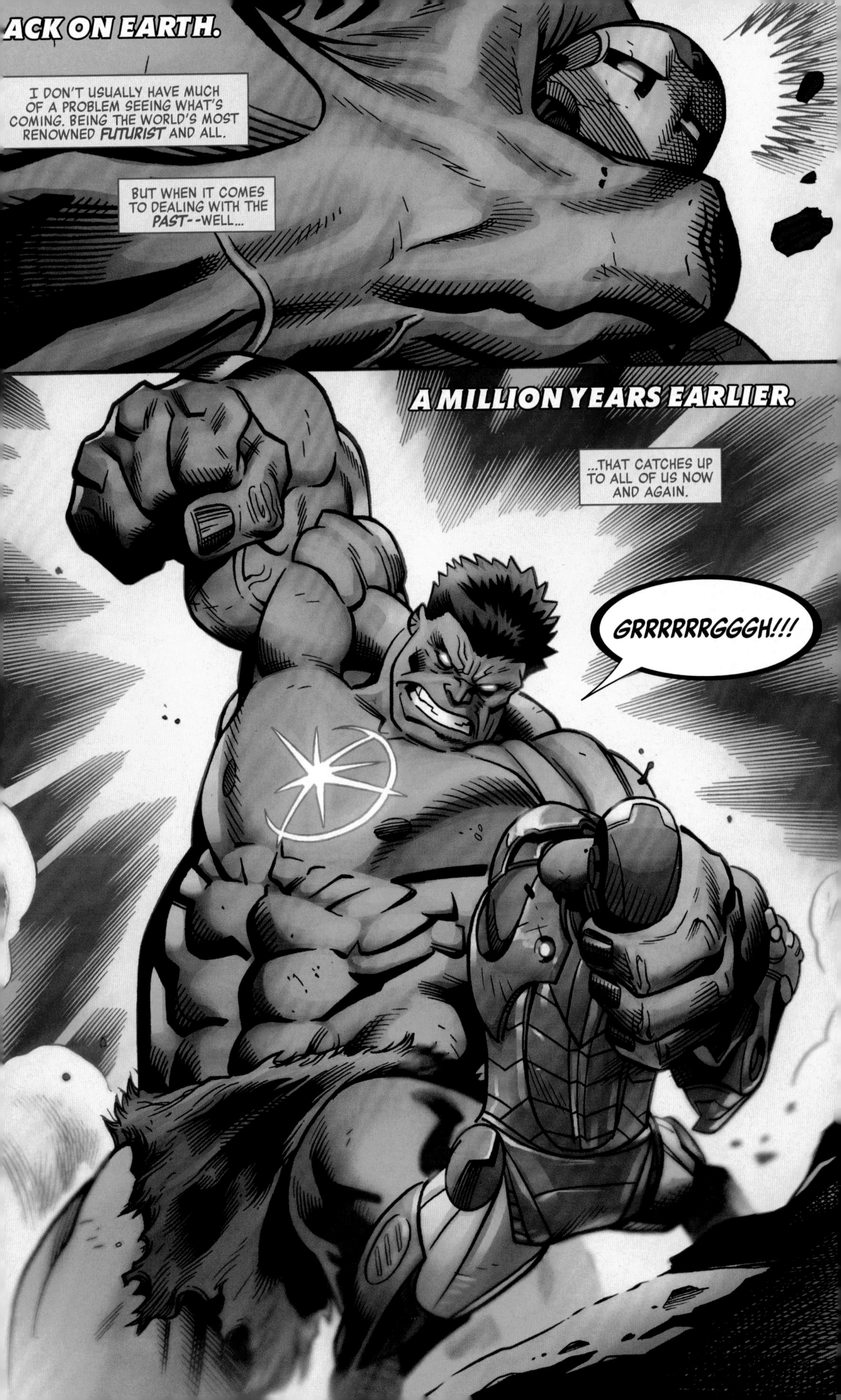
ACK ON EARTH.
I DON'T USUALLY HAVE MUCH OF A PROBLEM SEEING WHAT'S COMING. BEING THE WORLD'S MOST RENOWNED FUTURIST AND ALL.
BUT WHEN IT COMES TO DEALING WITH THE PAST--WELL...
A MILLION YEARS EARLIER.
...THAT CATCHES UP TO ALL OF US NOW AND AGAIN.
GRRRRRRGGGH!!!

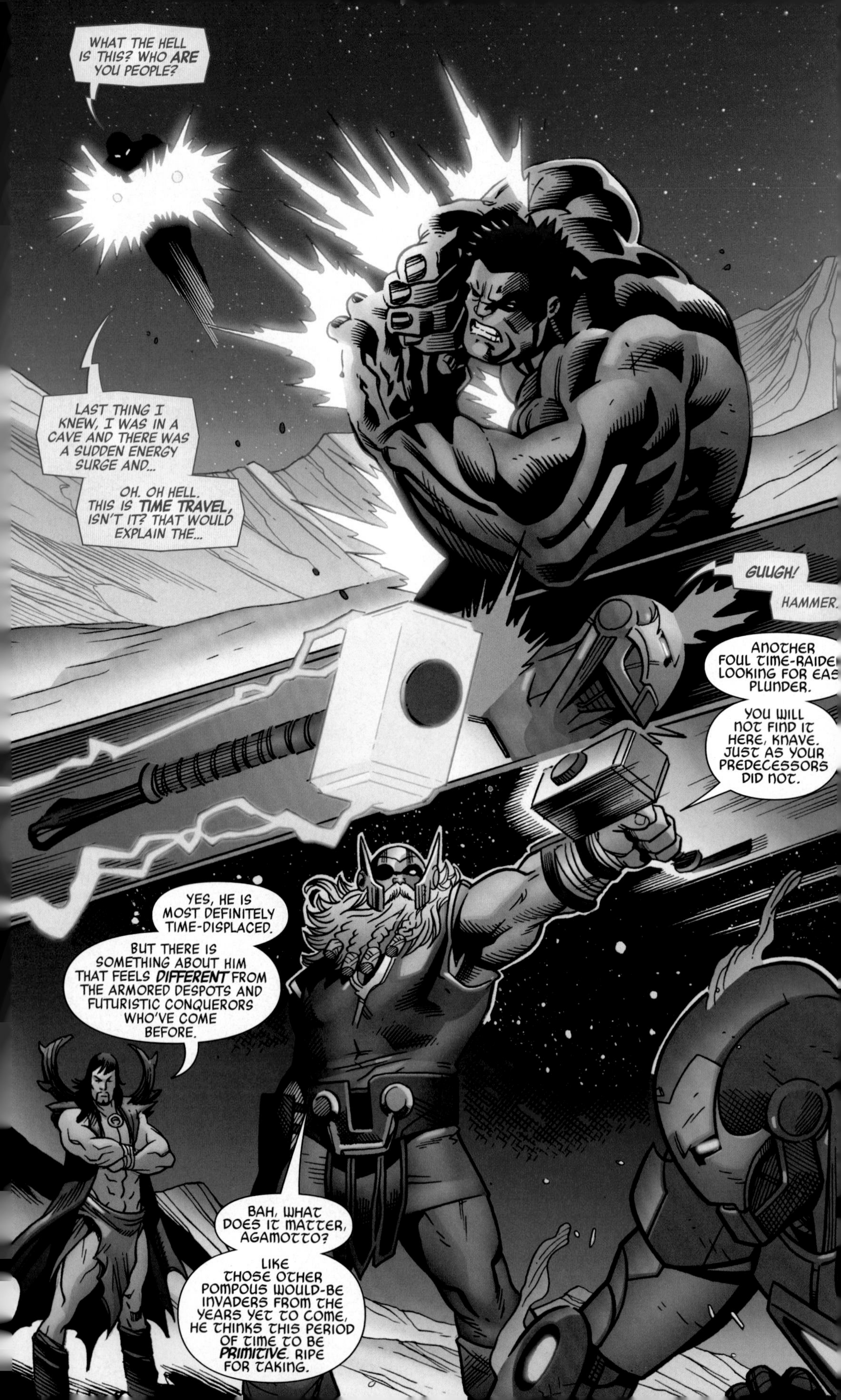

WHAT THE HELL IS THIS? WHO ARE YOU PEOPLE?
LAST THING I KNEW, I WAS IN A CAVE AND THERE WAS A SUDDEN ENERGY SURGE AND...
OH. OH HELL. THIS IS TIME TRAVEL, ISN'T IT? THAT WOULD EXPLAIN THE...
GUUGH!
HAMMER.
ANOTHER FOUL TIME-RAIDE LOOKING FOR EAS PLUNDER.
YOU WILL NOT FIND IT HERE, KNAVE. JUST AS YOUR PREDECESSORS DID NOT.
YES, HE IS MOST DEFINITELY TIME-DISPLACED.
BUT THERE IS SOMETHING ABOUT HIM THAT FEELS DIFFERENT FROM THE ARMORED DESPOTS AND FUTURISTIC CONQUERORS WHO'VE COME BEFORE.
BAH, WHAT DOES IT MATTER, AGAMOTTO?
LIKE THOSE OTHER POMPOUS WOULD-BE INVADERS FROM THE YEARS YET TO COME, HE THINKS THIS PERIOD OF TIME TO BE PRIMITIVE. RIPE FOR TAKING.

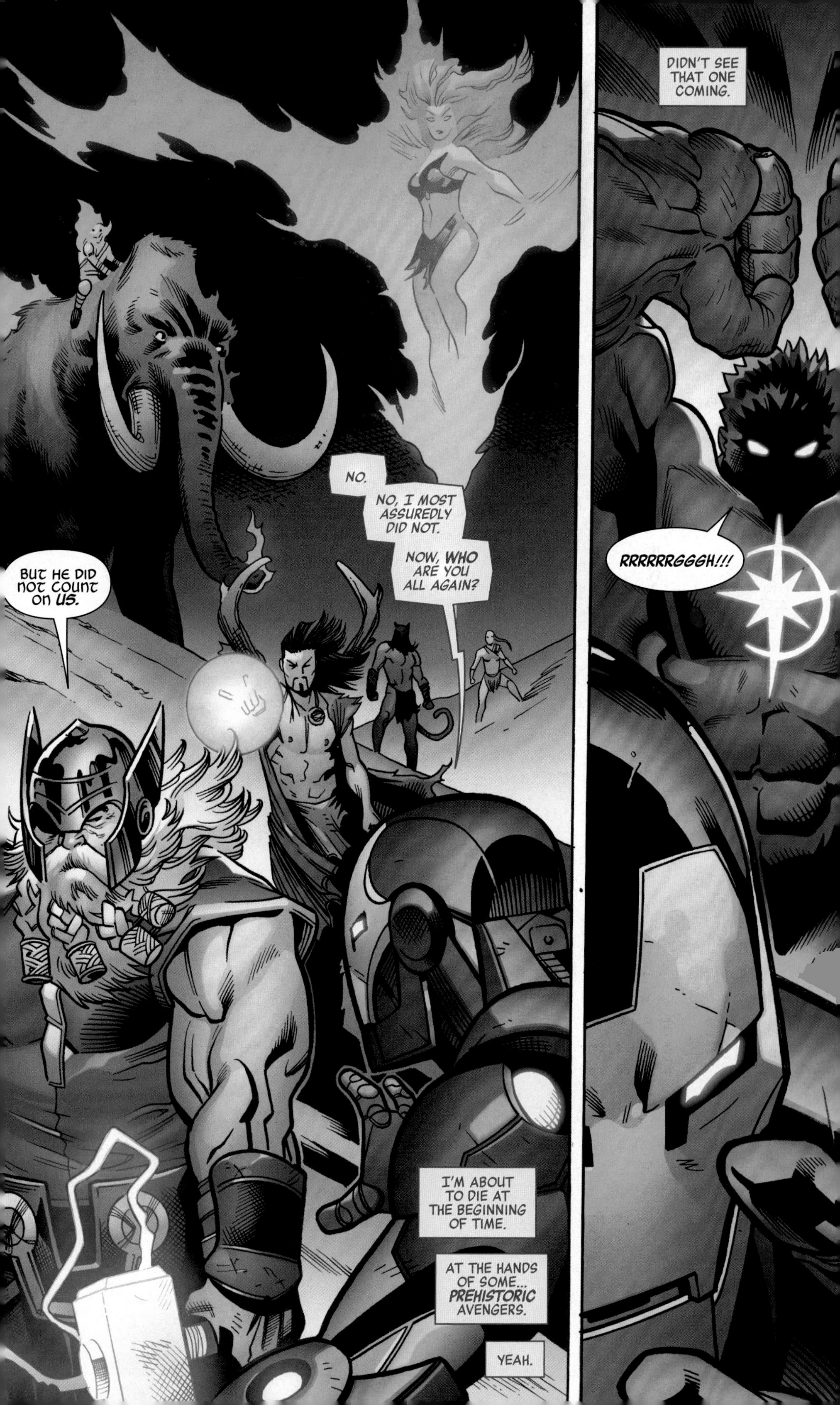

BUT HE DID NOT COUNT ON US.
NO.
NO, I MOST ASSUREDLY DID NOT.
NOW, WHO ARE YOU ALL AGAIN?
I'M ABOUT TO DIE AT THE BEGINNING OF TIME.
AT THE HANDS OF SOME... PREHISTORIC AVENGERS.
YEAH.
DIDN'T SEE THAT ONE COMING.
RRRRRRGGGH!!!

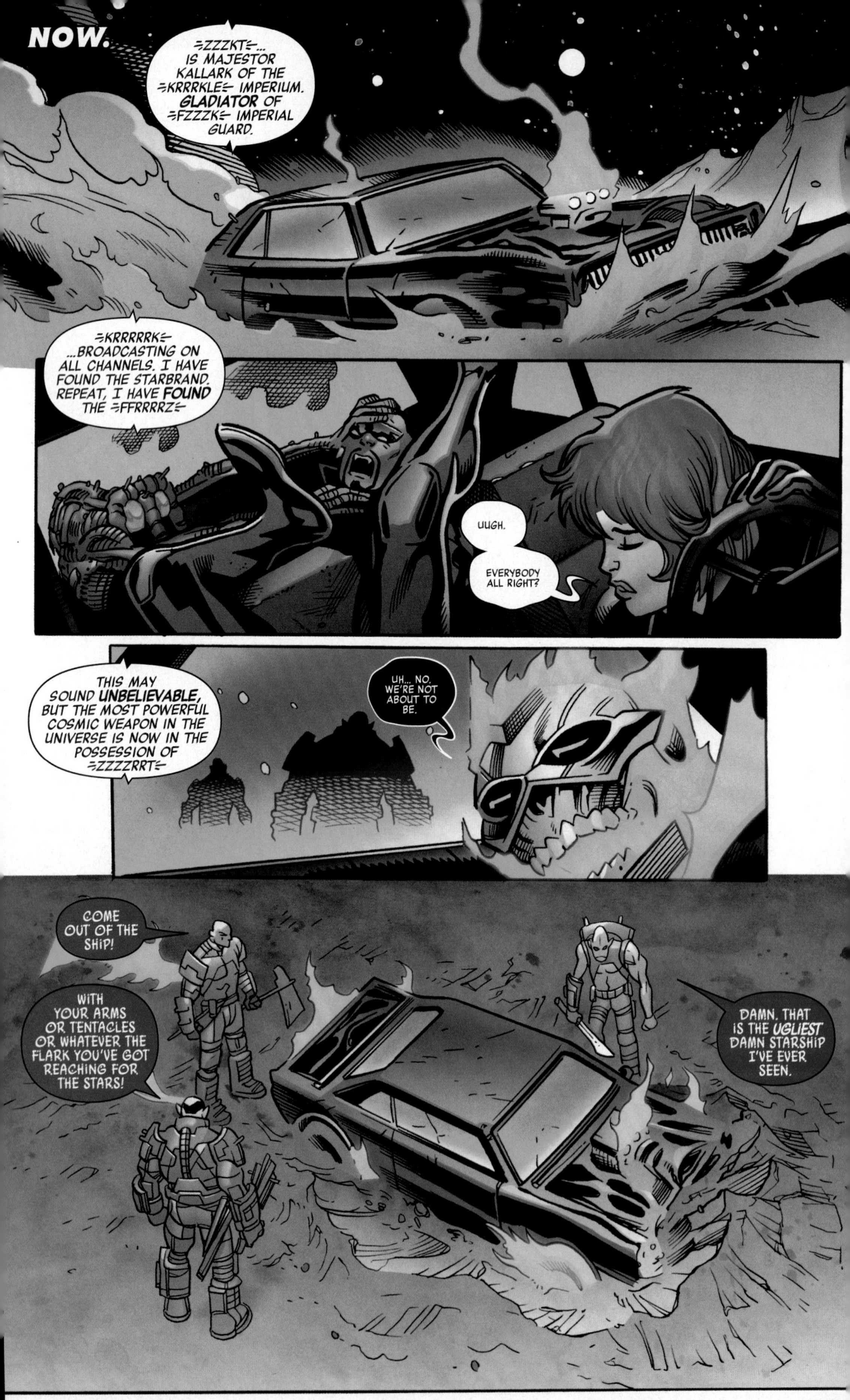
NOW.
=ZZZKT=... IS MAJESTOR KALLARK OF THE =KRRRKLE= IMPERIUM. GLADIATOR OF =FZZZK= IMPERIAL GUARD.
=KRRRRRK= ...BROADCASTING ON ALL CHANNELS. I HAVE FOUND THE STARBRAND. REPEAT, I HAVE FOUND THE =FFRRRRZ=
UUGH.
EVERYBODY ALL RIGHT?
THIS MAY SOUND UNBELIEVABLE, BUT THE MOST POWERFUL COSMIC WEAPON IN THE UNIVERSE IS NOW IN THE POSSESSION OF =ZZZZRRT=
UH... NO. WE'RE NOT ABOUT TO BE.
COME OUT OF THE SHIP!
WITH YOUR ARMS OR TENTACLES OR WHATEVER THE FLARK YOU'VE GOT REACHING FOR THE STARS!
DAMN. THAT IS THE UGLIEST DAMN STARSHIP I'VE EVER SEEN.

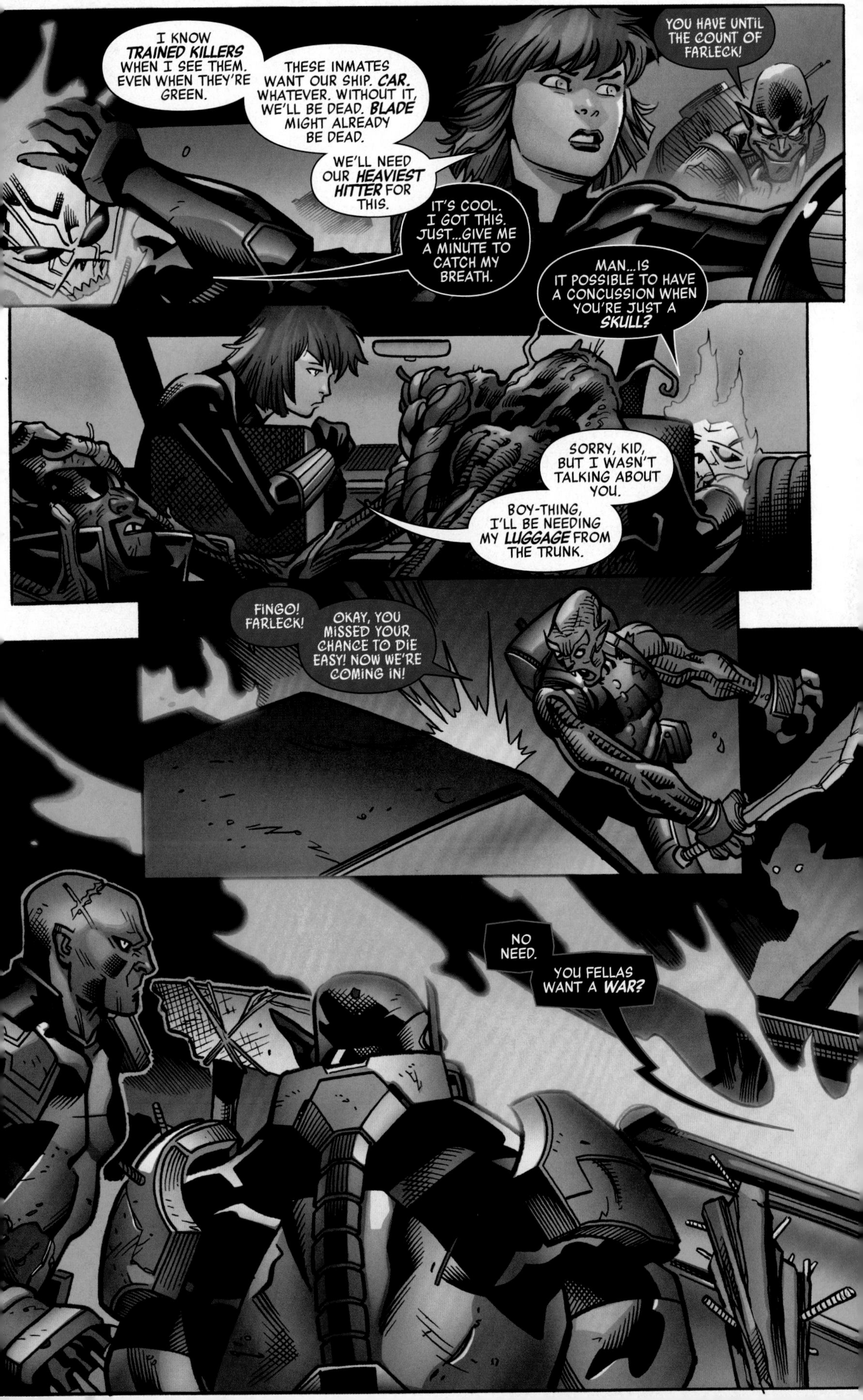
I KNOW TRAINED KILLERS WHEN I SEE THEM. EVEN WHEN THEY'RE GREEN.
THESE INMATES WANT OUR SHIP. CAR. WHATEVER. WITHOUT IT, WE'LL BE DEAD. BLADE MIGHT ALREADY BE DEAD.
WE'LL NEED OUR HEAVIEST HITTER FOR THIS.
YOU HAVE UNTIL THE COUNT OF FARLECK!
IT'S COOL. I GOT THIS. JUST...GIVE ME A MINUTE TO CATCH MY BREATH.
MAN...IS IT POSSIBLE TO HAVE A CONCUSSION WHEN YOU'RE JUST A SKULL?
SORRY, KID, BUT I WASN'T TALKING ABOUT YOU.
BOY-THING, I'LL BE NEEDING MY LUGGAGE FROM THE TRUNK.
FINGO! FARLECK!
OKAY, YOU MISSED YOUR CHANCE TO DIE EASY! NOW WE'RE COMING IN!
NO NEED.
YOU FELLAS WANT A WAR?

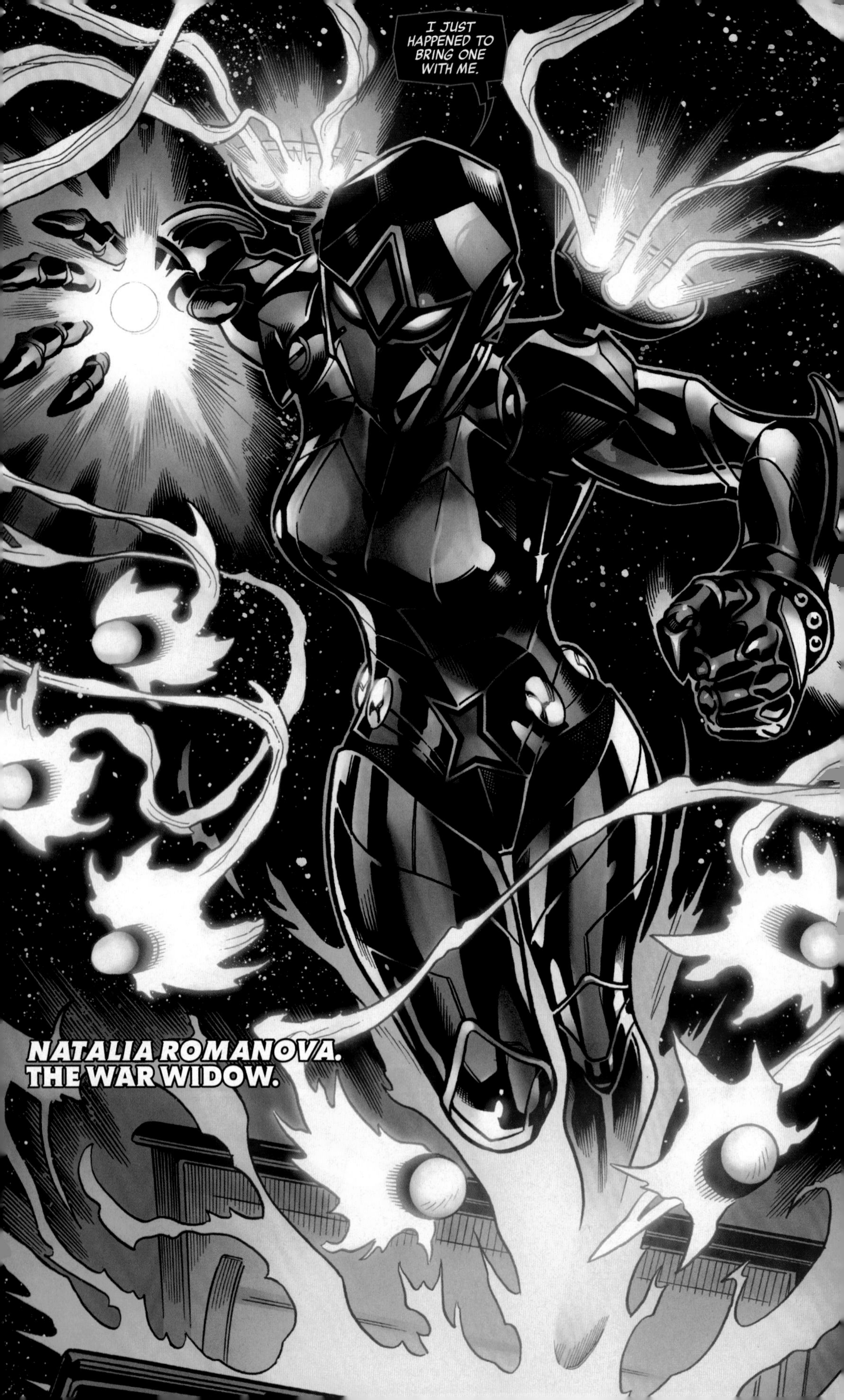
I JUST HAPPENED TO BRING ONE WITH ME.
NATALIA ROMANOVA. THE WAR WIDOW.

29 STARBRAND REBORN PART 3
THE BATTLE FOR THE BRAND

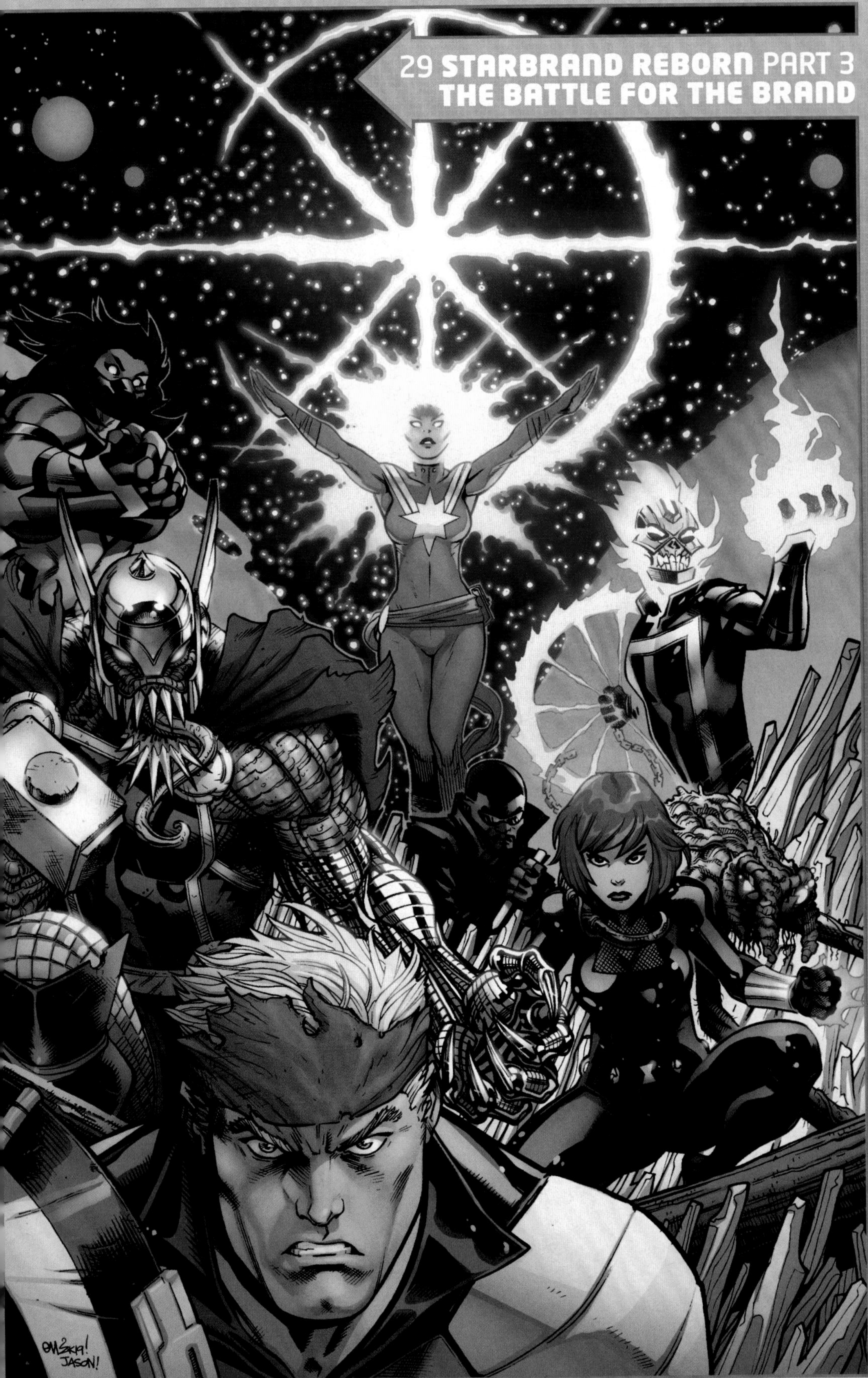

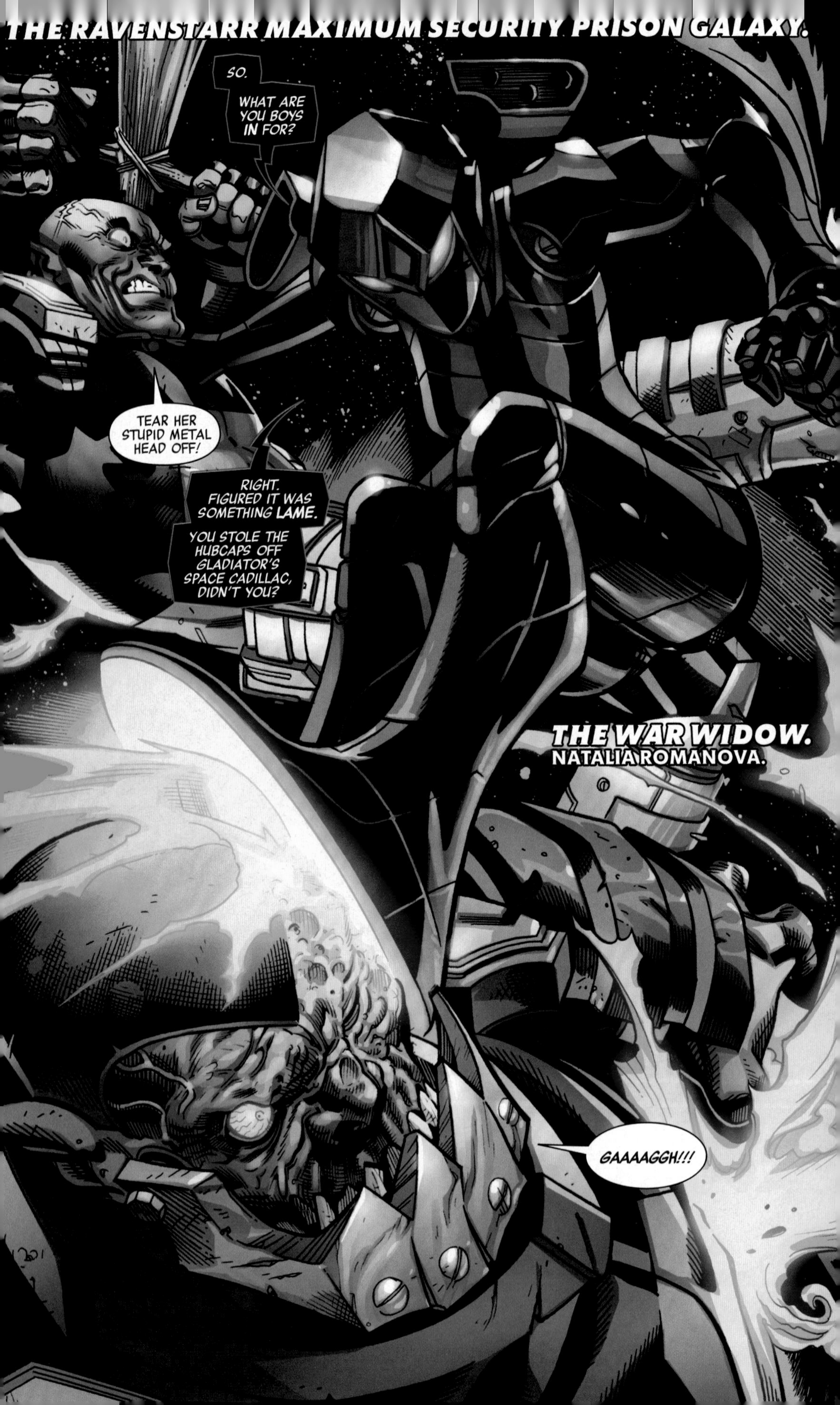
THE RAVENSTARR MAXIMUM SECURITY PRISON GALAXY.
SO.
WHAT ARE YOU BOYS IN FOR?
TEAR HER STUPID METAL HEAD OFF!
RIGHT. FIGURED IT WAS SOMETHING LAME.
YOU STOLE THE HUBCAPS OFF GLADIATOR'S SPACE CADILLAC, DIDN'T YOU?
THE WAR WIDOW.
NATALIA ROMANOVA.
GAAAAAGGH!!!

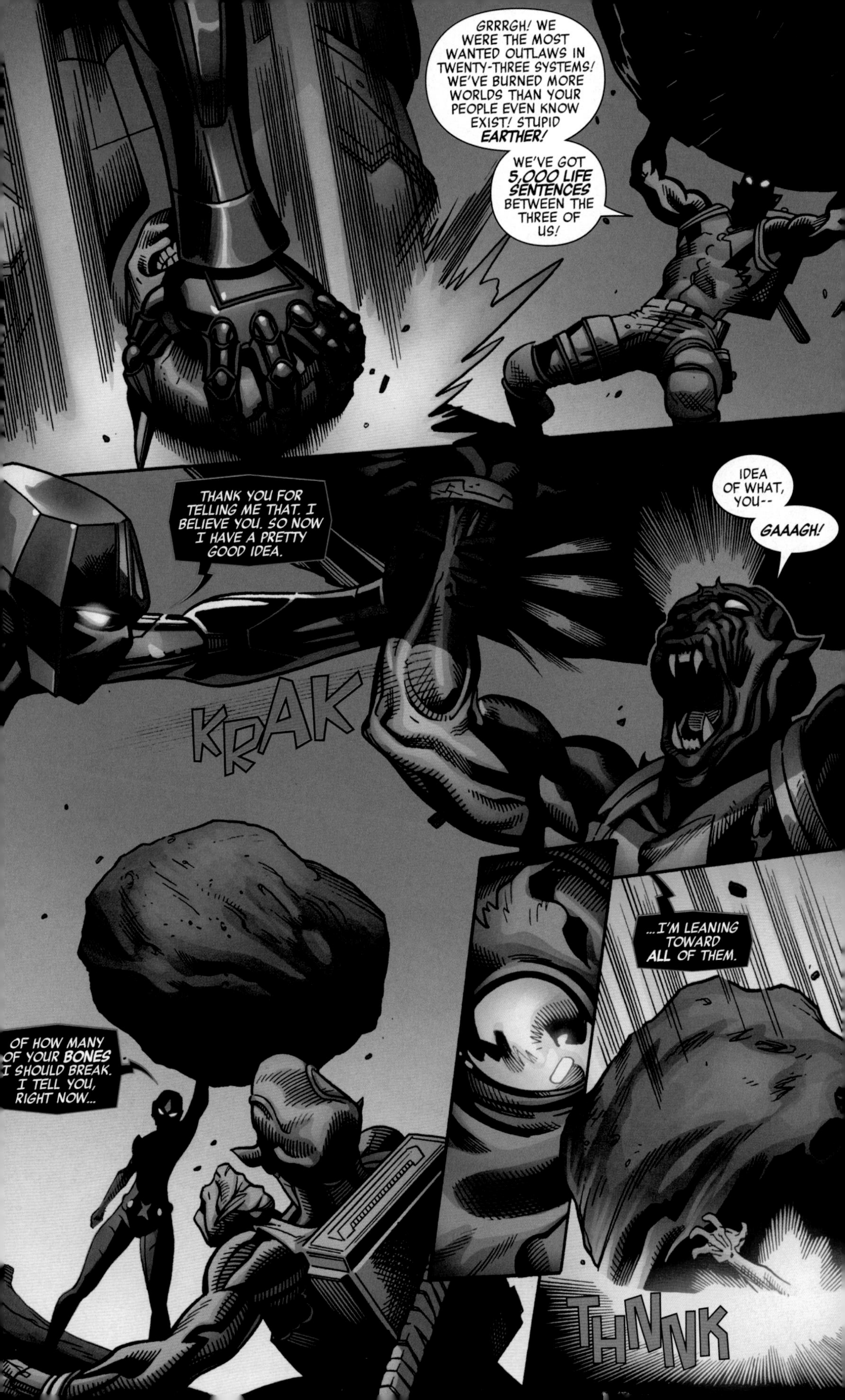
GRRRGH! WE WERE THE MOST WANTED OUTLAWS IN TWENTY-THREE SYSTEMS! WE'VE BURNED MORE WORLDS THAN YOUR PEOPLE EVEN KNOW EXIST! STUPID EARTHER!
WE'VE GOT 5,000 LIFE SENTENCES BETWEEN THE THREE OF US!
THANK YOU FOR TELLING ME THAT. I BELIEVE YOU. SO NOW I HAVE A PRETTY GOOD IDEA.
IDEA OF WHAT, YOU--
GAAAGH!
KRAK
OF HOW MANY OF YOUR BONES I SHOULD BREAK. I TELL YOU, RIGHT NOW...
...I'M LEANING TOWARD ALL OF THEM.
THNNK

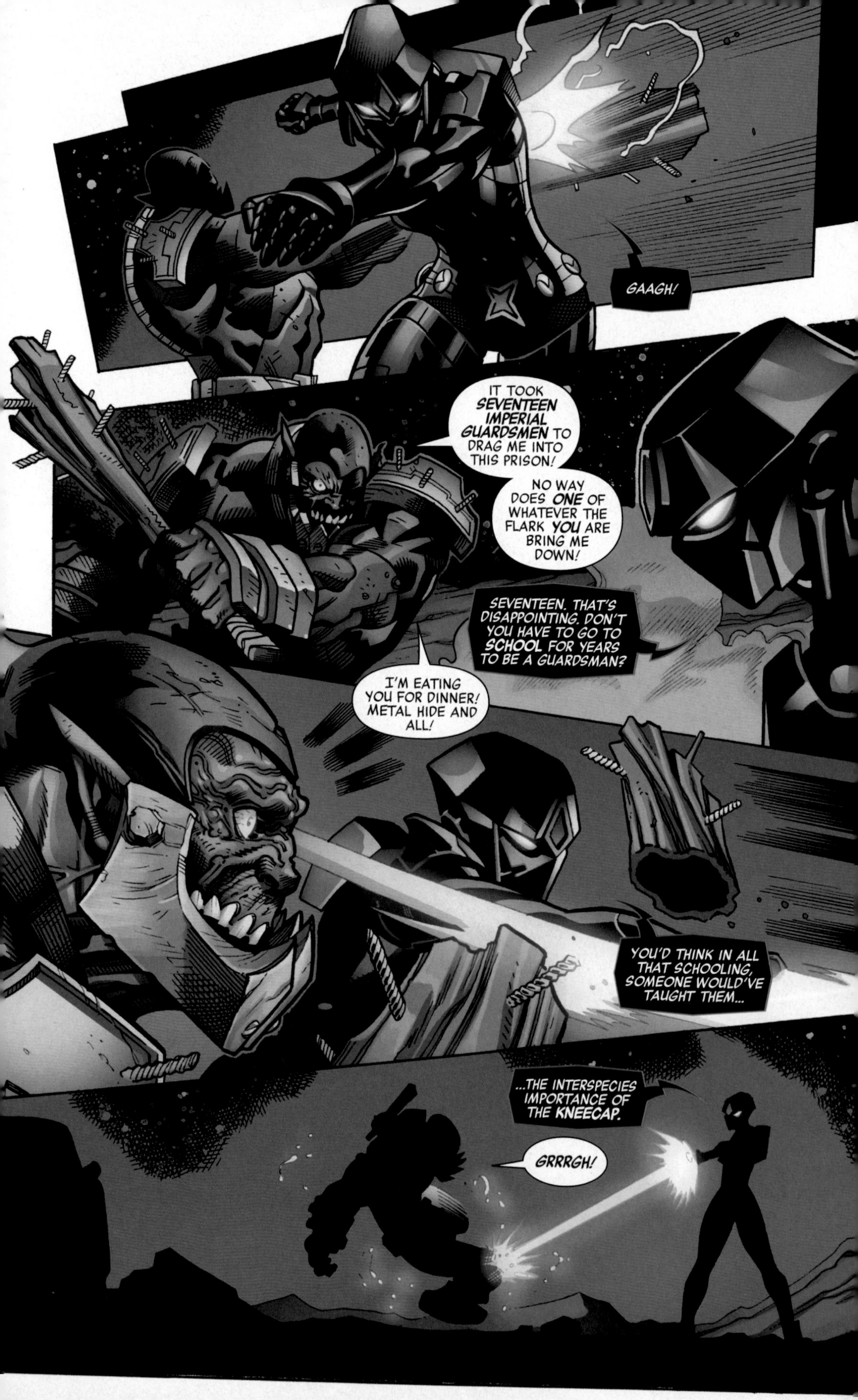
GAAGH!
IT TOOK SEVENTEEN IMPERIAL GUARDSMEN TO DRAG ME INTO THIS PRISON!
NO WAY DOES ONE OF WHATEVER THE FLARK YOU ARE BRING ME DOWN!
SEVENTEEN. THAT'S DISAPPOINTING. DON'T YOU HAVE TO GO TO SCHOOL FOR YEARS TO BE A GUARDSMAN?
I'M EATING YOU FOR DINNER! METAL HIDE AND ALL!
YOU'D THINK IN ALL THAT SCHOOLING, SOMEONE WOULD'VE TAUGHT THEM...
...THE INTERSPECIES IMPORTANCE OF THE KNEECAP.
GRRRGH!

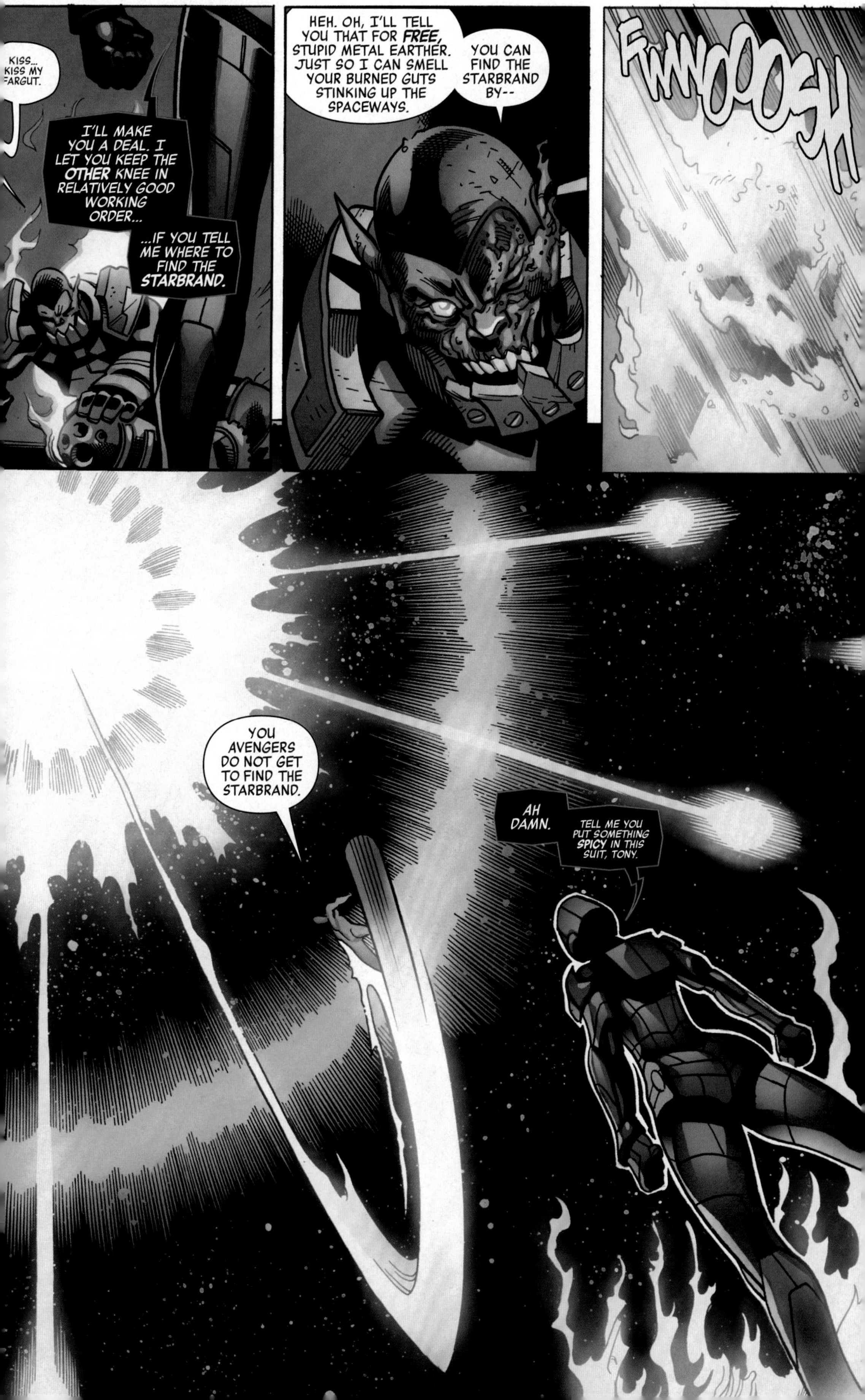
KISS... KISS MY FARGUT.
I'LL MAKE YOU A DEAL. I LET YOU KEEP THE OTHER KNEE IN RELATIVELY GOOD WORKING ORDER...
...IF YOU TELL ME WHERE TO FIND THE STARBRAND.
HEH. OH, I'LL TELL YOU THAT FOR FREE, STUPID METAL EARTHER. JUST SO I CAN SMELL YOUR BURNED GUTS STINKING UP THE SPACEWAYS.
YOU CAN FIND THE STARBRAND BY--
FWNOOOOSH
YOU AVENGERS DO NOT GET TO FIND THE STARBRAND.
AH DAMN.
TELL ME YOU PUT SOMETHING SPICY IN THIS SUIT, TONY.

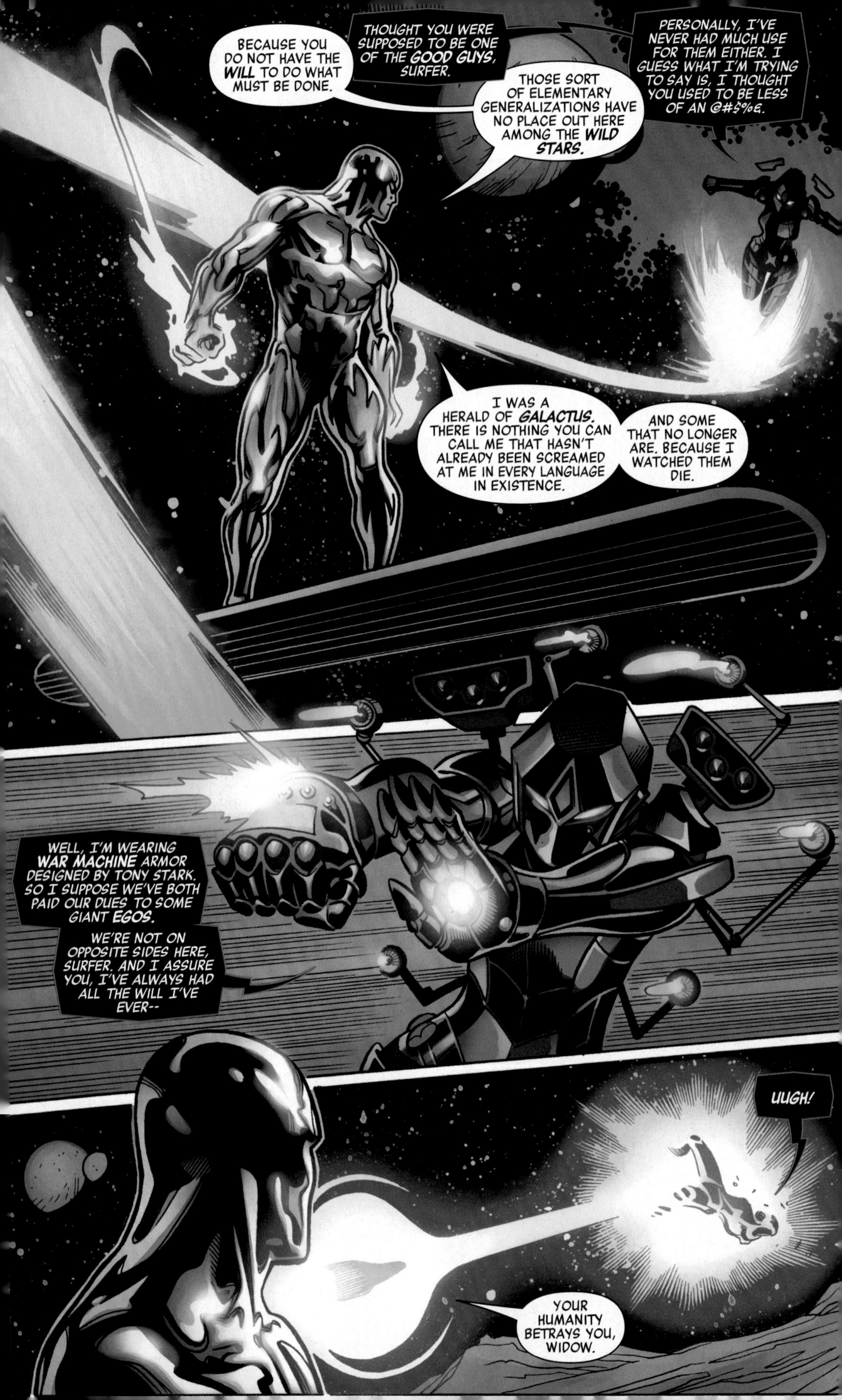
BECAUSE YOU DO NOT HAVE THE **WILL** TO DO WHAT MUST BE DONE.
THOUGHT YOU WERE SUPPOSED TO BE ONE OF THE **GOOD GUYS**, SURFER.
THOSE SORT OF ELEMENTARY GENERALIZATIONS HAVE NO PLACE OUT HERE AMONG THE **WILD STARS.**
PERSONALLY, I'VE NEVER HAD MUCH USE FOR THEM EITHER. I GUESS WHAT I'M TRYING TO SAY IS, I THOUGHT YOU USED TO BE LESS OF AN @#$%&.
I WAS A HERALD OF **GALACTUS.** THERE IS NOTHING YOU CAN CALL ME THAT HASN'T ALREADY BEEN SCREAMED AT ME IN EVERY LANGUAGE IN EXISTENCE.
AND SOME THAT NO LONGER ARE. BECAUSE I WATCHED THEM DIE.
WELL, I'M WEARING **WAR MACHINE** ARMOR DESIGNED BY TONY STARK. SO I SUPPOSE WE'VE BOTH PAID OUR DUES TO SOME GIANT **EGOS.**
WE'RE NOT ON OPPOSITE SIDES HERE, SURFER. AND I ASSURE YOU, I'VE ALWAYS HAD ALL THE WILL I'VE EVER--
UUGH!
YOUR HUMANITY BETRAYS YOU, WIDOW.

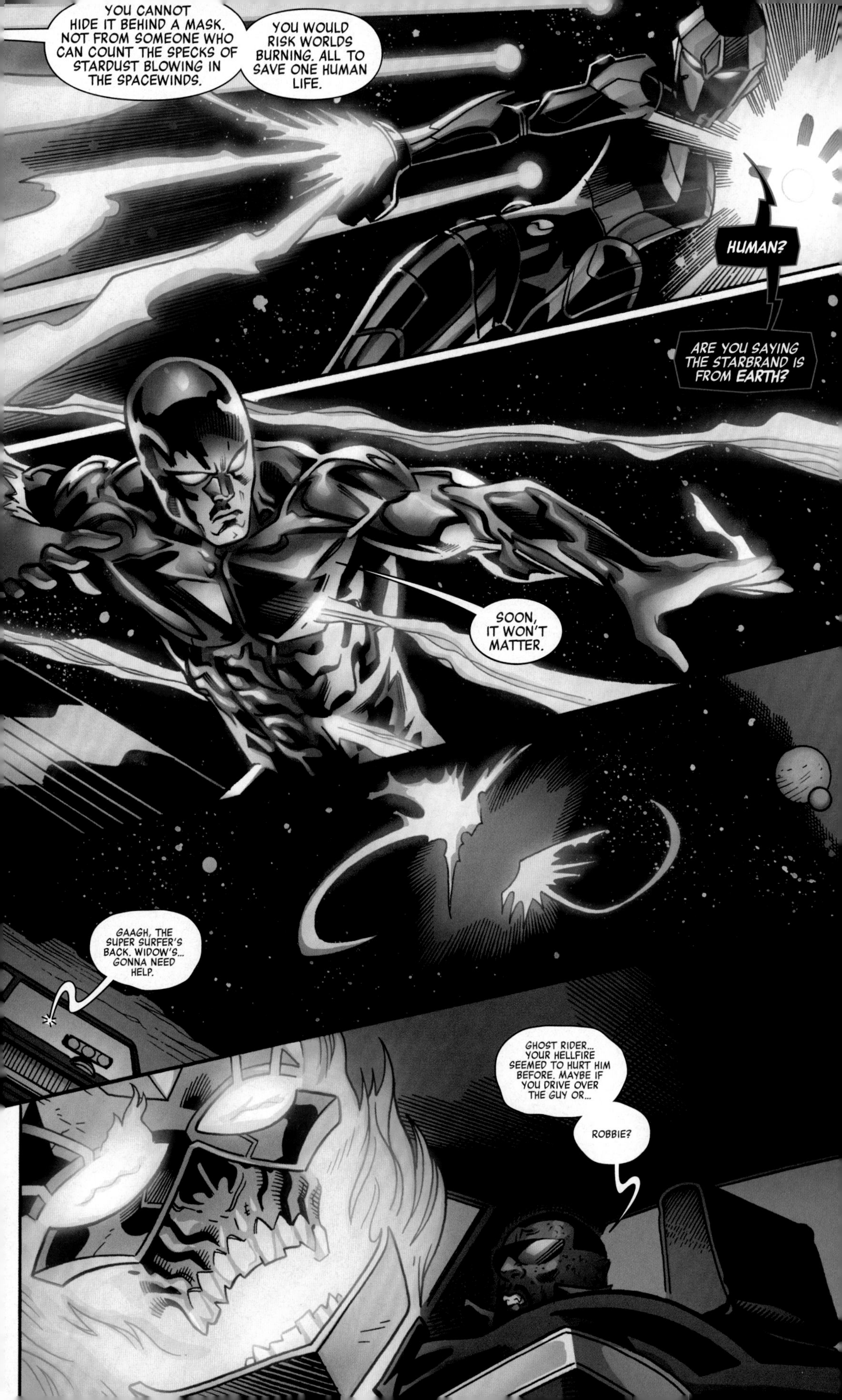

YOU CANNOT HIDE IT BEHIND A MASK. NOT FROM SOMEONE WHO CAN COUNT THE SPECKS OF STARDUST BLOWING IN THE SPACEWINDS.
YOU WOULD RISK WORLDS BURNING. ALL TO SAVE ONE HUMAN LIFE.
HUMAN?
ARE YOU SAYING THE STARBRAND IS FROM EARTH?
SOON, IT WON'T MATTER.
GAAGH, THE SUPER SURFER'S BACK. WIDOW'S... GONNA NEED HELP.
GHOST RIDER... YOUR HELLFIRE SEEMED TO HURT HIM BEFORE. MAYBE IF YOU DRIVE OVER THE GUY OR...
ROBBIE?

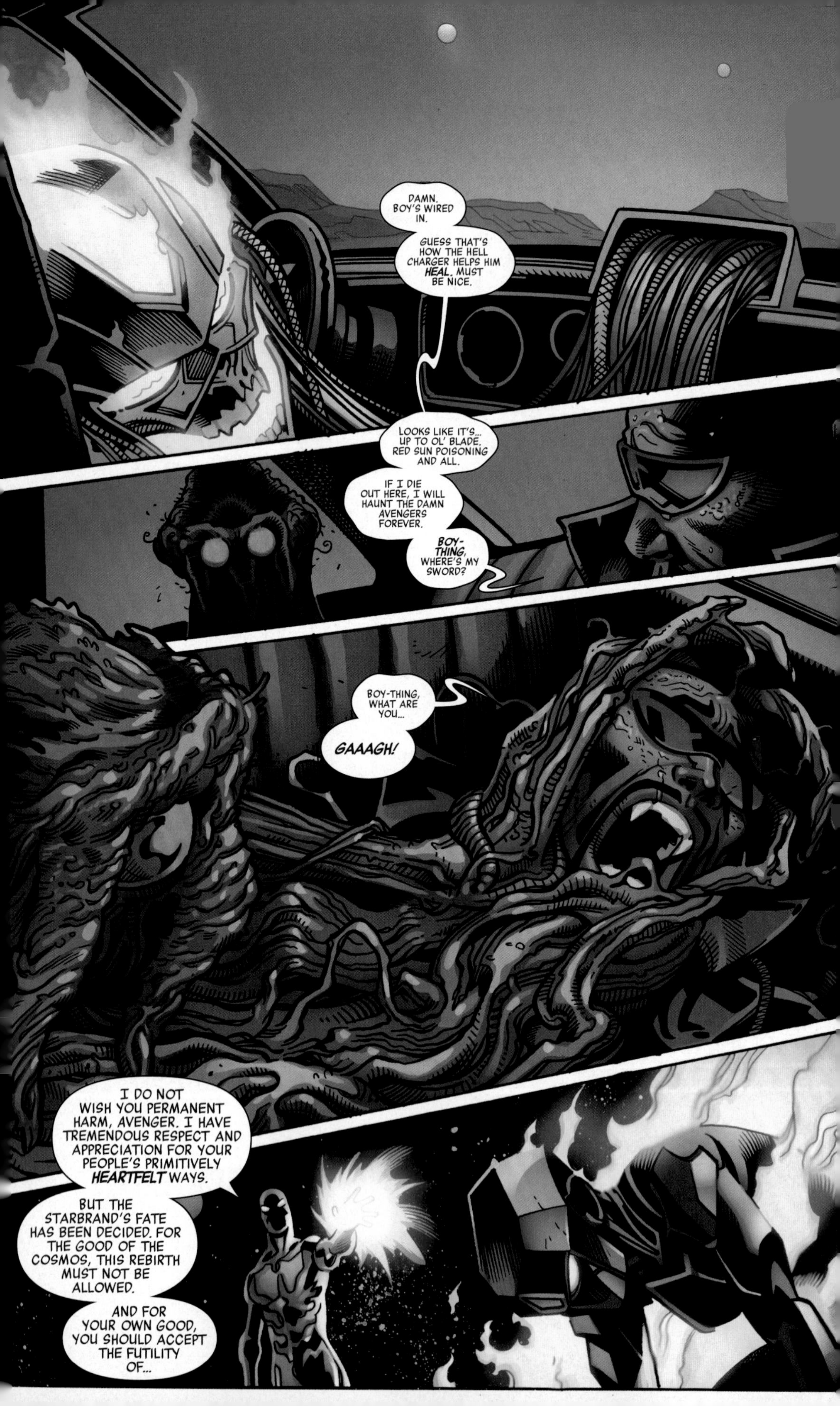

DAMN. BOY'S WIRED IN.
GUESS THAT'S HOW THE HELL CHARGER HELPS HIM HEAL. MUST BE NICE.
LOOKS LIKE IT'S... UP TO OL' BLADE. RED SUN POISONING AND ALL.
IF I DIE OUT HERE, I WILL HAUNT THE DAMN AVENGERS FOREVER.
BOY-THING, WHERE'S MY SWORD?
BOY-THING, WHAT ARE YOU...
GAAAGH!
I DO NOT WISH YOU PERMANENT HARM, AVENGER. I HAVE TREMENDOUS RESPECT AND APPRECIATION FOR YOUR PEOPLE'S PRIMITIVELY HEARTFELT WAYS.
BUT THE STARBRAND'S FATE HAS BEEN DECIDED. FOR THE GOOD OF THE COSMOS, THIS REBIRTH MUST NOT BE ALLOWED.
AND FOR YOUR OWN GOOD, YOU SHOULD ACCEPT THE FUTILITY OF...

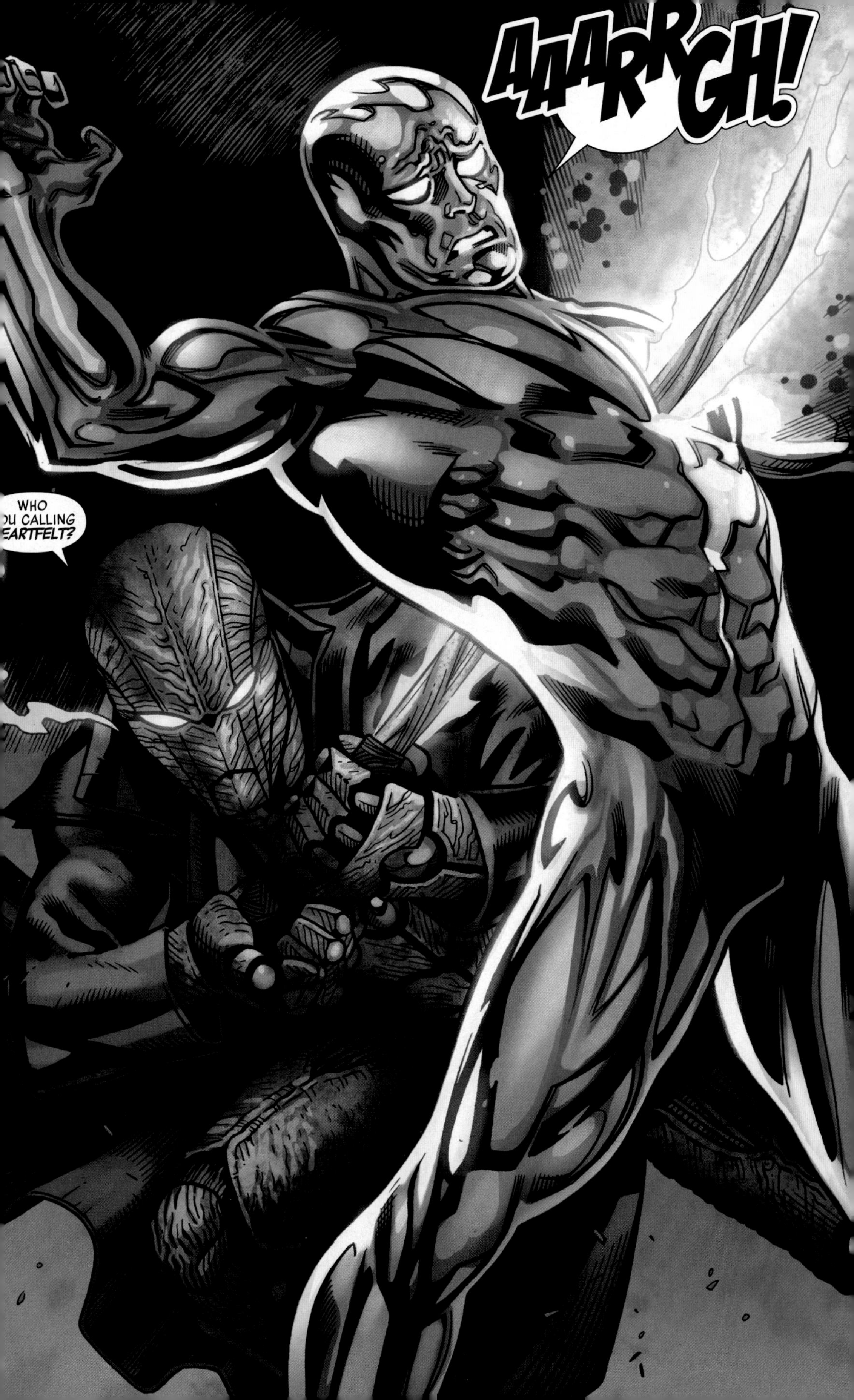
AAARRGH!
WHO OU CALLING EARTFELT?

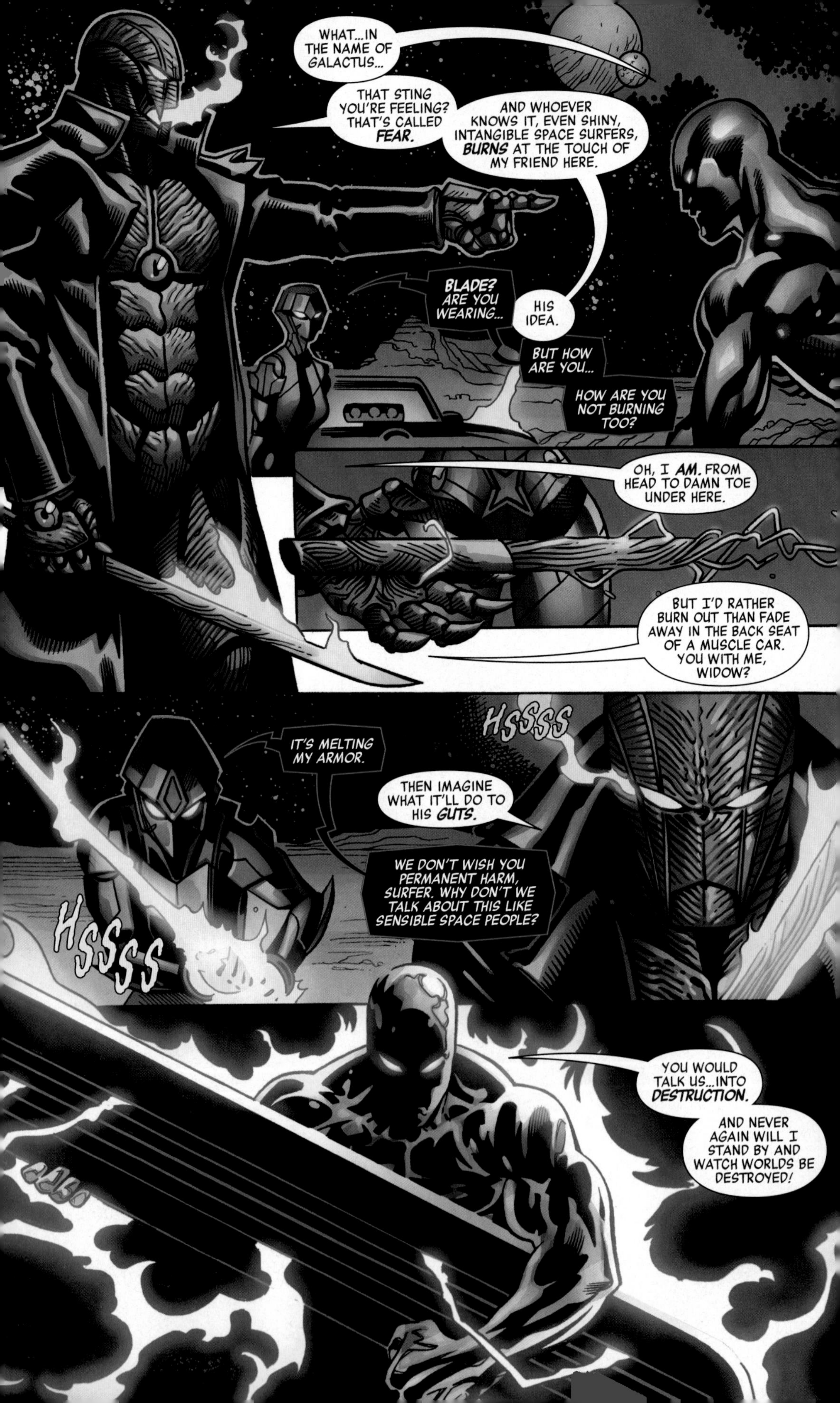
WHAT...IN THE NAME OF GALACTUS...
THAT STING YOU'RE FEELING? THAT'S CALLED FEAR.
AND WHOEVER KNOWS IT, EVEN SHINY, INTANGIBLE SPACE SURFERS, BURNS AT THE TOUCH OF MY FRIEND HERE.
BLADE? ARE YOU WEARING...
HIS IDEA.
BUT HOW ARE YOU...
HOW ARE YOU NOT BURNING TOO?
OH, I AM. FROM HEAD TO DAMN TOE UNDER HERE.
BUT I'D RATHER BURN OUT THAN FADE AWAY IN THE BACK SEAT OF A MUSCLE CAR. YOU WITH ME, WIDOW?
HSSSS
IT'S MELTING MY ARMOR.
THEN IMAGINE WHAT IT'LL DO TO HIS GUTS.
WE DON'T WISH YOU PERMANENT HARM, SURFER. WHY DON'T WE TALK ABOUT THIS LIKE SENSIBLE SPACE PEOPLE?
HSSSSS
YOU WOULD TALK US...INTO DESTRUCTION.
AND NEVER AGAIN WILL I STAND BY AND WATCH WORLDS BE DESTROYED!

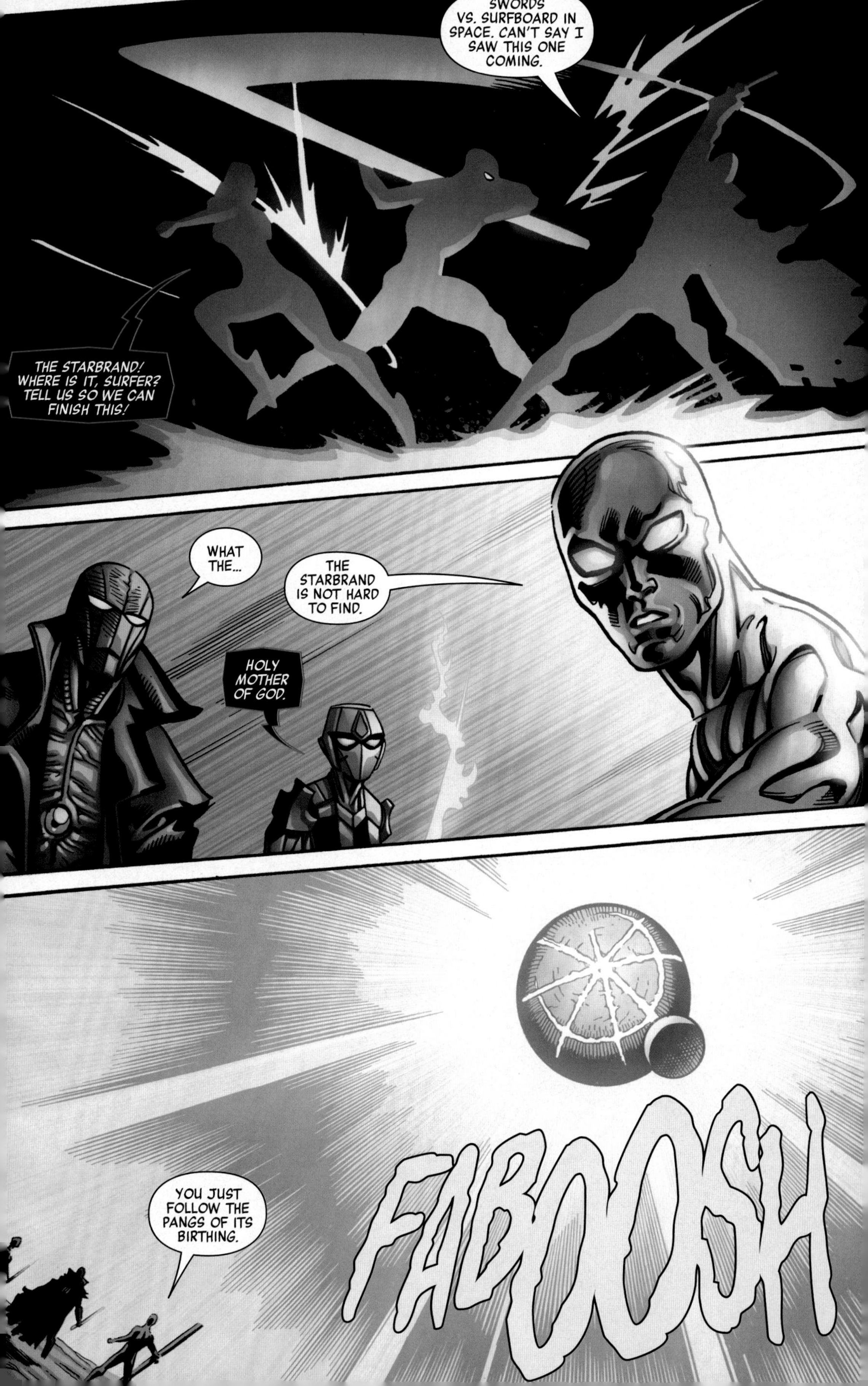
SWORDS VS. SURFBOARD IN SPACE. CAN'T SAY I SAW THIS ONE COMING.
THE STARBRAND! WHERE IS IT, SURFER? TELL US SO WE CAN FINISH THIS!
WHAT THE...
THE STARBRAND IS NOT HARD TO FIND.
HOLY MOTHER OF GOD.
YOU JUST FOLLOW THE PANGS OF ITS BIRTHING.
FABOOSH

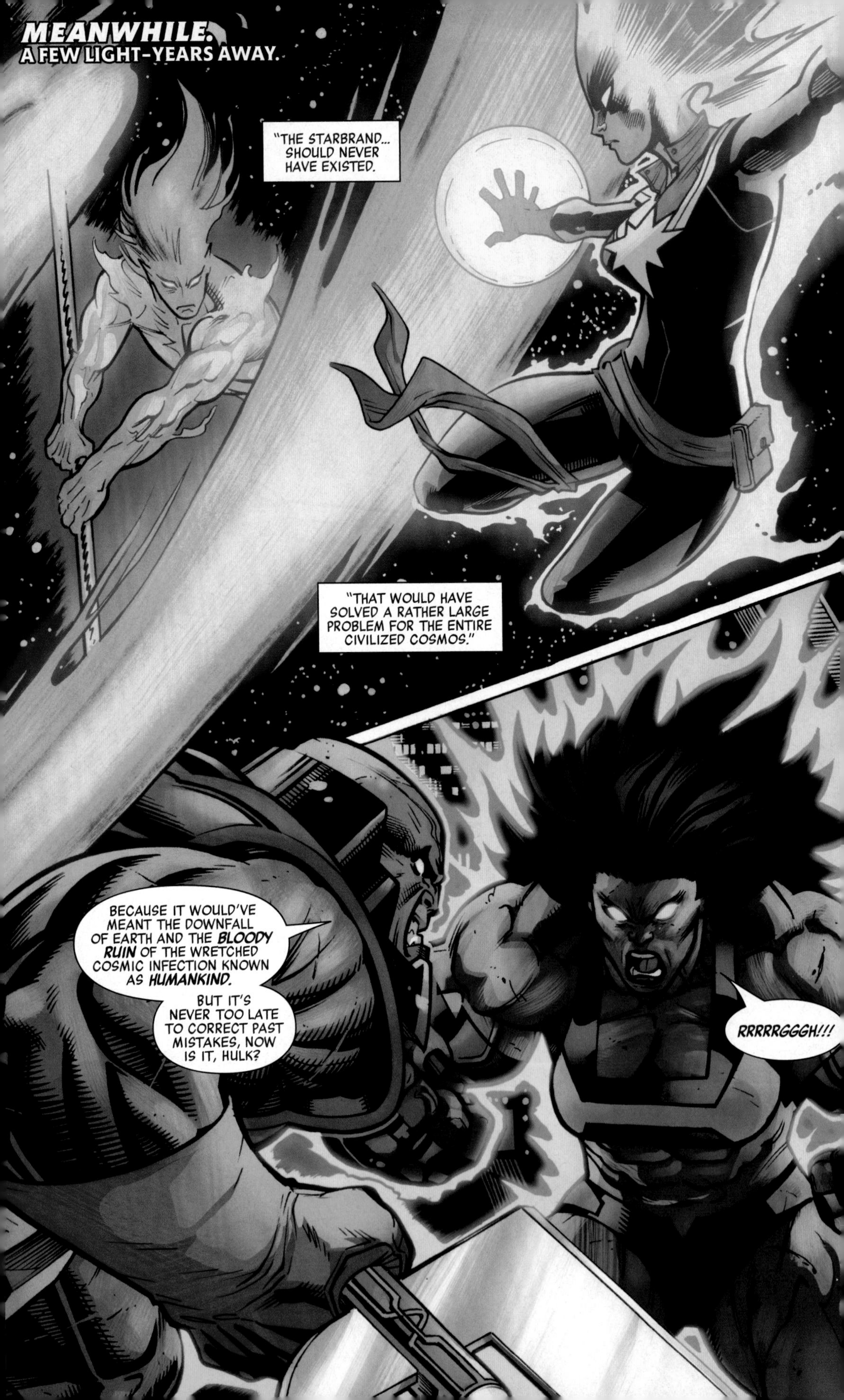
MEANWHILE.
A FEW LIGHT-YEARS AWAY.
"THE STARBRAND... SHOULD NEVER HAVE EXISTED.
"THAT WOULD HAVE SOLVED A RATHER LARGE PROBLEM FOR THE ENTIRE CIVILIZED COSMOS."
BECAUSE IT WOULD'VE MEANT THE DOWNFALL OF EARTH AND THE BLOODY RUIN OF THE WRETCHED COSMIC INFECTION KNOWN AS HUMANKIND.
BUT IT'S NEVER TOO LATE TO CORRECT PAST MISTAKES, NOW IS IT, HULK?
RRRRRGGGH!!!

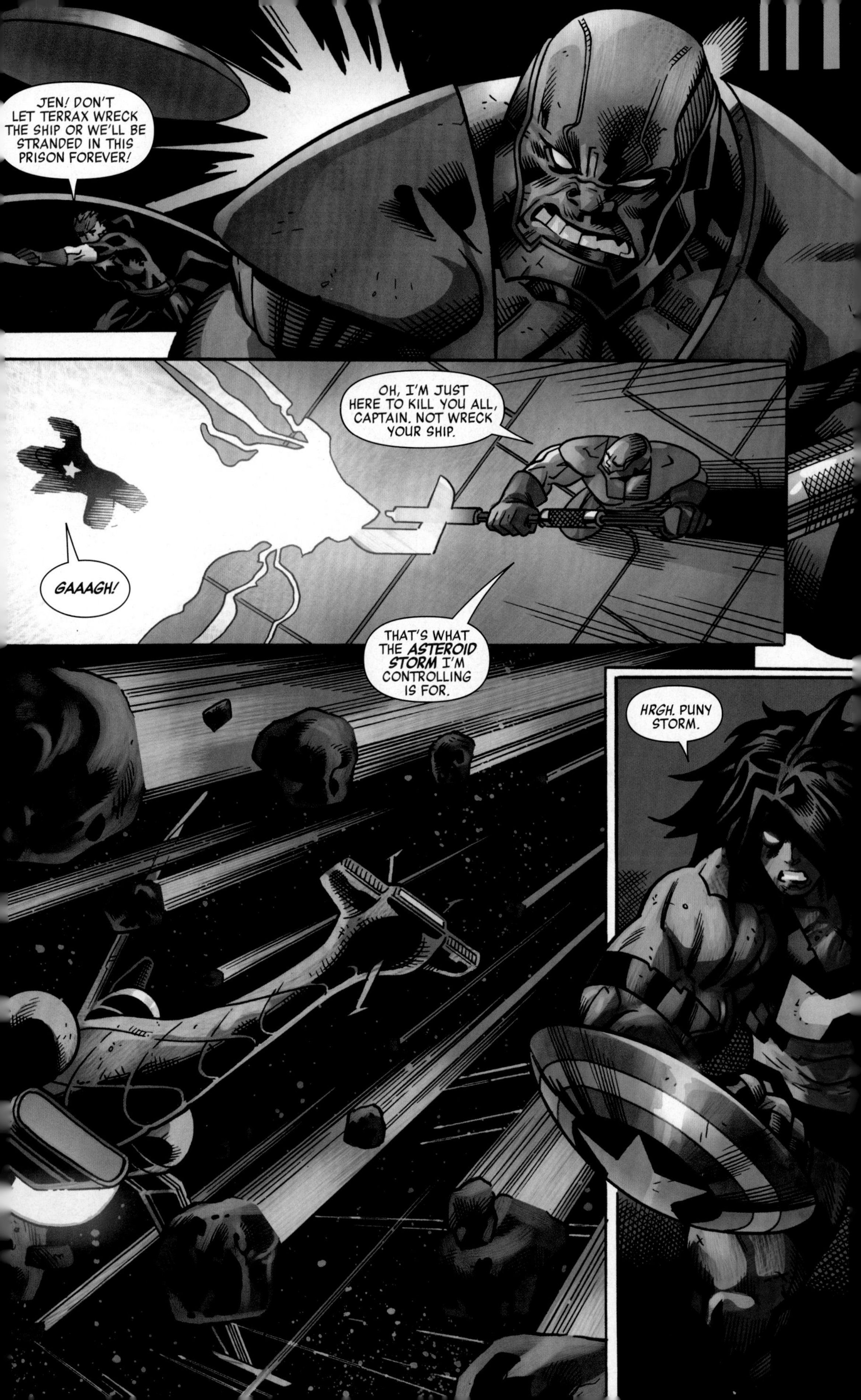
JEN! DON'T LET TERRAX WRECK THE SHIP OR WE'LL BE STRANDED IN THIS PRISON FOREVER!
OH, I'M JUST HERE TO KILL YOU ALL, CAPTAIN. NOT WRECK YOUR SHIP.
GAAAGH!
THAT'S WHAT THE ASTEROID STORM I'M CONTROLLING IS FOR.
HRGH. PUNY STORM.

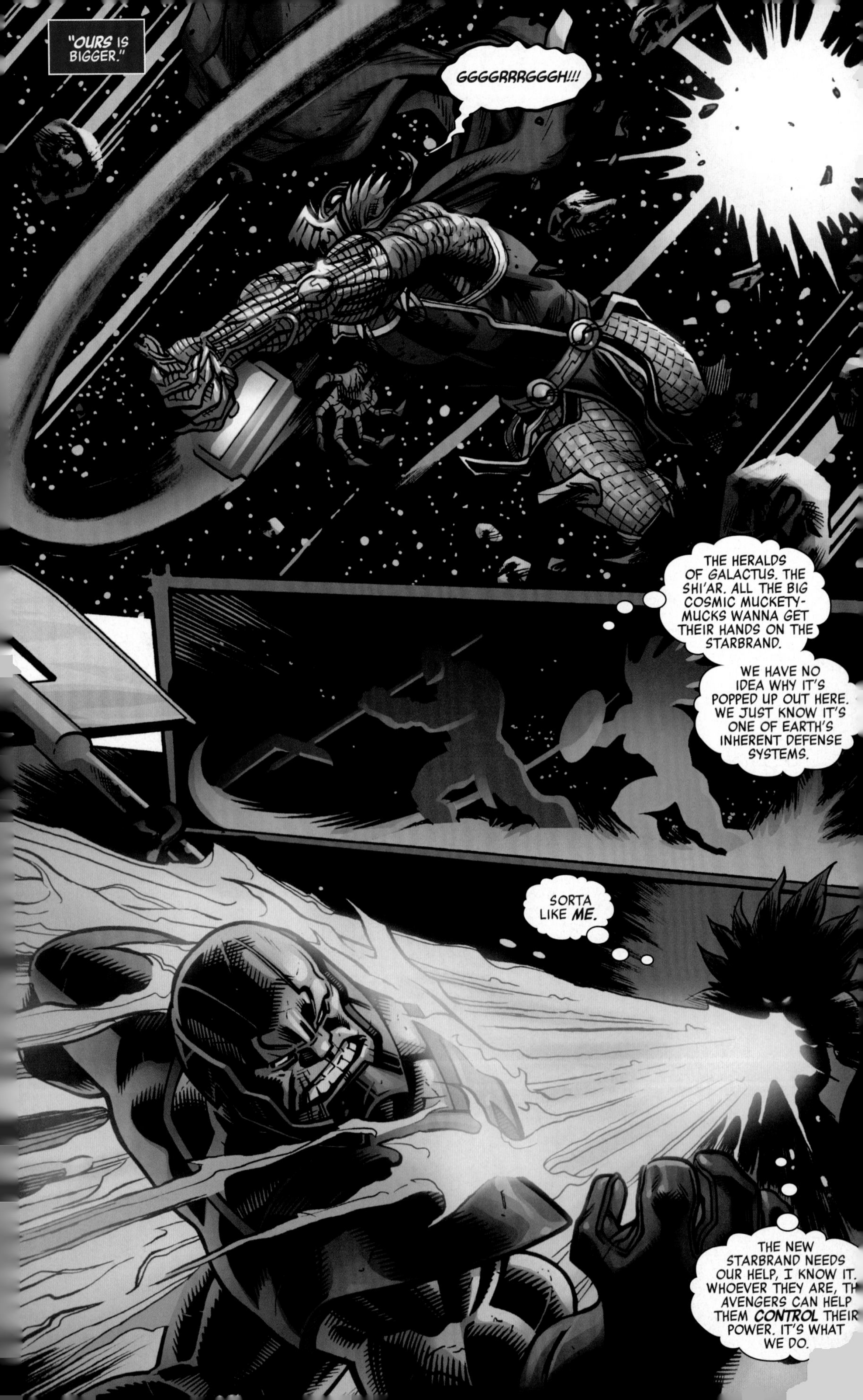
"OURS IS BIGGER."
GGGGRRRGGGH!!!
THE HERALDS OF GALACTUS. THE SHI'AR. ALL THE BIG COSMIC MUCKETY-MUCKS WANNA GET THEIR HANDS ON THE STARBRAND.
WE HAVE NO IDEA WHY IT'S POPPED UP OUT HERE. WE JUST KNOW IT'S ONE OF EARTH'S INHERENT DEFENSE SYSTEMS.
SORTA LIKE ME.
THE NEW STARBRAND NEEDS OUR HELP, I KNOW IT. WHOEVER THEY ARE, TH AVENGERS CAN HELP THEM CONTROL THEIR POWER. IT'S WHAT WE DO.

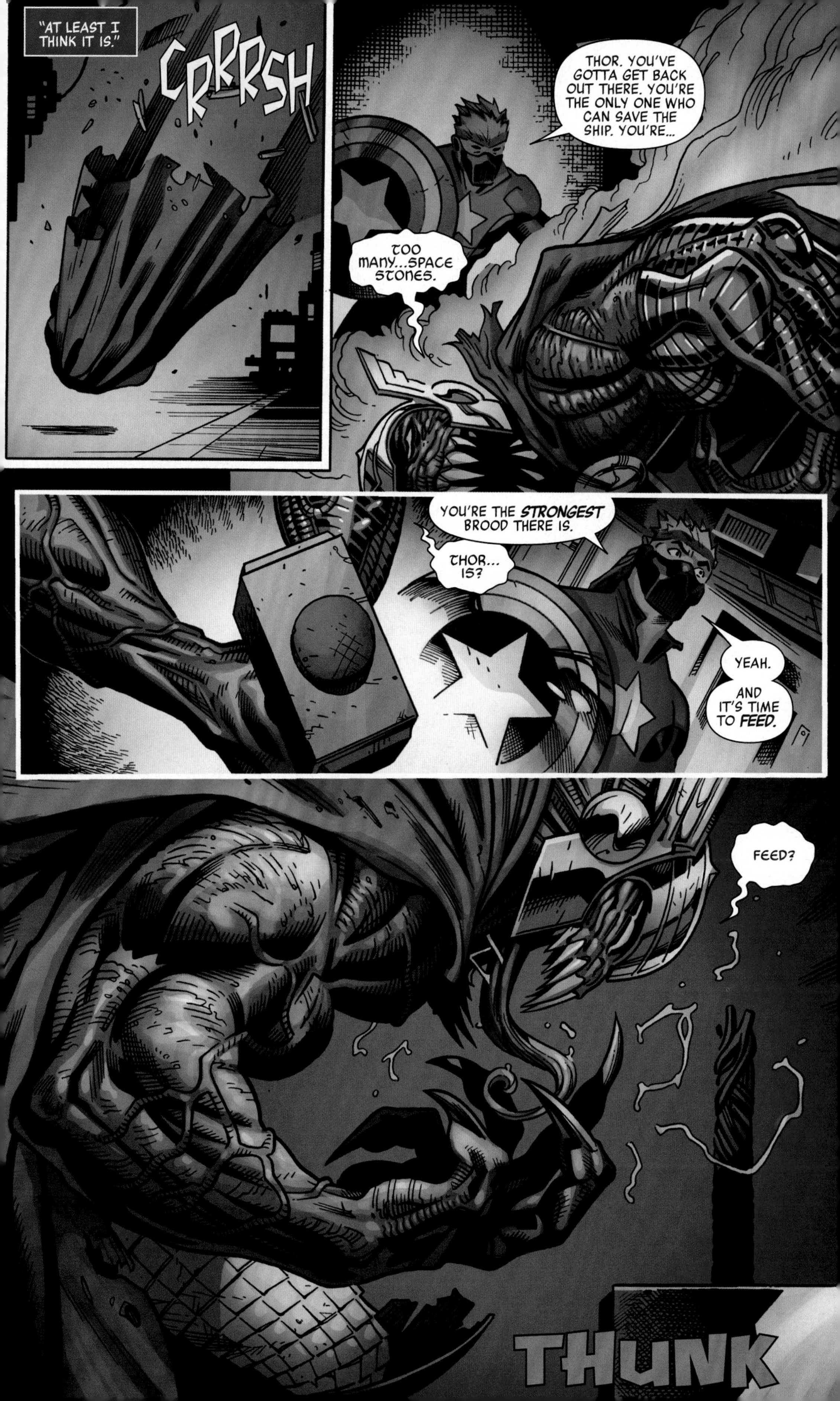
"AT LEAST I THINK IT IS."
CRRRSH
THOR. YOU'VE GOTTA GET BACK OUT THERE. YOU'RE THE ONLY ONE WHO CAN SAVE THE SHIP. YOU'RE...
TOO MANY...SPACE STONES.
YOU'RE THE STRONGEST BROOD THERE IS.
THOR... IS?
YEAH.
AND IT'S TIME TO FEED.
FEED?
THUNK

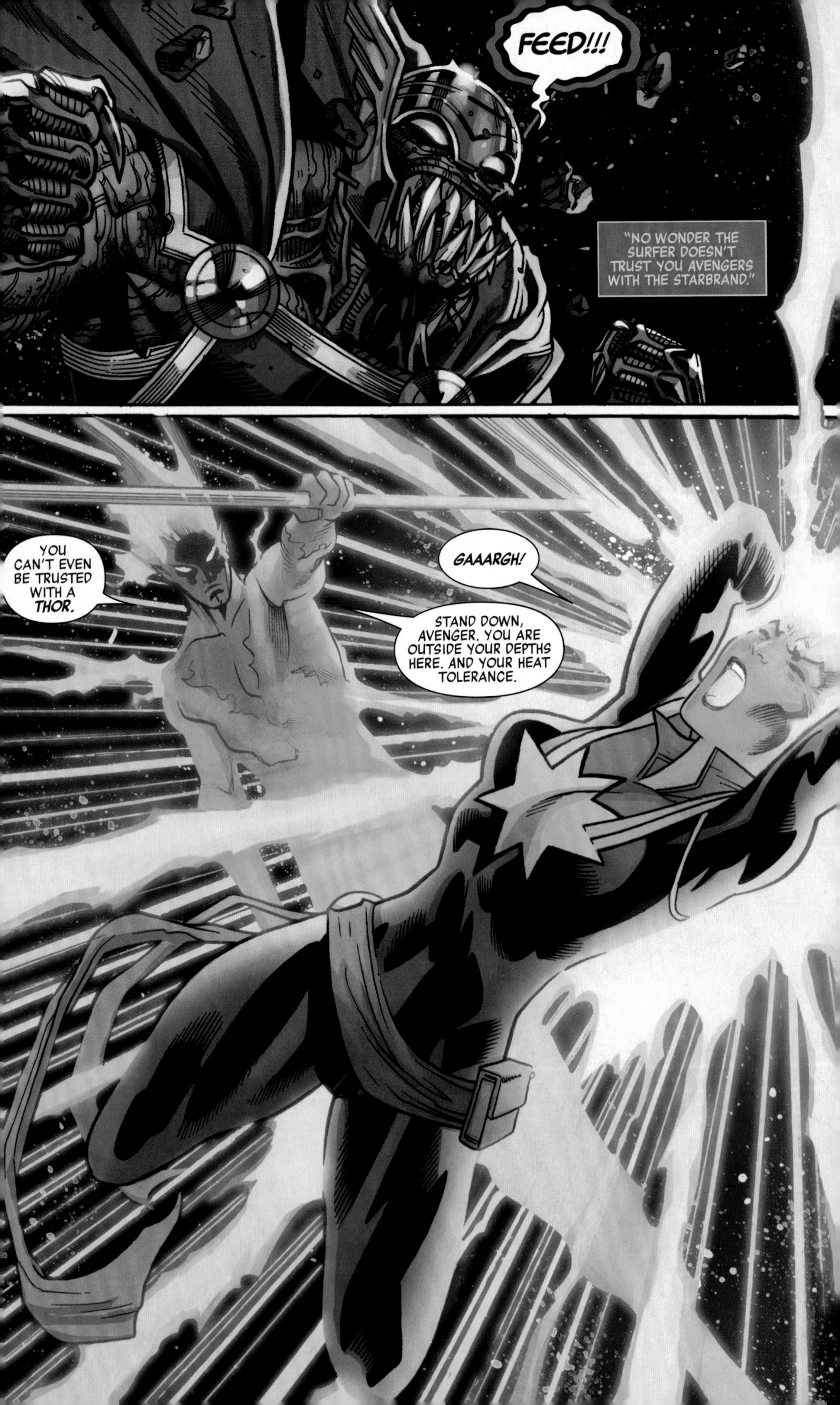
FEED!!!
"NO WONDER THE SURFER DOESN'T TRUST YOU AVENGERS WITH THE STARBRAND."
YOU CAN'T EVEN BE TRUSTED WITH A THOR.
GAAARGH!
STAND DOWN, AVENGER. YOU ARE OUTSIDE YOUR DEPTHS HERE. AND YOUR HEAT TOLERANCE.

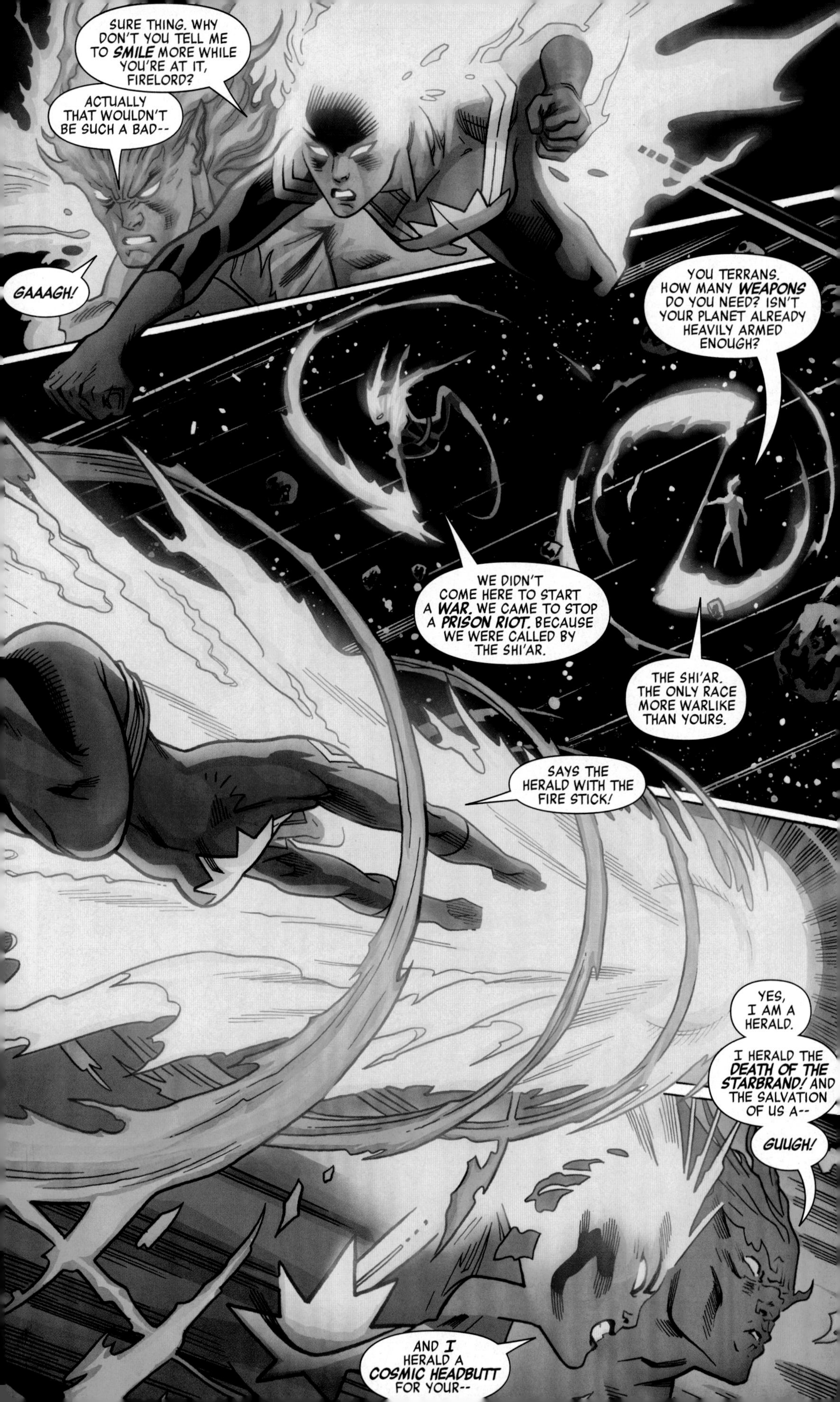
SURE THING. WHY DON'T YOU TELL ME TO SMILE MORE WHILE YOU'RE AT IT, FIRELORD?
ACTUALLY THAT WOULDN'T BE SUCH A BAD--
GAAAGH!
YOU TERRANS. HOW MANY WEAPONS DO YOU NEED? ISN'T YOUR PLANET ALREADY HEAVILY ARMED ENOUGH?
WE DIDN'T COME HERE TO START A WAR. WE CAME TO STOP A PRISON RIOT. BECAUSE WE WERE CALLED BY THE SHI'AR.
THE SHI'AR. THE ONLY RACE MORE WARLIKE THAN YOURS.
SAYS THE HERALD WITH THE FIRE STICK!
YES, I AM A HERALD.
I HERALD THE DEATH OF THE STARBRAND! AND THE SALVATION OF US A--
GUUGH!
AND I HERALD A COSMIC HEADBUTT FOR YOUR--

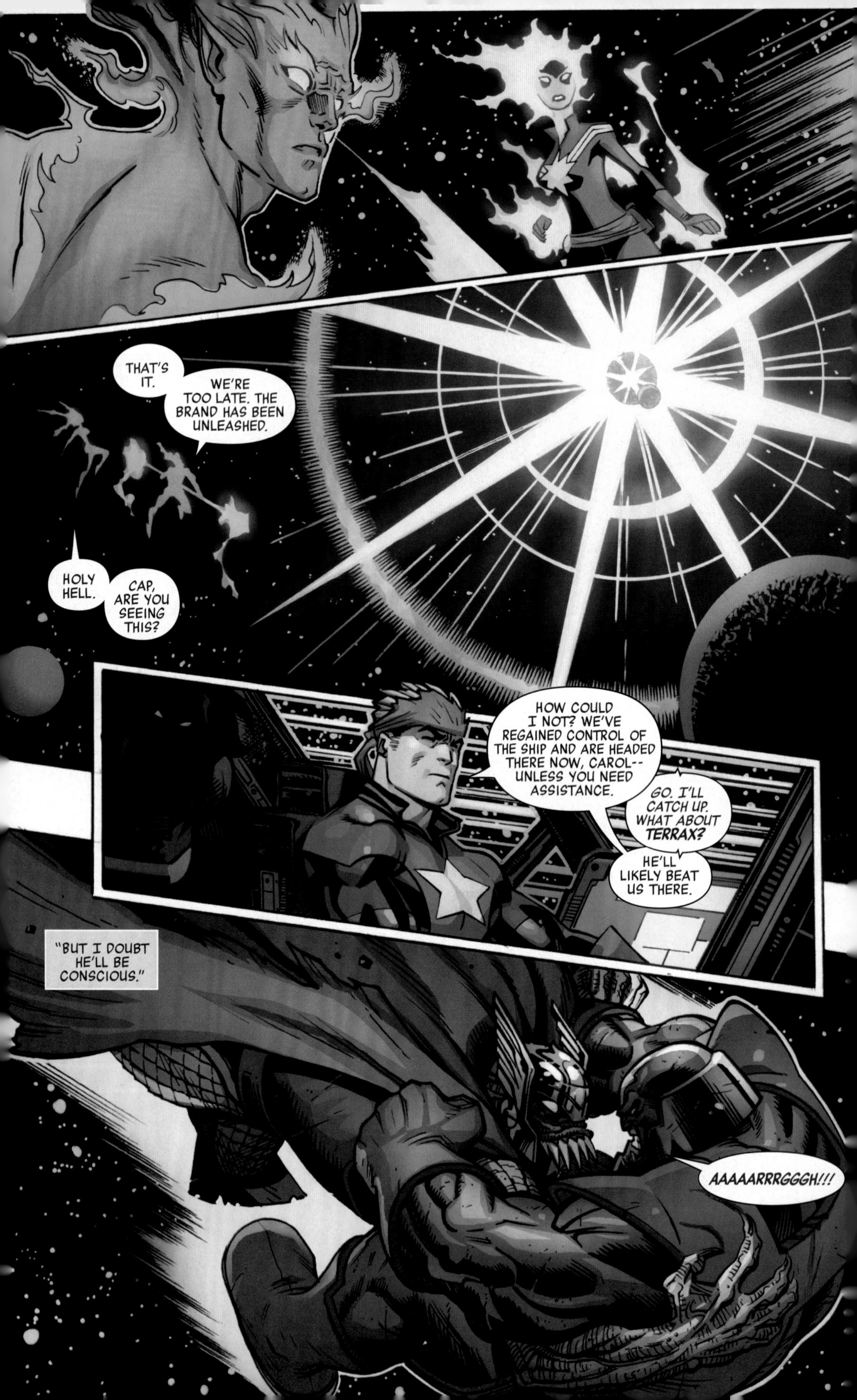
THAT'S IT.
WE'RE TOO LATE. THE BRAND HAS BEEN UNLEASHED.
HOLY HELL.
CAP, ARE YOU SEEING THIS?
HOW COULD I NOT? WE'VE REGAINED CONTROL OF THE SHIP AND ARE HEADED THERE NOW, CAROL-- UNLESS YOU NEED ASSISTANCE.
GO. I'LL CATCH UP. WHAT ABOUT TERRAX?
HE'LL LIKELY BEAT US THERE.
"BUT I DOUBT HE'LL BE CONSCIOUS."
AAAAARRRGGGH!!!

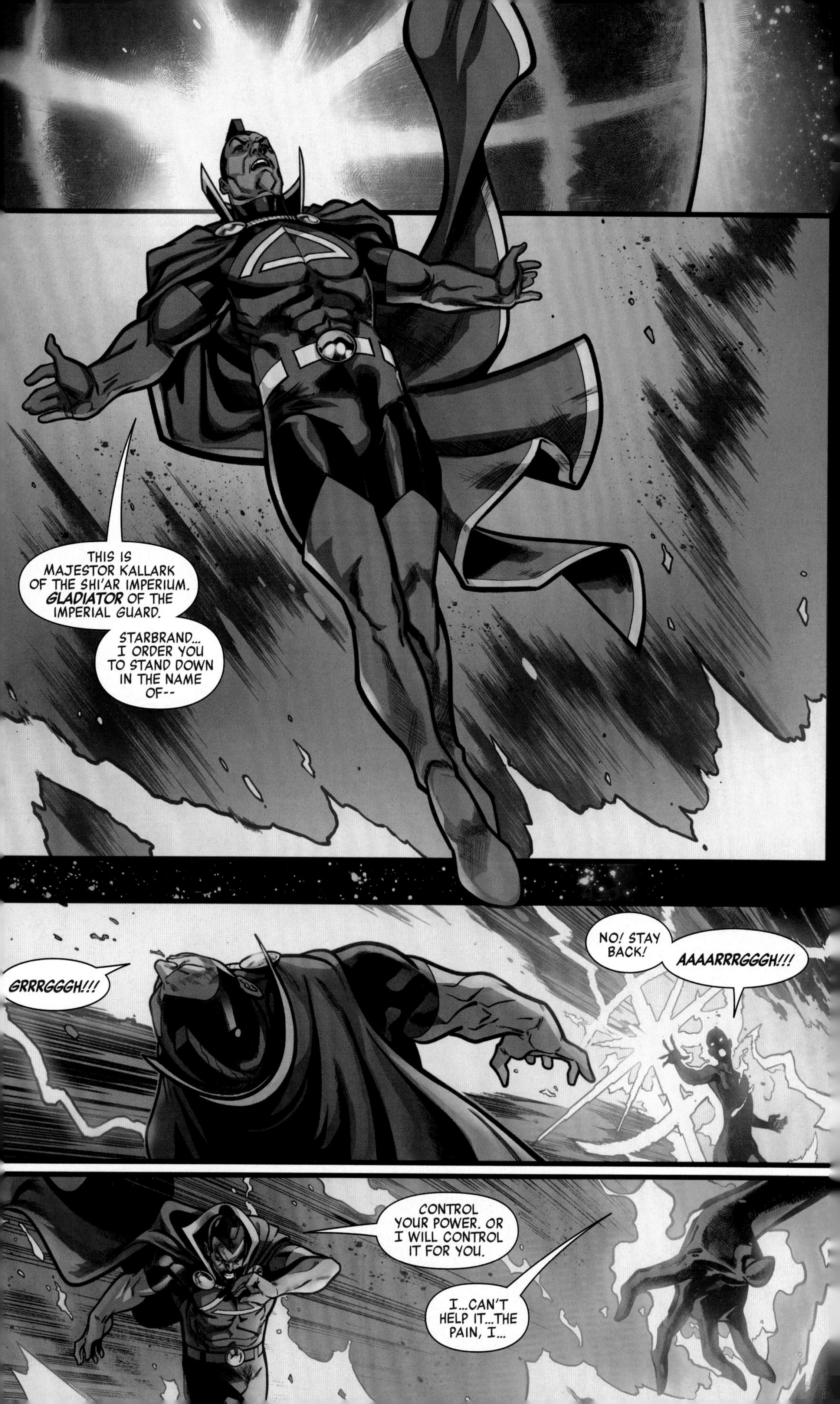
THIS IS MAJESTOR KALLARK OF THE SHI'AR IMPERIUM. GLADIATOR OF THE IMPERIAL GUARD.
STARBRAND... I ORDER YOU TO STAND DOWN IN THE NAME OF--
GRRRGGGH!!!
NO! STAY BACK!
AAAARRRGGGH!!!
CONTROL YOUR POWER. OR I WILL CONTROL IT FOR YOU.
I...CAN'T HELP IT...THE PAIN, I...

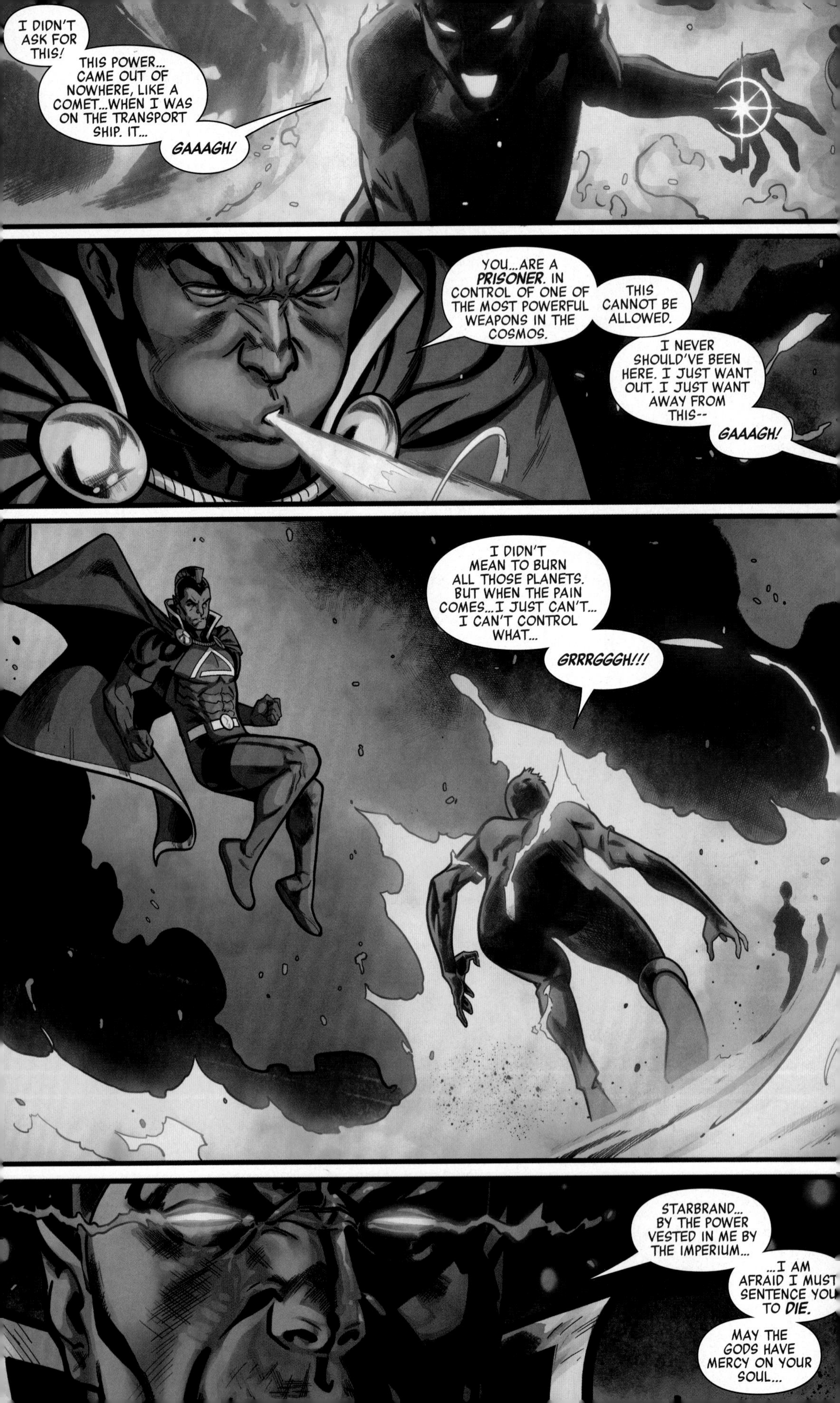
I DIDN'T ASK FOR THIS!
THIS POWER... CAME OUT OF NOWHERE, LIKE A COMET...WHEN I WAS ON THE TRANSPORT SHIP. IT...
GAAAGH!
YOU...ARE A PRISONER. IN CONTROL OF ONE OF THE MOST POWERFUL WEAPONS IN THE COSMOS.
THIS CANNOT BE ALLOWED.
I NEVER SHOULD'VE BEEN HERE. I JUST WANT OUT. I JUST WANT AWAY FROM THIS--
GAAAGH!
I DIDN'T MEAN TO BURN ALL THOSE PLANETS. BUT WHEN THE PAIN COMES...I JUST CAN'T... I CAN'T CONTROL WHAT...
GRRRGGGH!!!
STARBRAND... BY THE POWER VESTED IN ME BY THE IMPERIUM...
...I AM AFRAID I MUST SENTENCE YOU TO DIE.
MAY THE GODS HAVE MERCY ON YOUR SOUL...

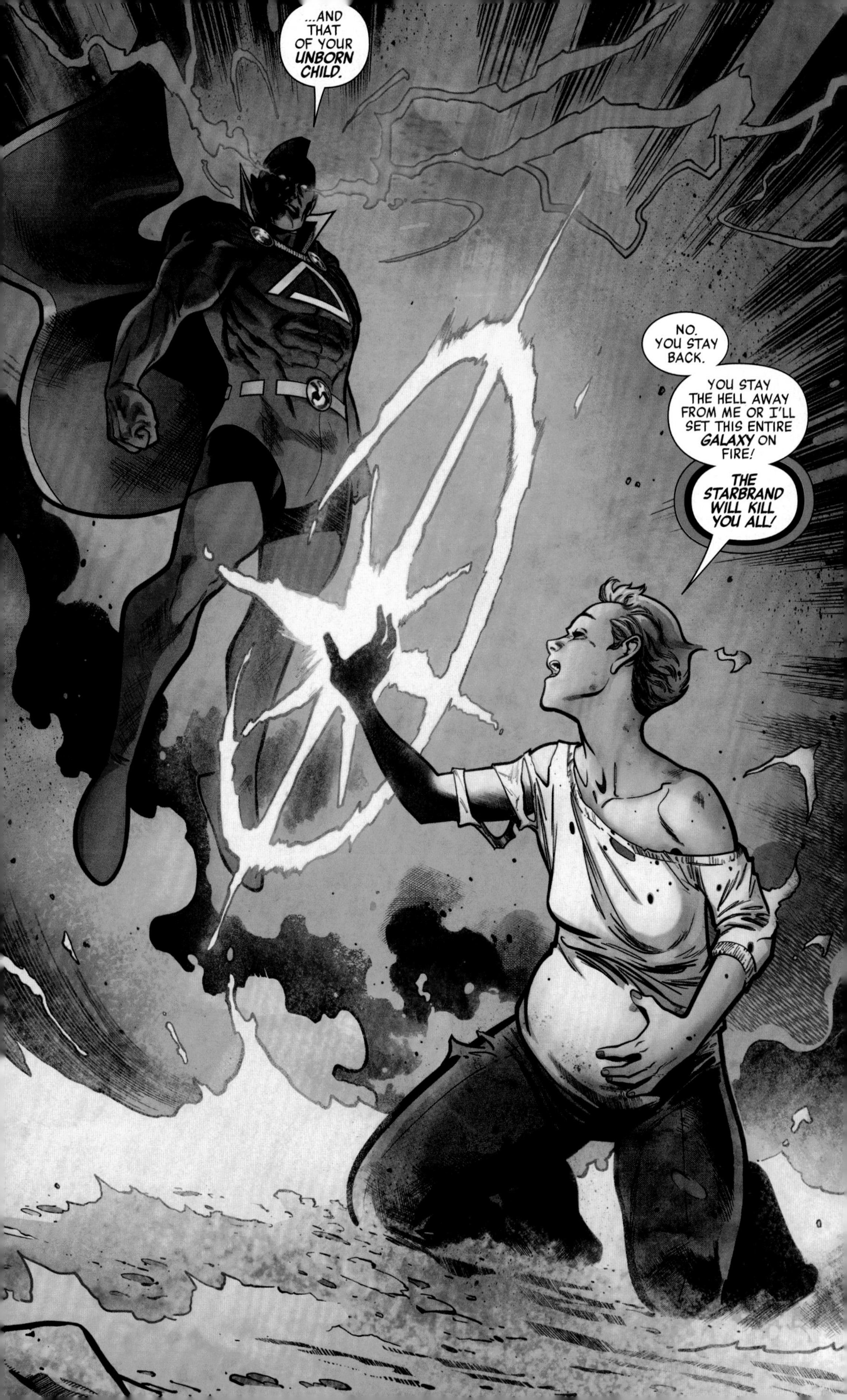
...AND THAT OF YOUR UNBORN CHILD.
NO. YOU STAY BACK.
YOU STAY THE HELL AWAY FROM ME OR I'LL SET THIS ENTIRE GALAXY ON FIRE!
THE STARBRAND WILL KILL YOU ALL!

30 STARBRAND REBORN PART 4
NATIVITY IN THE STARS

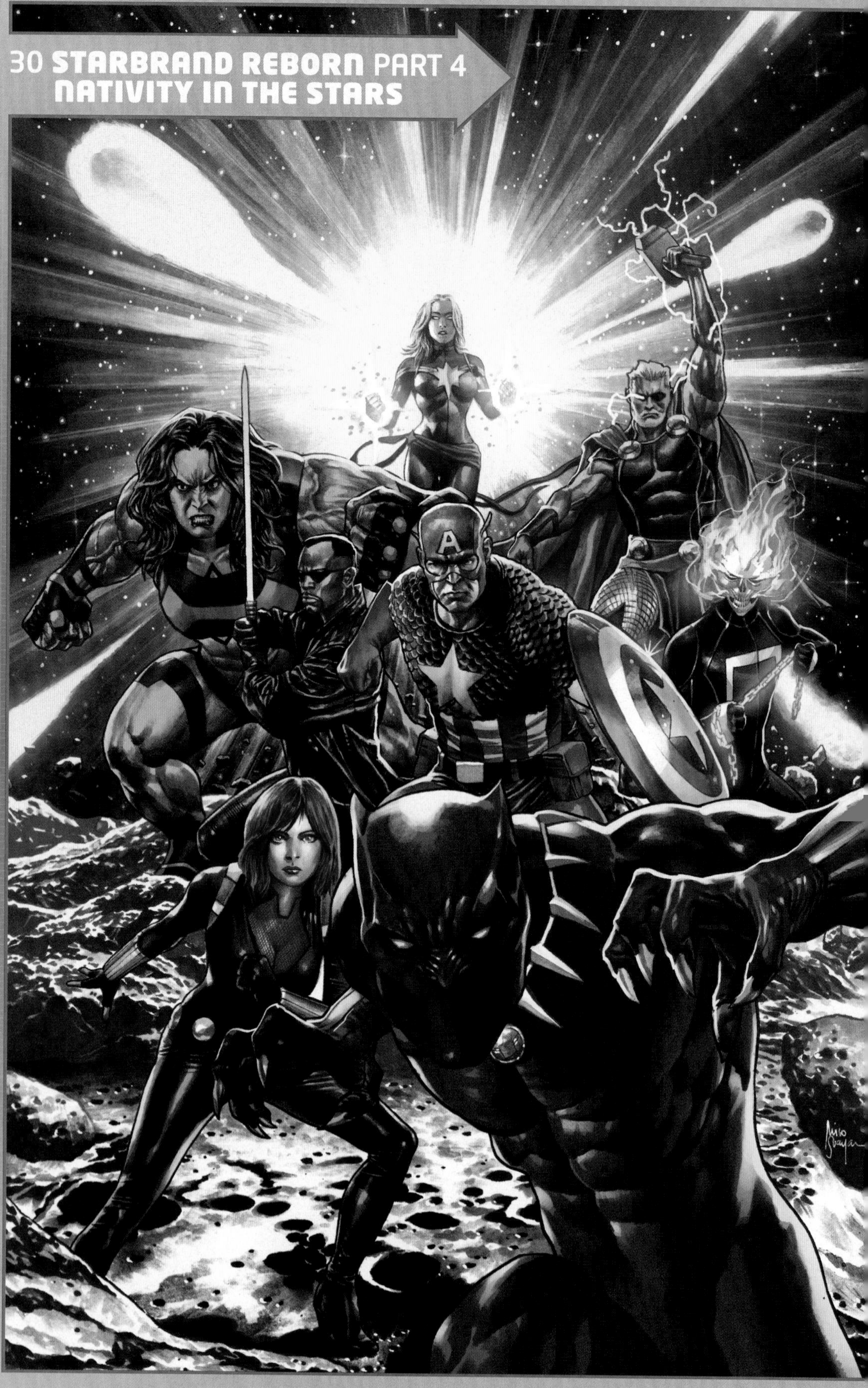

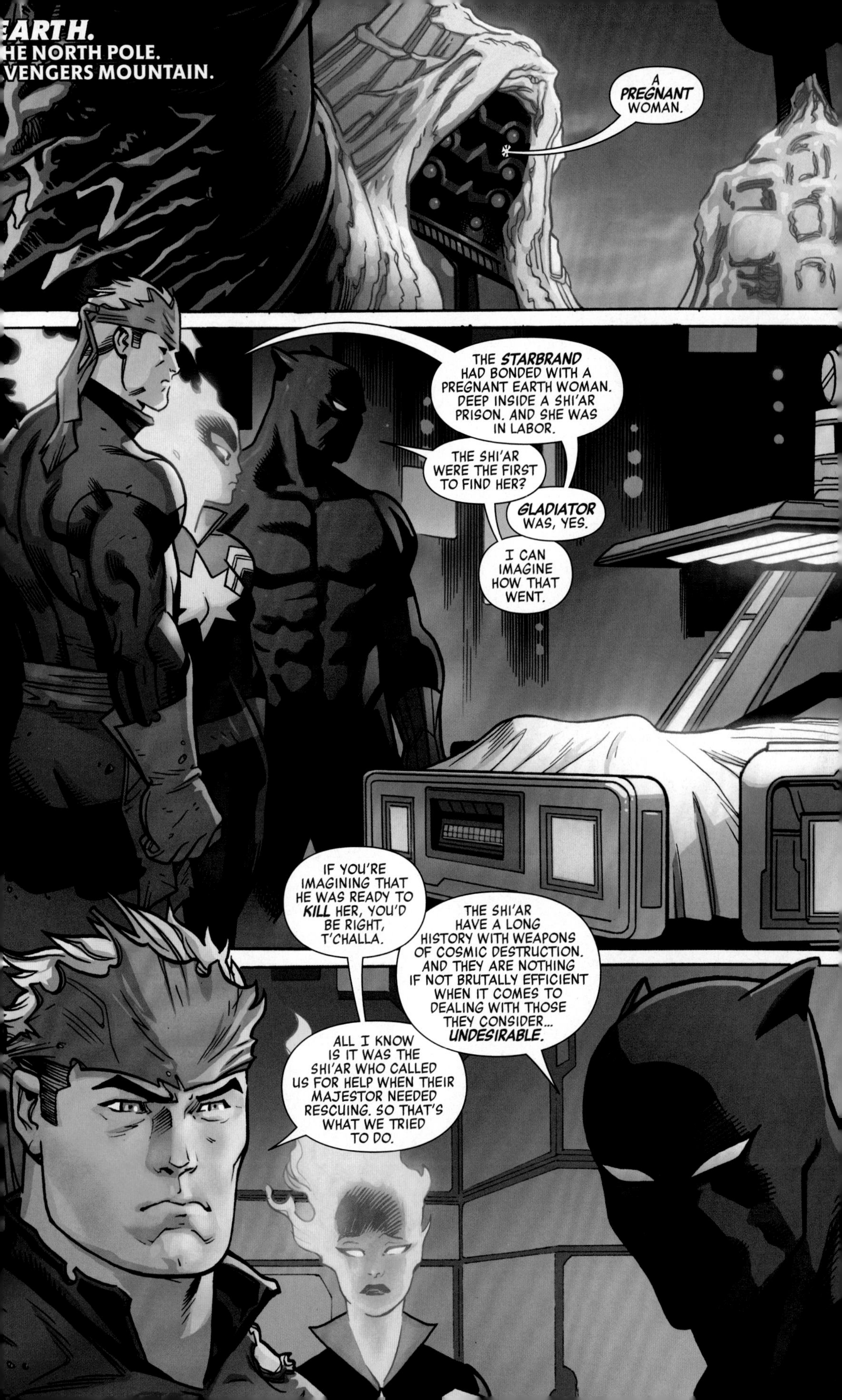
EARTH.
THE NORTH POLE.
AVENGERS MOUNTAIN.
A PREGNANT WOMAN.
THE STARBRAND HAD BONDED WITH A PREGNANT EARTH WOMAN. DEEP INSIDE A SHI'AR PRISON. AND SHE WAS IN LABOR.
THE SHI'AR WERE THE FIRST TO FIND HER?
GLADIATOR WAS, YES.
I CAN IMAGINE HOW THAT WENT.
IF YOU'RE IMAGINING THAT HE WAS READY TO KILL HER, YOU'D BE RIGHT, T'CHALLA.
THE SHI'AR HAVE A LONG HISTORY WITH WEAPONS OF COSMIC DESTRUCTION. AND THEY ARE NOTHING IF NOT BRUTALLY EFFICIENT WHEN IT COMES TO DEALING WITH THOSE THEY CONSIDER... UNDESIRABLE.
ALL I KNOW IS IT WAS THE SHI'AR WHO CALLED US FOR HELP WHEN THEIR MAJESTOR NEEDED RESCUING. SO THAT'S WHAT WE TRIED TO DO.

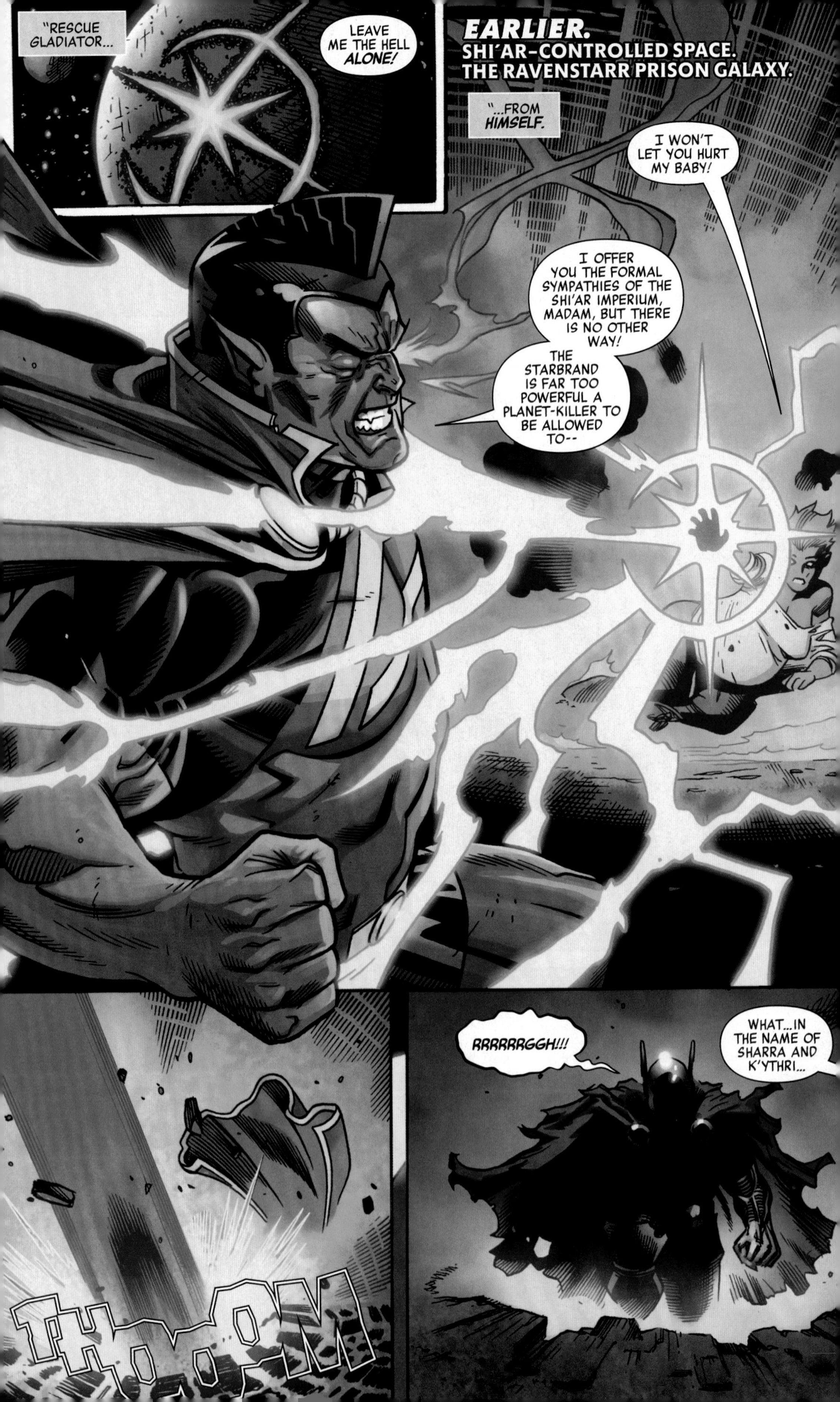
"RESCUE GLADIATOR...
LEAVE ME THE HELL ALONE!
EARLIER.
SHI'AR-CONTROLLED SPACE.
THE RAVENSTARR PRISON GALAXY.
"...FROM HIMSELF.
I WON'T LET YOU HURT MY BABY!
I OFFER YOU THE FORMAL SYMPATHIES OF THE SHI'AR IMPERIUM, MADAM, BUT THERE IS NO OTHER WAY!
THE STARBRAND IS FAR TOO POWERFUL A PLANET-KILLER TO BE ALLOWED TO--
THOOOOM
BRRRRRGGH!!!
WHAT...IN THE NAME OF SHARRA AND K'YTHRI...

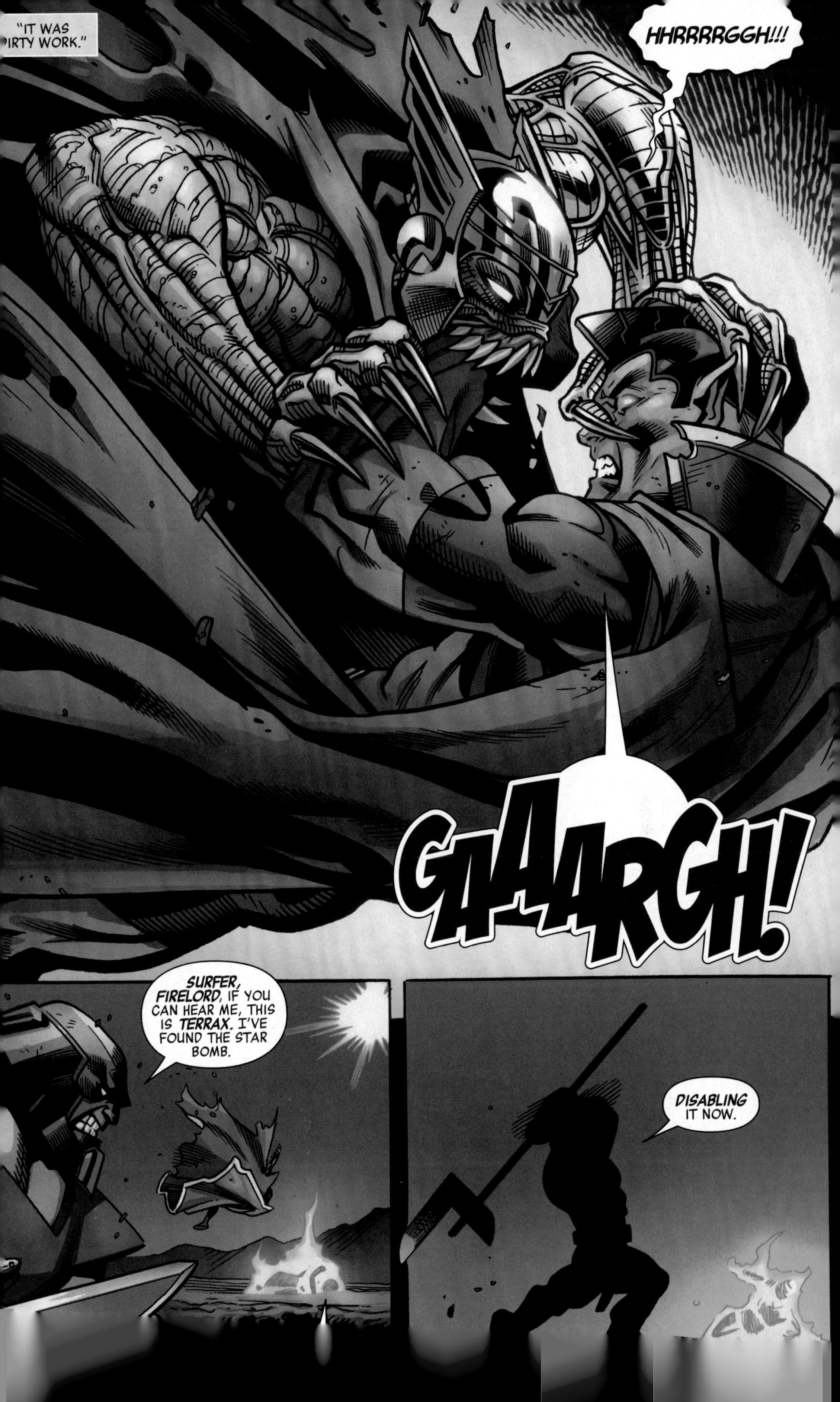
"IT WAS
DIRTY WORK."
HHRRRRGGH!!!
GAAARGH!
SURFER, FIRELORD, IF YOU CAN HEAR ME, THIS IS TERRAX. I'VE FOUND THE STAR BOMB.
DISABLING IT NOW.

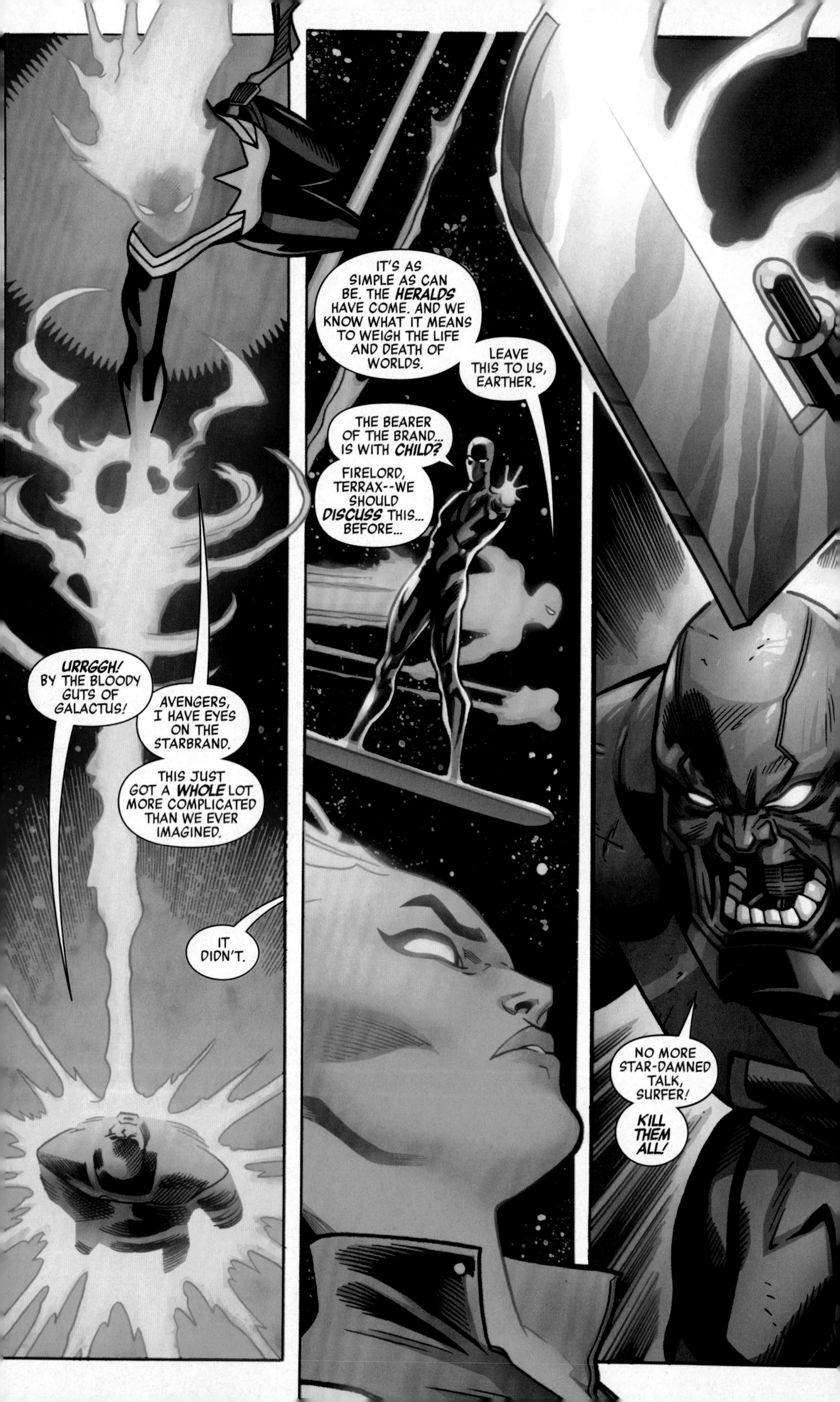
URRGGH! BY THE BLOODY GUTS OF GALACTUS!
AVENGERS, I HAVE EYES ON THE STARBRAND.
THIS JUST GOT A WHOLE LOT MORE COMPLICATED THAN WE EVER IMAGINED.
IT DIDN'T.
IT'S AS SIMPLE AS CAN BE. THE HERALDS HAVE COME. AND WE KNOW WHAT IT MEANS TO WEIGH THE LIFE AND DEATH OF WORLDS.
LEAVE THIS TO US, EARTHER.
THE BEARER OF THE BRAND... IS WITH CHILD?
FIRELORD, TERRAX--WE SHOULD DISCUSS THIS... BEFORE...
NO MORE STAR-DAMNED TALK, SURFER!
KILL THEM ALL!

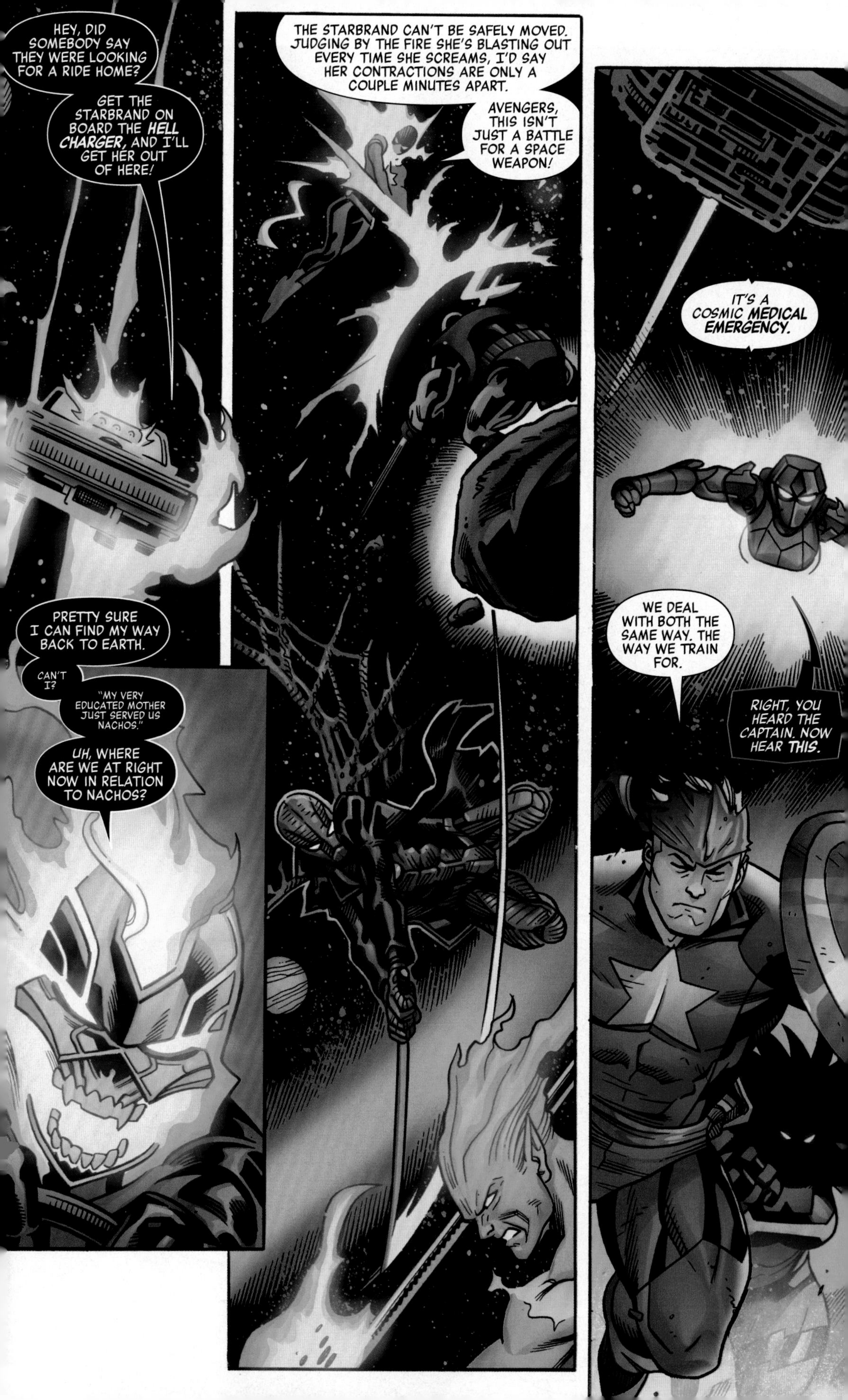
HEY, DID SOMEBODY SAY THEY WERE LOOKING FOR A RIDE HOME?
GET THE STARBRAND ON BOARD THE HELL CHARGER, AND I'LL GET HER OUT OF HERE!
PRETTY SURE I CAN FIND MY WAY BACK TO EARTH.
CAN'T I?
"MY VERY EDUCATED MOTHER JUST SERVED US NACHOS."
UH, WHERE ARE WE AT RIGHT NOW IN RELATION TO NACHOS?
THE STARBRAND CAN'T BE SAFELY MOVED. JUDGING BY THE FIRE SHE'S BLASTING OUT EVERY TIME SHE SCREAMS, I'D SAY HER CONTRACTIONS ARE ONLY A COUPLE MINUTES APART.
AVENGERS, THIS ISN'T JUST A BATTLE FOR A SPACE WEAPON!
IT'S A COSMIC MEDICAL EMERGENCY.
WE DEAL WITH BOTH THE SAME WAY. THE WAY WE TRAIN FOR.
RIGHT, YOU HEARD THE CAPTAIN. NOW HEAR THIS.

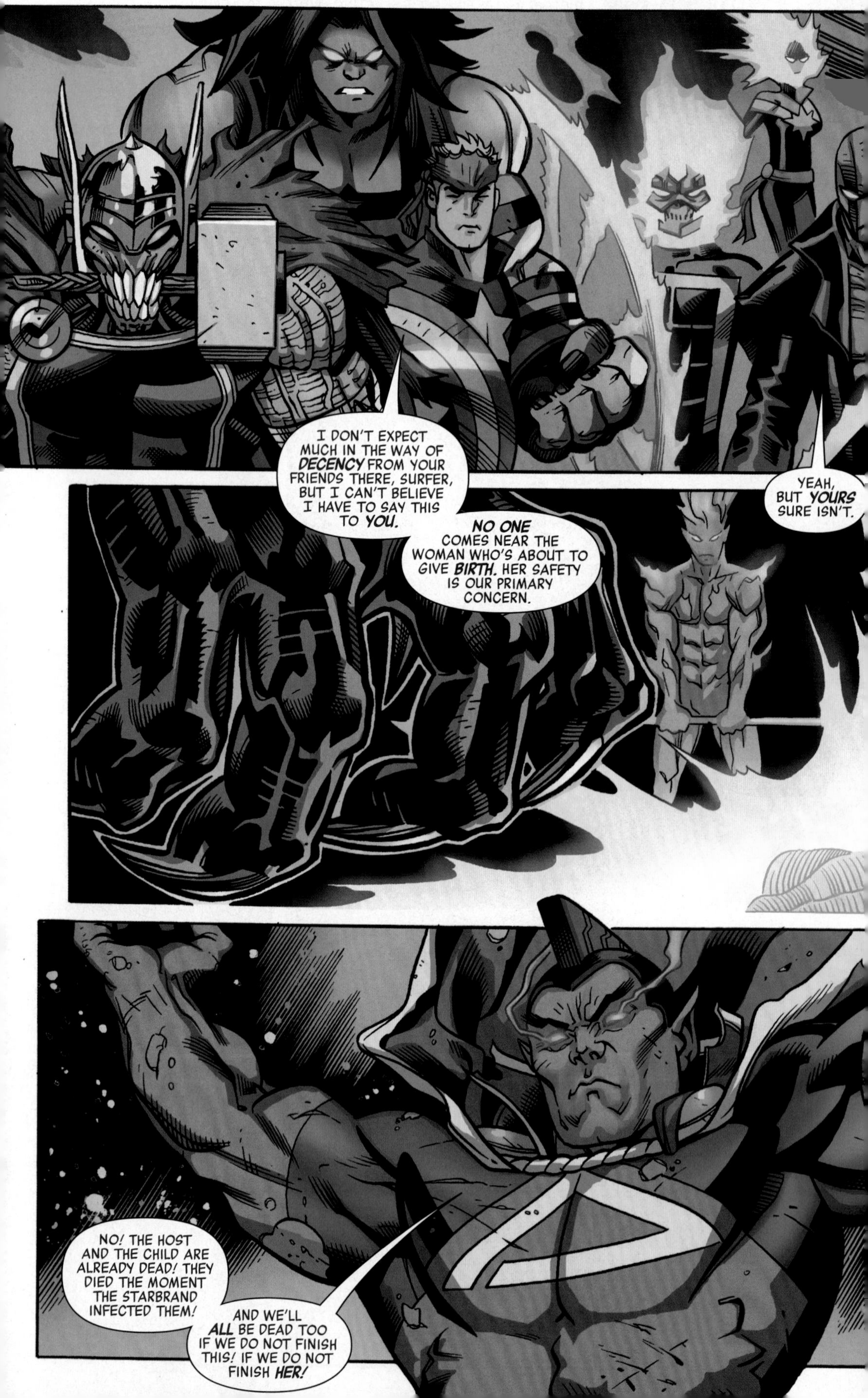

I DON'T EXPECT MUCH IN THE WAY OF DECENCY FROM YOUR FRIENDS THERE, SURFER, BUT I CAN'T BELIEVE I HAVE TO SAY THIS TO YOU.
NO ONE COMES NEAR THE WOMAN WHO'S ABOUT TO GIVE BIRTH. HER SAFETY IS OUR PRIMARY CONCERN.
YEAH, BUT YOURS SURE ISN'T.
NO! THE HOST AND THE CHILD ARE ALREADY DEAD! THEY DIED THE MOMENT THE STARBRAND INFECTED THEM!
AND WE'LL ALL BE DEAD TOO IF WE DO NOT FINISH THIS! IF WE DO NOT FINISH HER!

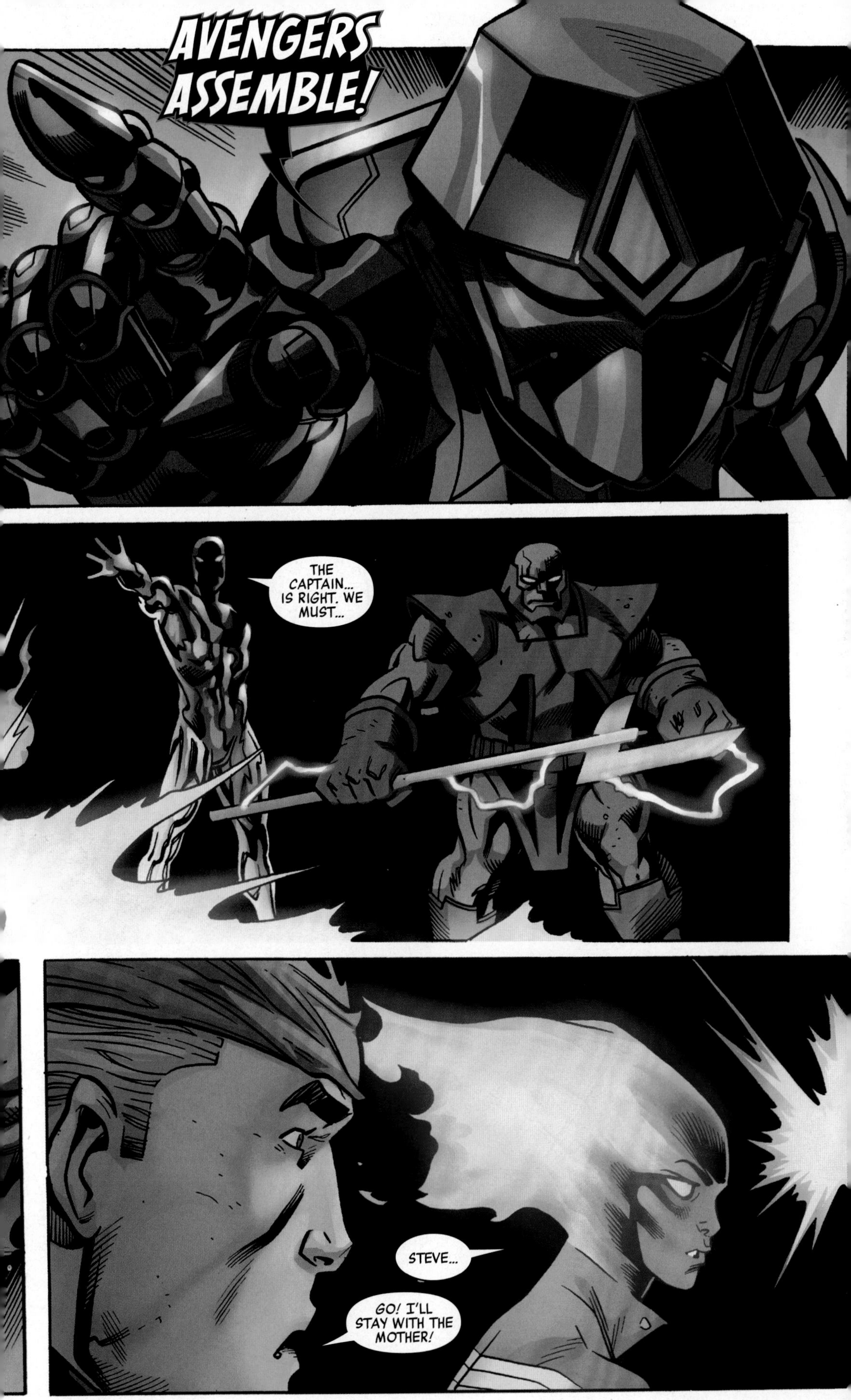
AVENGERS ASSEMBLE!
THE CAPTAIN... IS RIGHT. WE MUST...
STEVE...
GO! I'LL STAY WITH THE MOTHER!

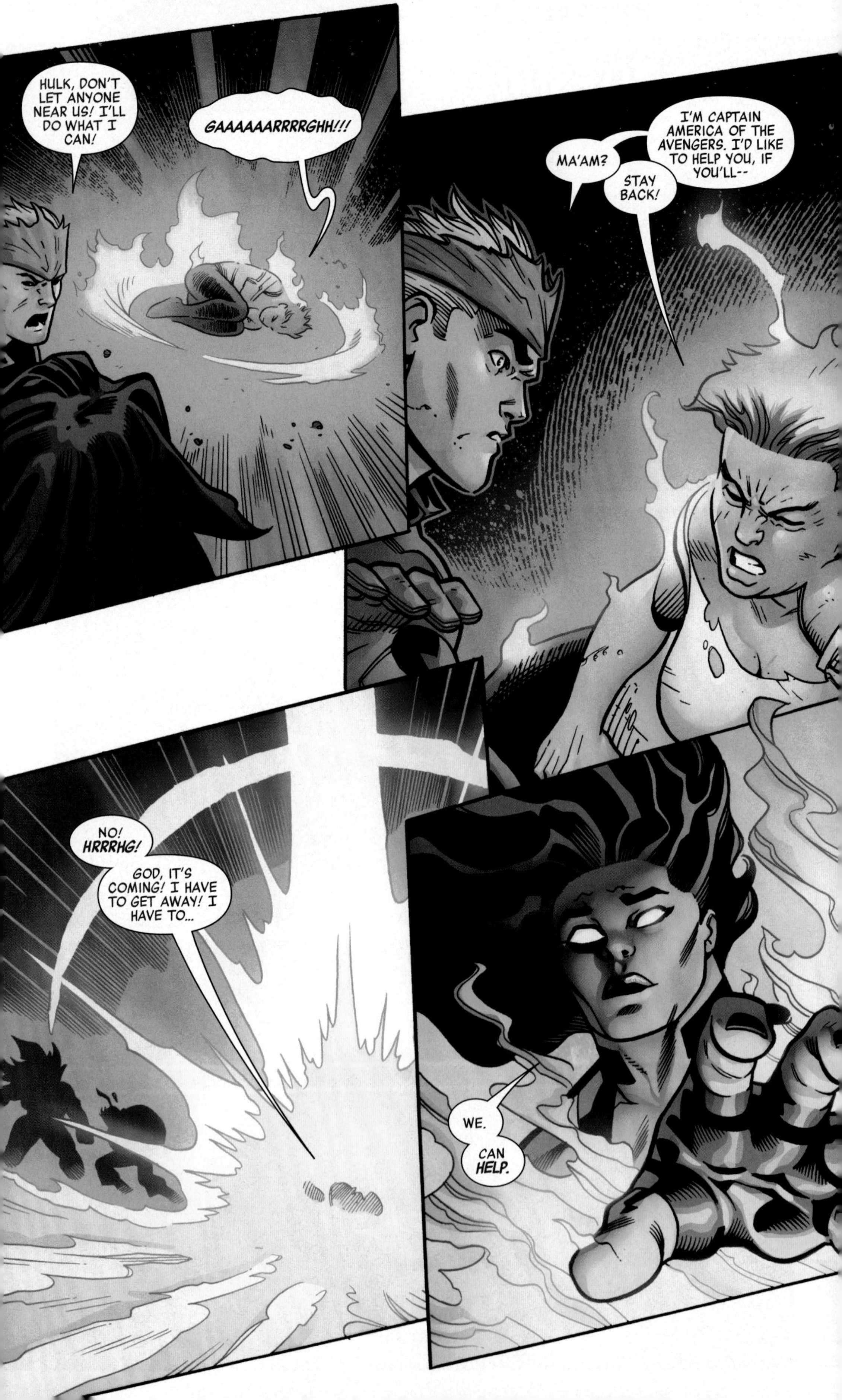

HULK, DON'T LET ANYONE NEAR US! I'LL DO WHAT I CAN!
GAAAAAARRRRGHH!!!
MA'AM?
I'M CAPTAIN AMERICA OF THE AVENGERS. I'D LIKE TO HELP YOU, IF YOU'LL--
STAY BACK!
NO! HRRRHG!
GOD, IT'S COMING! I HAVE TO GET AWAY! I HAVE TO...
WE.
CAN HELP.

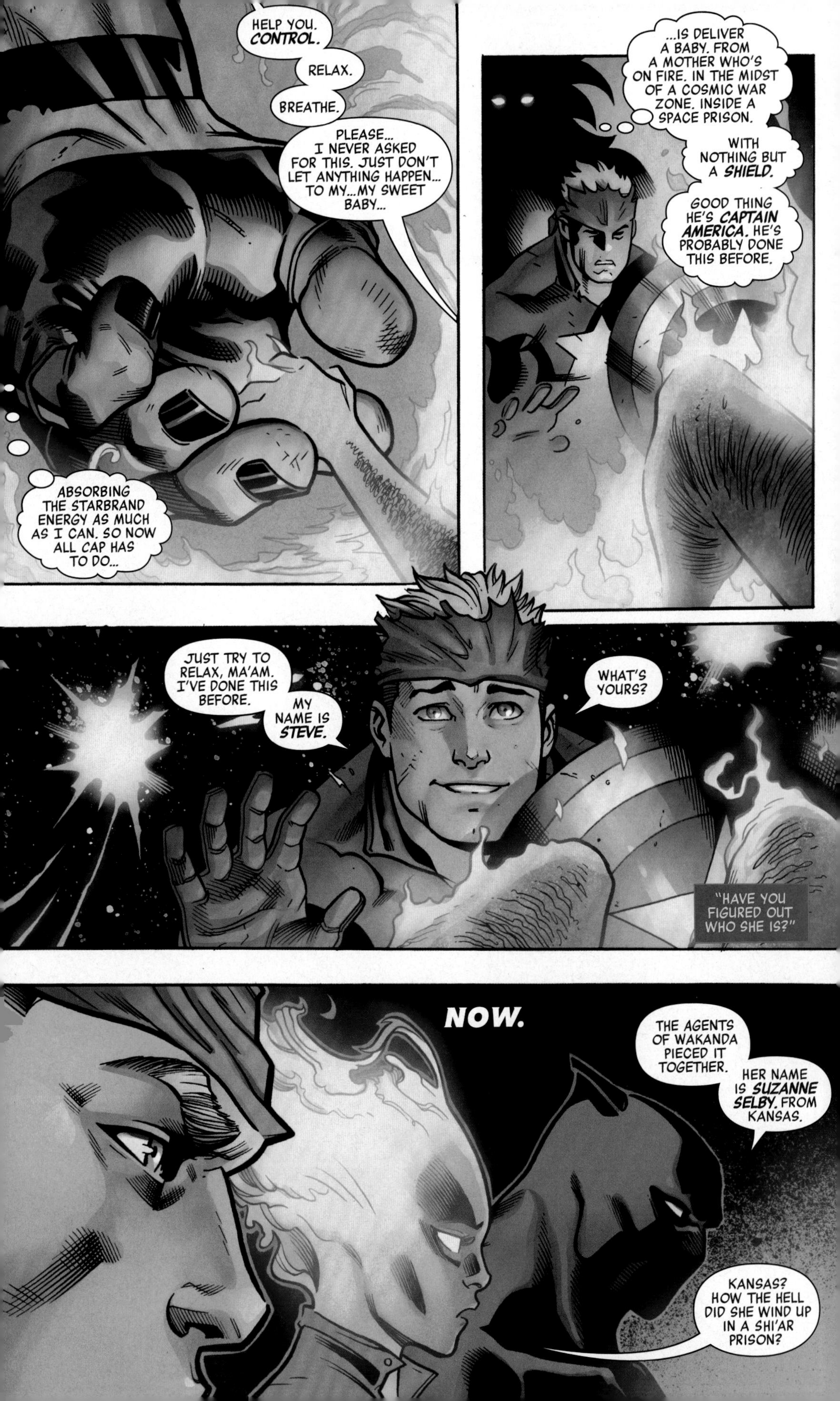
HELP YOU. CONTROL.
RELAX.
BREATHE.
PLEASE... I NEVER ASKED FOR THIS. JUST DON'T LET ANYTHING HAPPEN... TO MY...MY SWEET BABY...
ABSORBING THE STARBRAND ENERGY AS MUCH AS I CAN. SO NOW ALL CAP HAS TO DO...
...IS DELIVER A BABY. FROM A MOTHER WHO'S ON FIRE. IN THE MIDST OF A COSMIC WAR ZONE. INSIDE A SPACE PRISON.
WITH NOTHING BUT A SHIELD.
GOOD THING HE'S CAPTAIN AMERICA. HE'S PROBABLY DONE THIS BEFORE.
JUST TRY TO RELAX, MA'AM. I'VE DONE THIS BEFORE.
MY NAME IS STEVE.
WHAT'S YOURS?
"HAVE YOU FIGURED OUT WHO SHE IS?"
NOW.
THE AGENTS OF WAKANDA PIECED IT TOGETHER.
HER NAME IS SUZANNE SELBY. FROM KANSAS.
KANSAS? HOW THE HELL DID SHE WIND UP IN A SHI'AR PRISON?

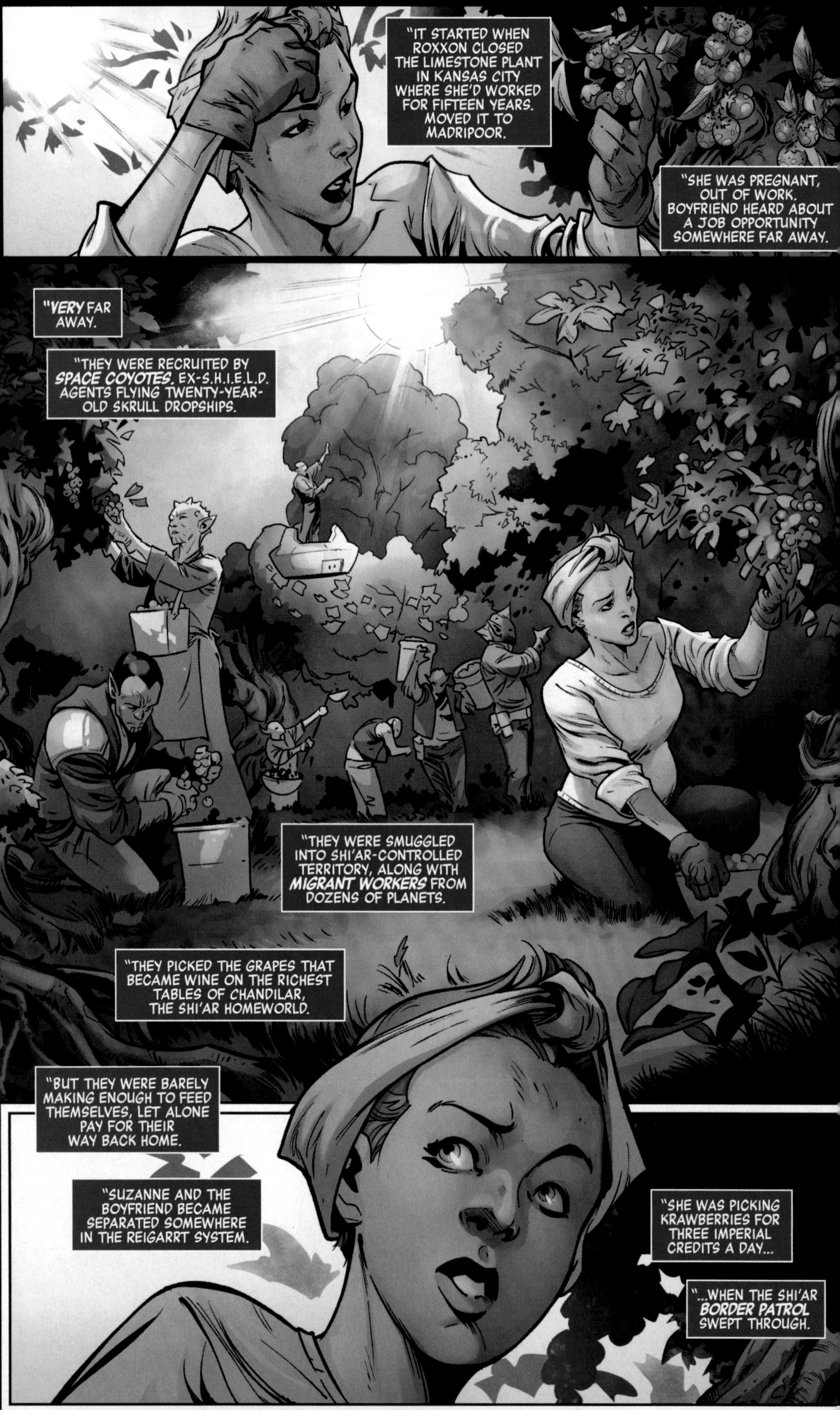
"IT STARTED WHEN ROXXON CLOSED THE LIMESTONE PLANT IN KANSAS CITY WHERE SHE'D WORKED FOR FIFTEEN YEARS. MOVED IT TO MADRIPOOR.
"SHE WAS PREGNANT, OUT OF WORK. BOYFRIEND HEARD ABOUT A JOB OPPORTUNITY SOMEWHERE FAR AWAY.
"VERY FAR AWAY.
"THEY WERE RECRUITED BY SPACE COYOTES. EX-S.H.I.E.L.D. AGENTS FLYING TWENTY-YEAR-OLD SKRULL DROPSHIPS.
"THEY WERE SMUGGLED INTO SHI'AR-CONTROLLED TERRITORY, ALONG WITH MIGRANT WORKERS FROM DOZENS OF PLANETS.
"THEY PICKED THE GRAPES THAT BECAME WINE ON THE RICHEST TABLES OF CHANDILAR, THE SHI'AR HOMEWORLD.
"BUT THEY WERE BARELY MAKING ENOUGH TO FEED THEMSELVES, LET ALONE PAY FOR THEIR WAY BACK HOME.
"SUZANNE AND THE BOYFRIEND BECAME SEPARATED SOMEWHERE IN THE REIGARRT SYSTEM.
"SHE WAS PICKING KRAWBERRIES FOR THREE IMPERIAL CREDITS A DAY...
"...WHEN THE SHI'AR BORDER PATROL SWEPT THROUGH.

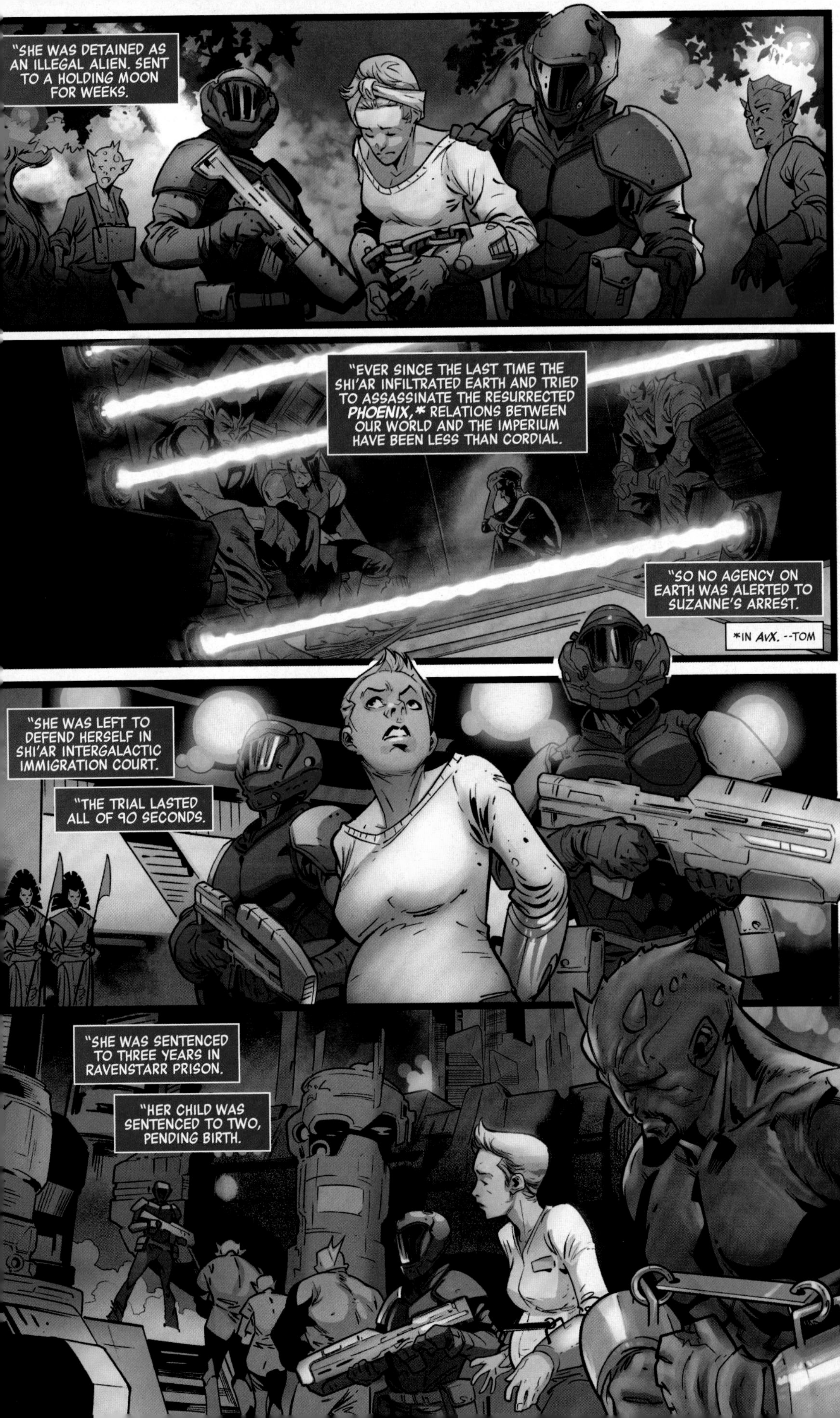
"SHE WAS DETAINED AS AN ILLEGAL ALIEN. SENT TO A HOLDING MOON FOR WEEKS.
"EVER SINCE THE LAST TIME THE SHI'AR INFILTRATED EARTH AND TRIED TO ASSASSINATE THE RESURRECTED PHOENIX,* RELATIONS BETWEEN OUR WORLD AND THE IMPERIUM HAVE BEEN LESS THAN CORDIAL.
"SO NO AGENCY ON EARTH WAS ALERTED TO SUZANNE'S ARREST.
*IN AvX. --TOM
"SHE WAS LEFT TO DEFEND HERSELF IN SHI'AR INTERGALACTIC IMMIGRATION COURT.
"THE TRIAL LASTED ALL OF 90 SECONDS.
"SHE WAS SENTENCED TO THREE YEARS IN RAVENSTARR PRISON.
"HER CHILD WAS SENTENCED TO TWO, PENDING BIRTH.

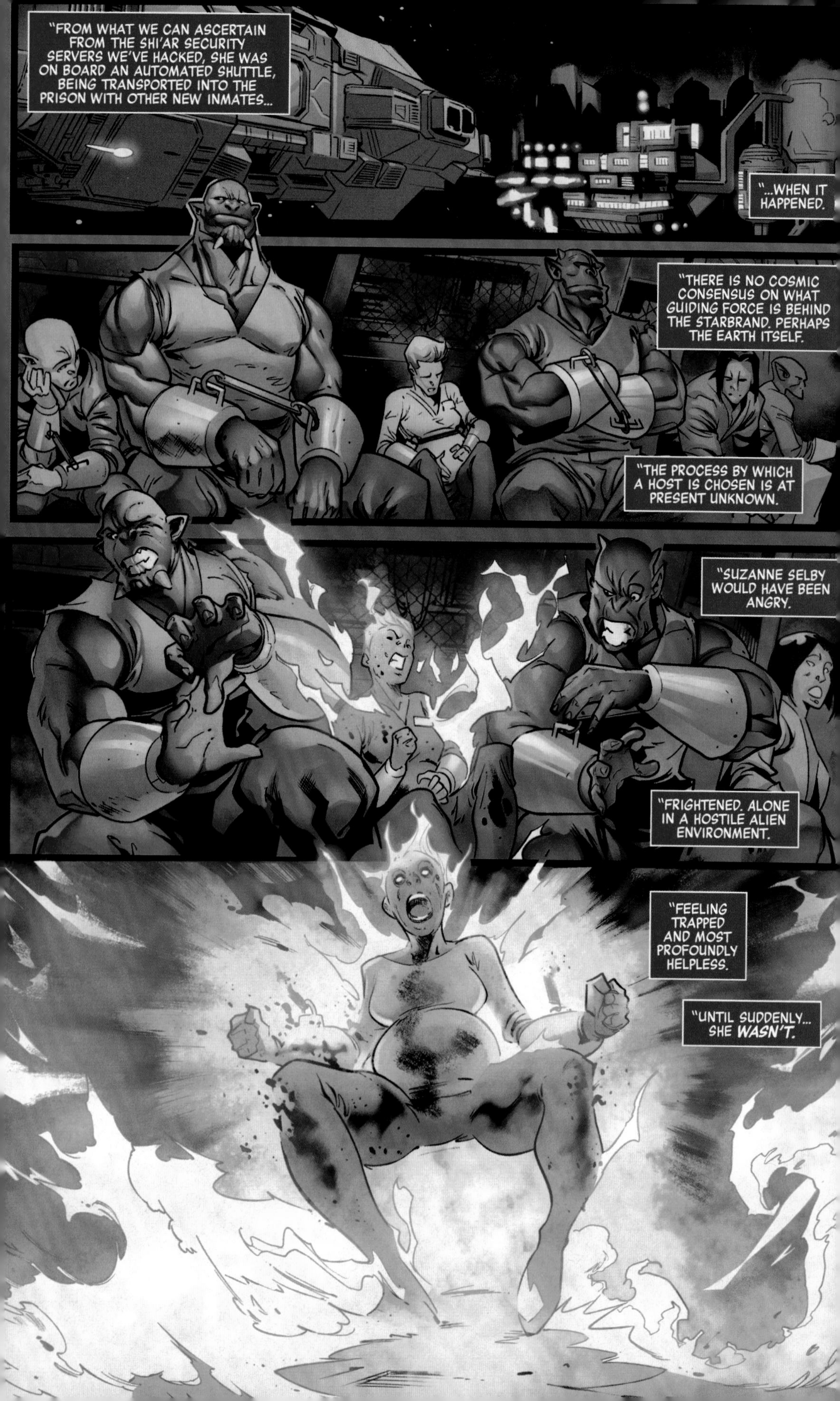
"FROM WHAT WE CAN ASCERTAIN FROM THE SHI'AR SECURITY SERVERS WE'VE HACKED, SHE WAS ON BOARD AN AUTOMATED SHUTTLE, BEING TRANSPORTED INTO THE PRISON WITH OTHER NEW INMATES...
"...WHEN IT HAPPENED.
"THERE IS NO COSMIC CONSENSUS ON WHAT GUIDING FORCE IS BEHIND THE STARBRAND. PERHAPS THE EARTH ITSELF.
"THE PROCESS BY WHICH A HOST IS CHOSEN IS AT PRESENT UNKNOWN.
"SUZANNE SELBY WOULD HAVE BEEN ANGRY.
"FRIGHTENED. ALONE IN A HOSTILE ALIEN ENVIRONMENT.
"FEELING TRAPPED AND MOST PROFOUNDLY HELPLESS.
"UNTIL SUDDENLY... SHE ***WASN'T.***

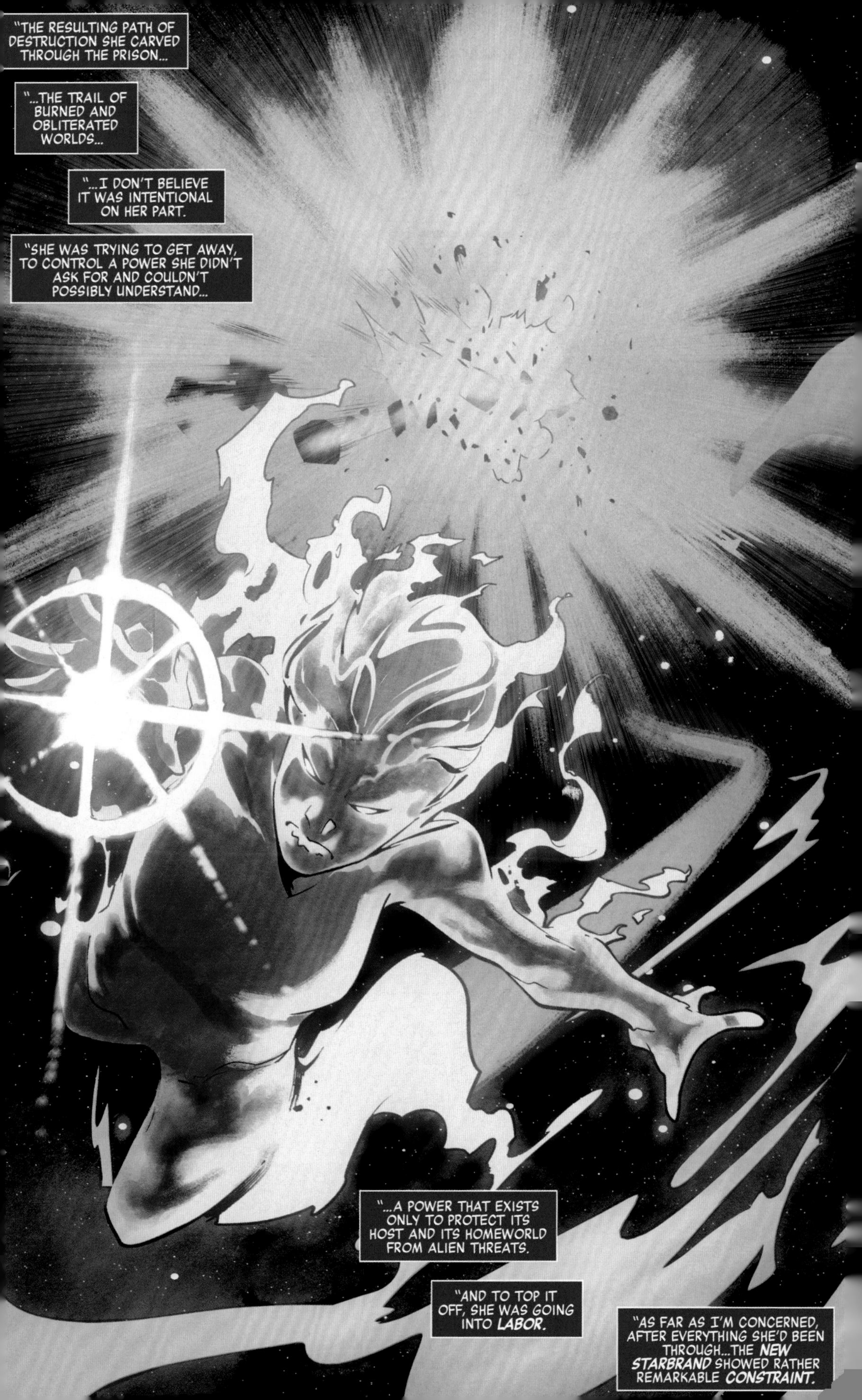
"THE RESULTING PATH OF DESTRUCTION SHE CARVED THROUGH THE PRISON...
"...THE TRAIL OF BURNED AND OBLITERATED WORLDS...
"...I DON'T BELIEVE IT WAS INTENTIONAL ON HER PART.
"SHE WAS TRYING TO GET AWAY, TO CONTROL A POWER SHE DIDN'T ASK FOR AND COULDN'T POSSIBLY UNDERSTAND...
"...A POWER THAT EXISTS ONLY TO PROTECT ITS HOST AND ITS HOMEWORLD FROM ALIEN THREATS.
"AND TO TOP IT OFF, SHE WAS GOING INTO ***LABOR.***
"AS FAR AS I'M CONCERNED, AFTER EVERYTHING SHE'D BEEN THROUGH...THE ***NEW STARBRAND*** SHOWED RATHER REMARKABLE ***CONSTRAINT.***

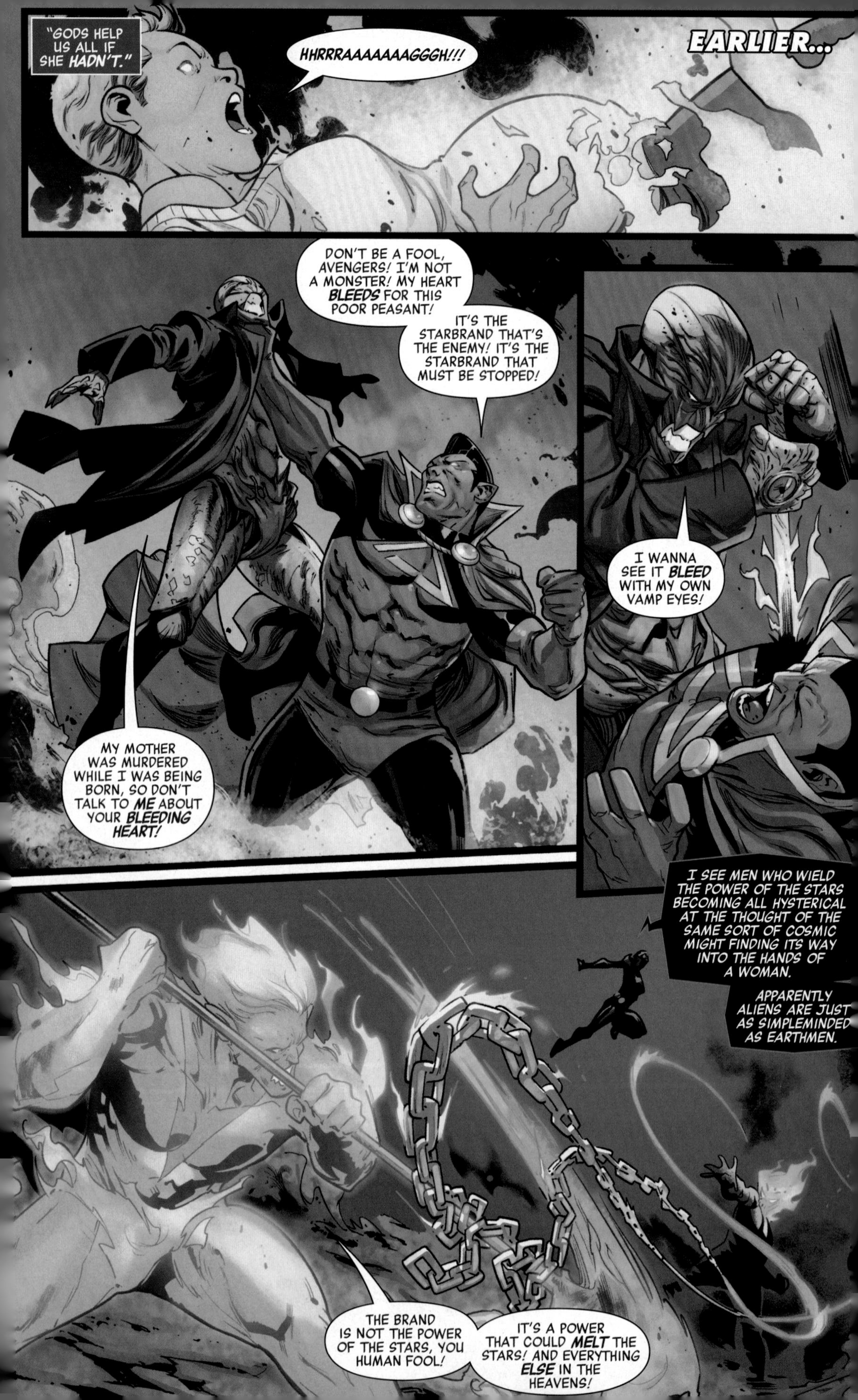

"GODS HELP US ALL IF SHE HADN'T."
HHRRRAAAAAAAGGGH!!!
EARLIER...
DON'T BE A FOOL, AVENGERS! I'M NOT A MONSTER! MY HEART BLEEDS FOR THIS POOR PEASANT!
IT'S THE STARBRAND THAT'S THE ENEMY! IT'S THE STARBRAND THAT MUST BE STOPPED!
MY MOTHER WAS MURDERED WHILE I WAS BEING BORN, SO DON'T TALK TO ME ABOUT YOUR BLEEDING HEART!
I WANNA SEE IT BLEED WITH MY OWN VAMP EYES!
I SEE MEN WHO WIELD THE POWER OF THE STARS BECOMING ALL HYSTERICAL AT THE THOUGHT OF THE SAME SORT OF COSMIC MIGHT FINDING ITS WAY INTO THE HANDS OF A WOMAN.
APPARENTLY ALIENS ARE JUST AS SIMPLEMINDED AS EARTHMEN.
THE BRAND IS NOT THE POWER OF THE STARS, YOU HUMAN FOOL!
IT'S A POWER THAT COULD MELT THE STARS! AND EVERYTHING ELSE IN THE HEAVENS!

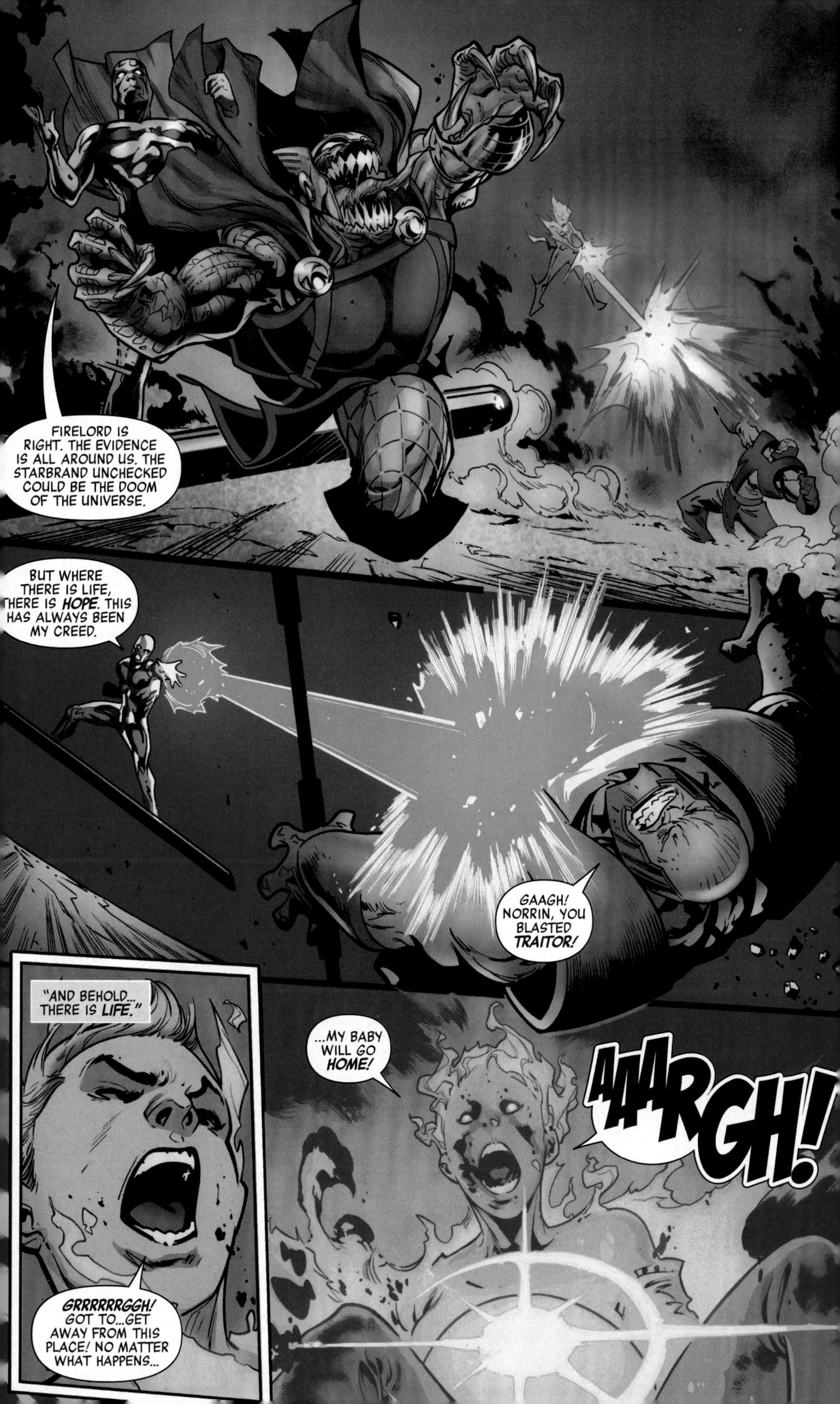

FIRELORD IS RIGHT. THE EVIDENCE IS ALL AROUND US. THE STARBRAND UNCHECKED COULD BE THE DOOM OF THE UNIVERSE.
BUT WHERE THERE IS LIFE, THERE IS HOPE. THIS HAS ALWAYS BEEN MY CREED.
GAAGH! NORRIN, YOU BLASTED TRAITOR!
"AND BEHOLD... THERE IS LIFE."
GRRRRRRGGH! GOT TO...GET AWAY FROM THIS PLACE! NO MATTER WHAT HAPPENS...
...MY BABY WILL GO HOME!
AAAARGH!

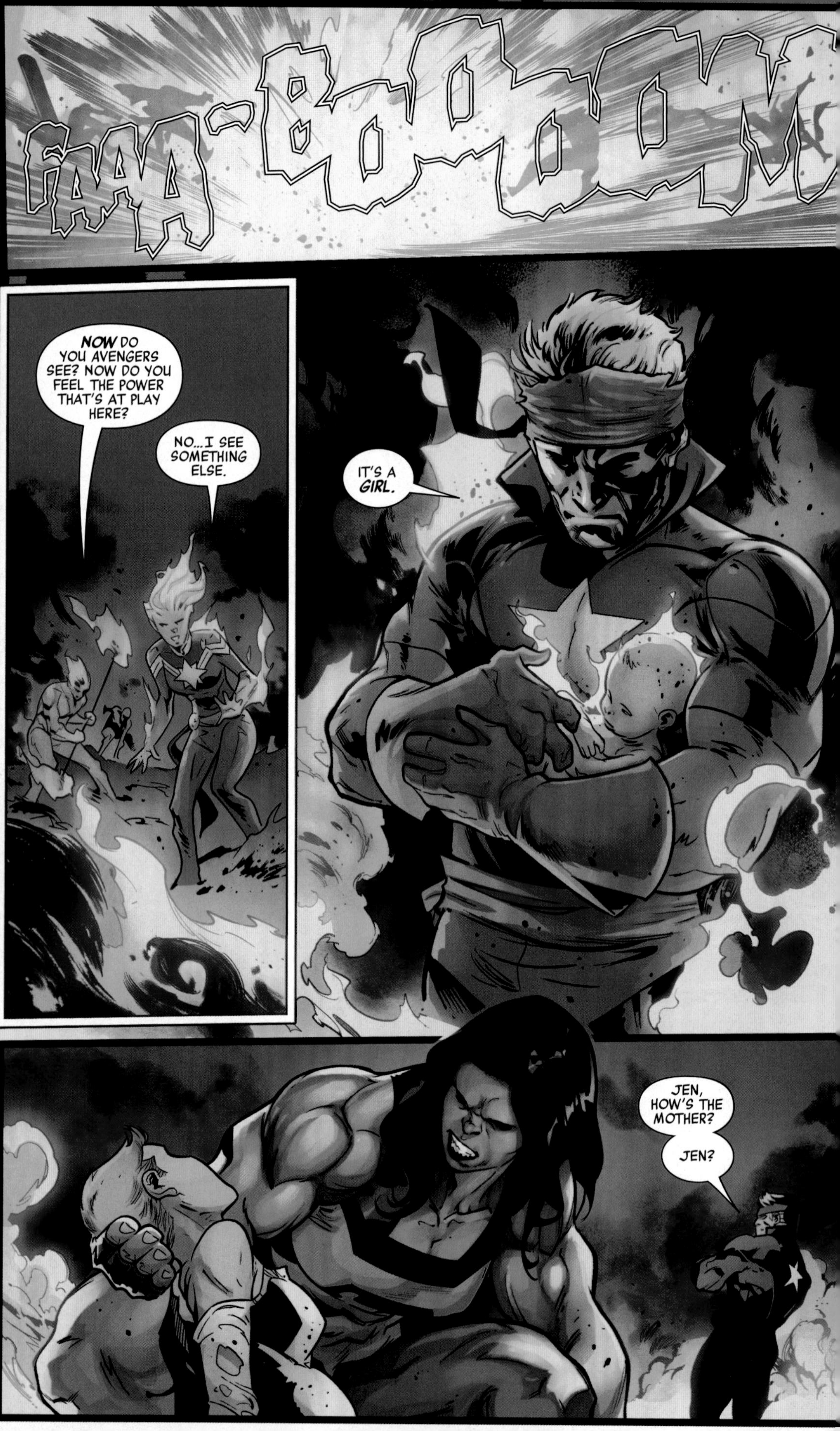
FAAA-BOOOOOM
NOW DO YOU AVENGERS SEE? NOW DO YOU FEEL THE POWER THAT'S AT PLAY HERE?
NO...I SEE SOMETHING ELSE.
IT'S A GIRL.
JEN, HOW'S THE MOTHER?
JEN?

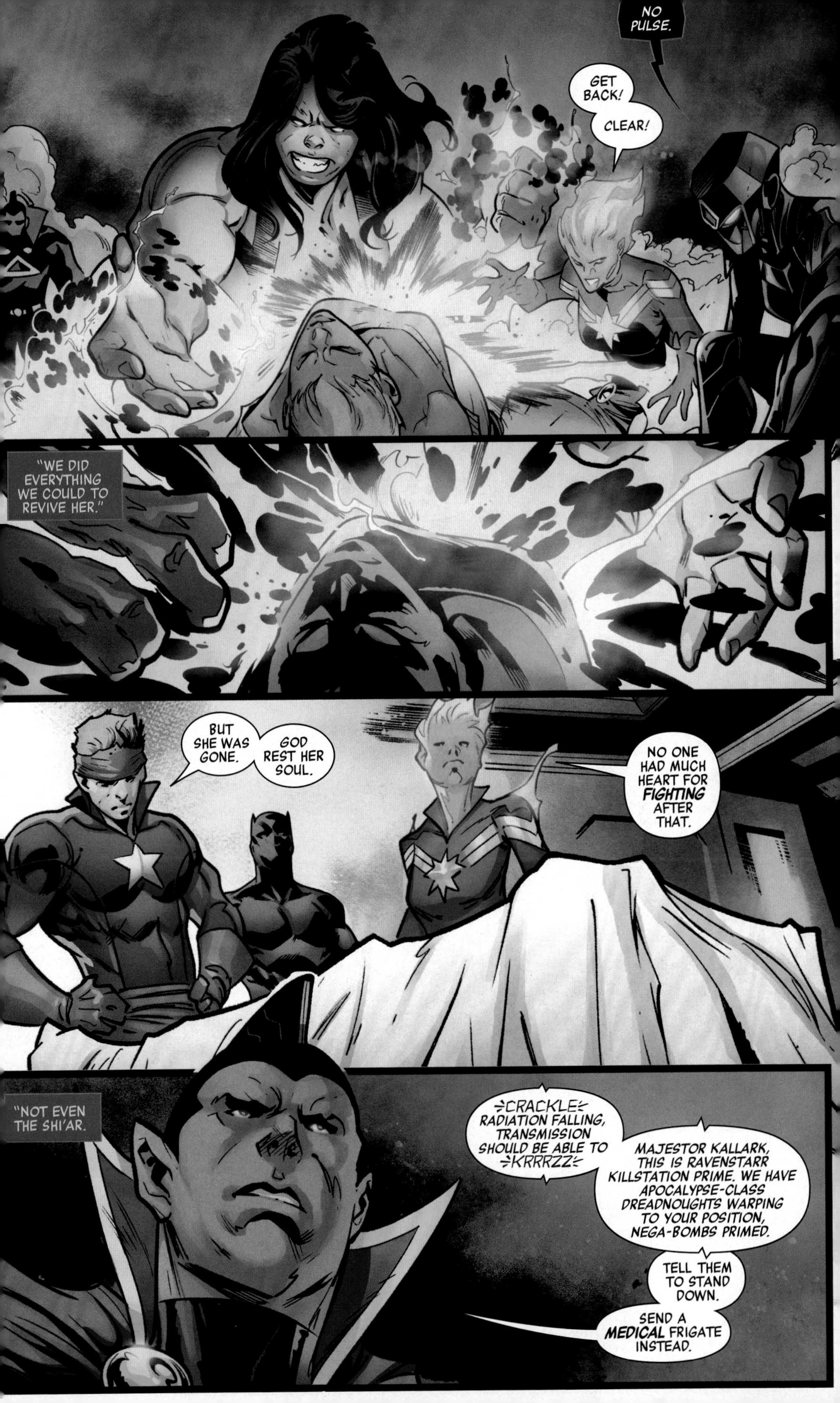

NO PULSE.
GET BACK!
CLEAR!
"WE DID EVERYTHING WE COULD TO REVIVE HER."
BUT SHE WAS GONE.
GOD REST HER SOUL.
NO ONE HAD MUCH HEART FOR FIGHTING AFTER THAT.
"NOT EVEN THE SHI'AR.
CRACKLE RADIATION FALLING, TRANSMISSION SHOULD BE ABLE TO KRRRZZ
MAJESTOR KALLARK, THIS IS RAVENSTARR KILLSTATION PRIME. WE HAVE APOCALYPSE-CLASS DREADNOUGHTS WARPING TO YOUR POSITION, NEGA-BOMBS PRIMED.
TELL THEM TO STAND DOWN.
SEND A MEDICAL FRIGATE INSTEAD.

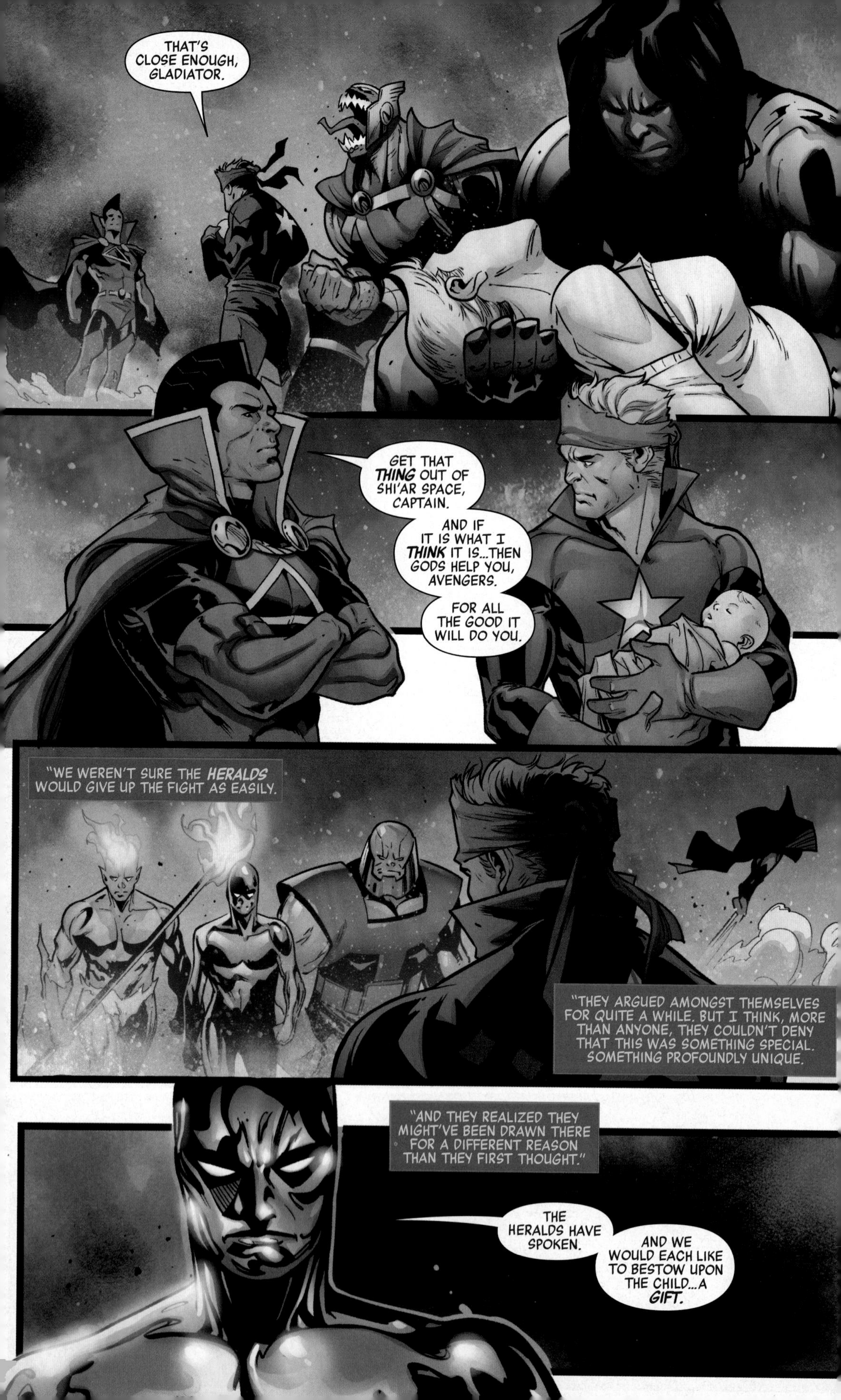
THAT'S CLOSE ENOUGH, GLADIATOR.
GET THAT THING OUT OF SHI'AR SPACE, CAPTAIN.
AND IF IT IS WHAT I THINK IT IS...THEN GODS HELP YOU, AVENGERS.
FOR ALL THE GOOD IT WILL DO YOU.
"WE WEREN'T SURE THE HERALDS WOULD GIVE UP THE FIGHT AS EASILY.
"THEY ARGUED AMONGST THEMSELVES FOR QUITE A WHILE. BUT I THINK, MORE THAN ANYONE, THEY COULDN'T DENY THAT THIS WAS SOMETHING SPECIAL. SOMETHING PROFOUNDLY UNIQUE.
"AND THEY REALIZED THEY MIGHT'VE BEEN DRAWN THERE FOR A DIFFERENT REASON THAN THEY FIRST THOUGHT."
THE HERALDS HAVE SPOKEN.
AND WE WOULD EACH LIKE TO BESTOW UPON THE CHILD...A GIFT.

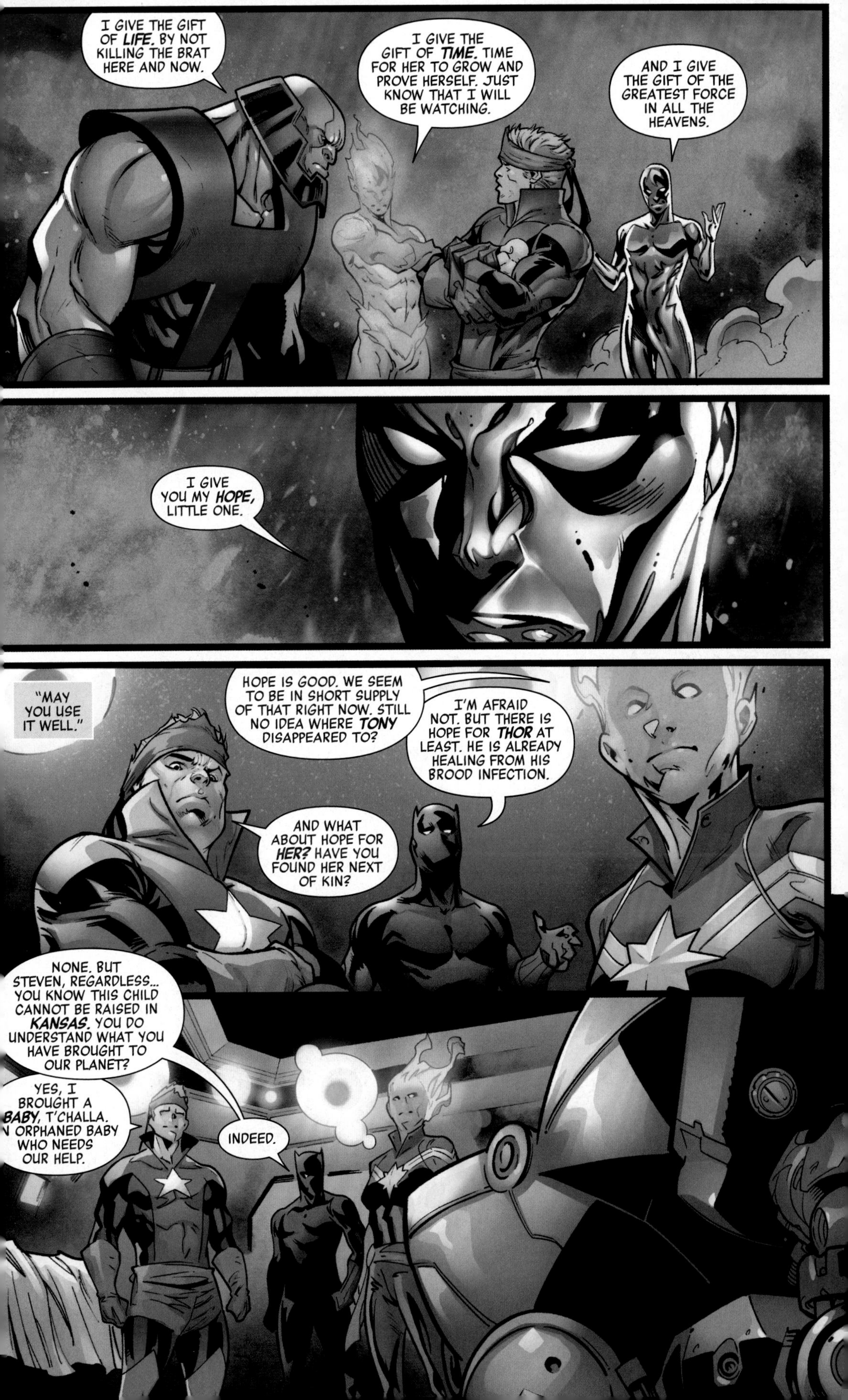
I GIVE THE GIFT OF LIFE. BY NOT KILLING THE BRAT HERE AND NOW.
I GIVE THE GIFT OF TIME. TIME FOR HER TO GROW AND PROVE HERSELF. JUST KNOW THAT I WILL BE WATCHING.
AND I GIVE THE GIFT OF THE GREATEST FORCE IN ALL THE HEAVENS.
I GIVE YOU MY HOPE, LITTLE ONE.
"MAY YOU USE IT WELL."
HOPE IS GOOD. WE SEEM TO BE IN SHORT SUPPLY OF THAT RIGHT NOW. STILL NO IDEA WHERE TONY DISAPPEARED TO?
I'M AFRAID NOT. BUT THERE IS HOPE FOR THOR AT LEAST. HE IS ALREADY HEALING FROM HIS BROOD INFECTION.
AND WHAT ABOUT HOPE FOR HER? HAVE YOU FOUND HER NEXT OF KIN?
NONE. BUT STEVEN, REGARDLESS... YOU KNOW THIS CHILD CANNOT BE RAISED IN KANSAS. YOU DO UNDERSTAND WHAT YOU HAVE BROUGHT TO OUR PLANET?
YES, I BROUGHT A BABY, T'CHALLA. N ORPHANED BABY WHO NEEDS OUR HELP.
INDEED.

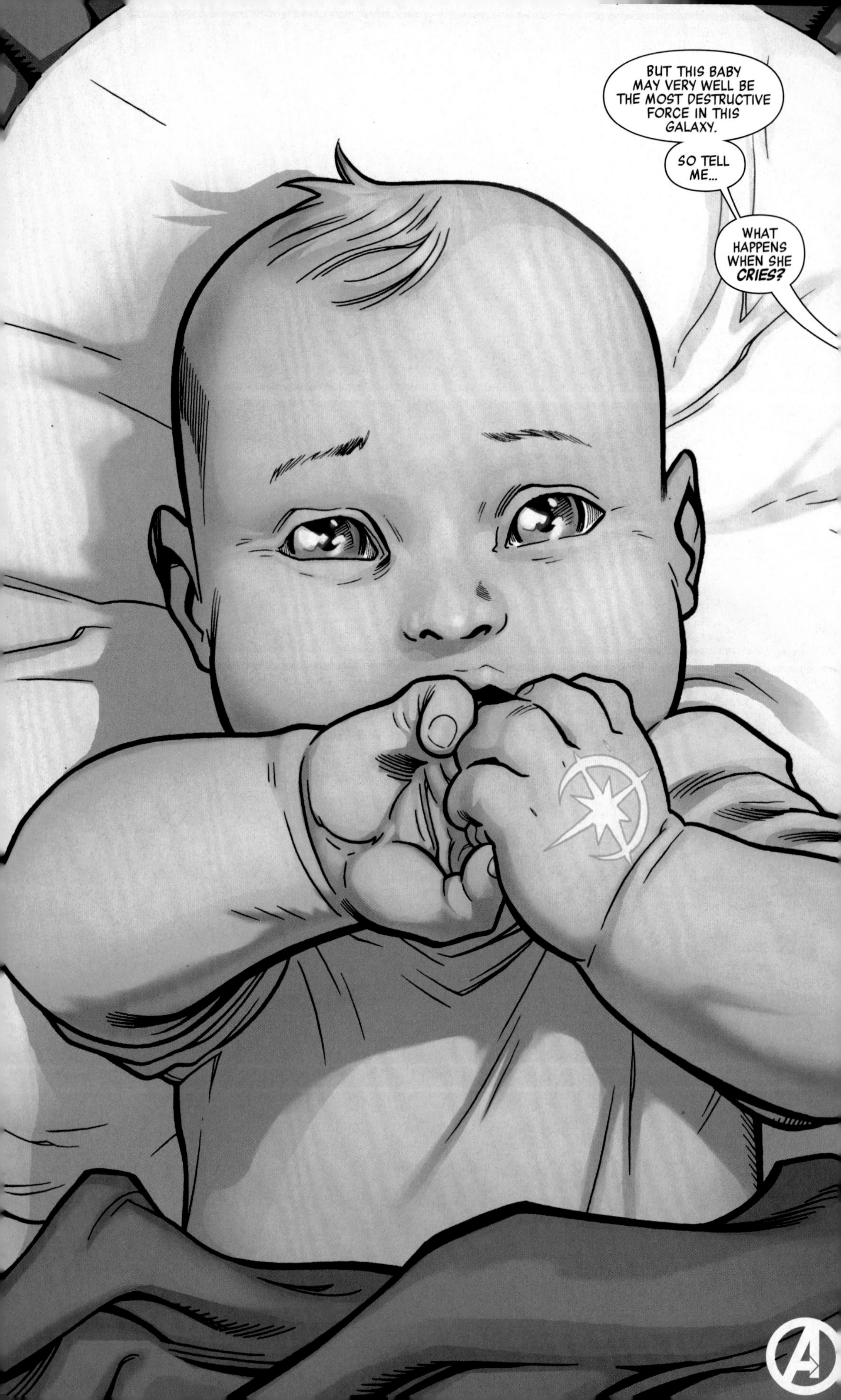
BUT THIS BABY MAY VERY WELL BE THE MOST DESTRUCTIVE FORCE IN THIS GALAXY.
SO TELL ME...
WHAT HAPPENS WHEN SHE *CRIES?*

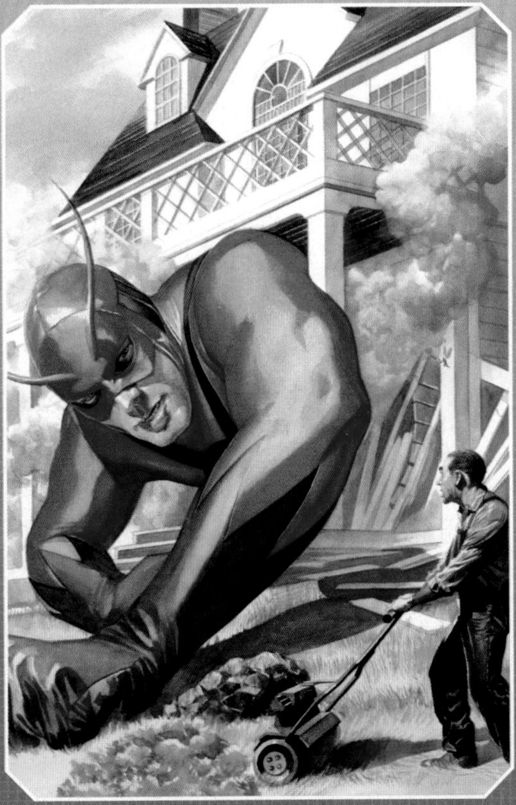

ALEX ROSS
26 MARVELS 25TH ANNIVERSARY
VARIANT

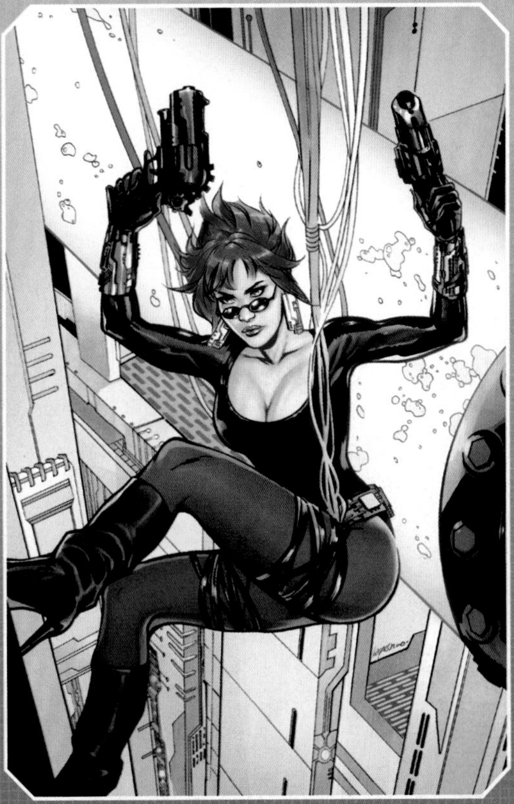

EMA LUPACCHINO
& JASON KEITH
28 2020 VARIANT

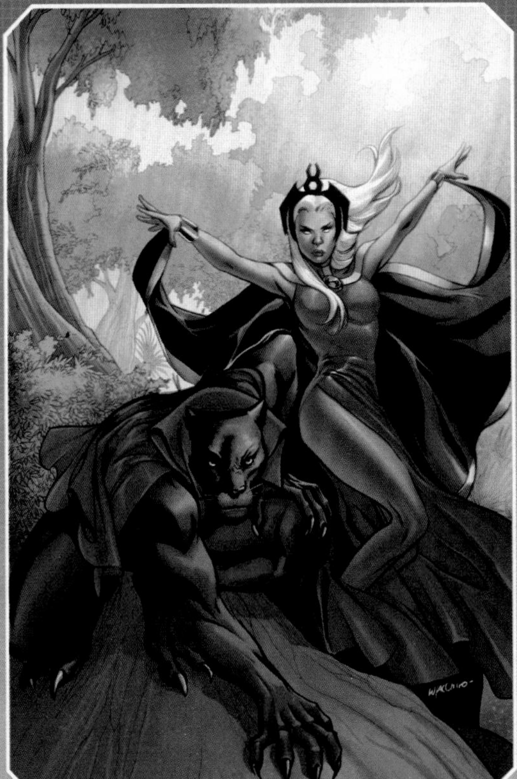

EMA LUPACCHINO & RACHELLE ROSENBERG
29 MARVELS X VARIANT

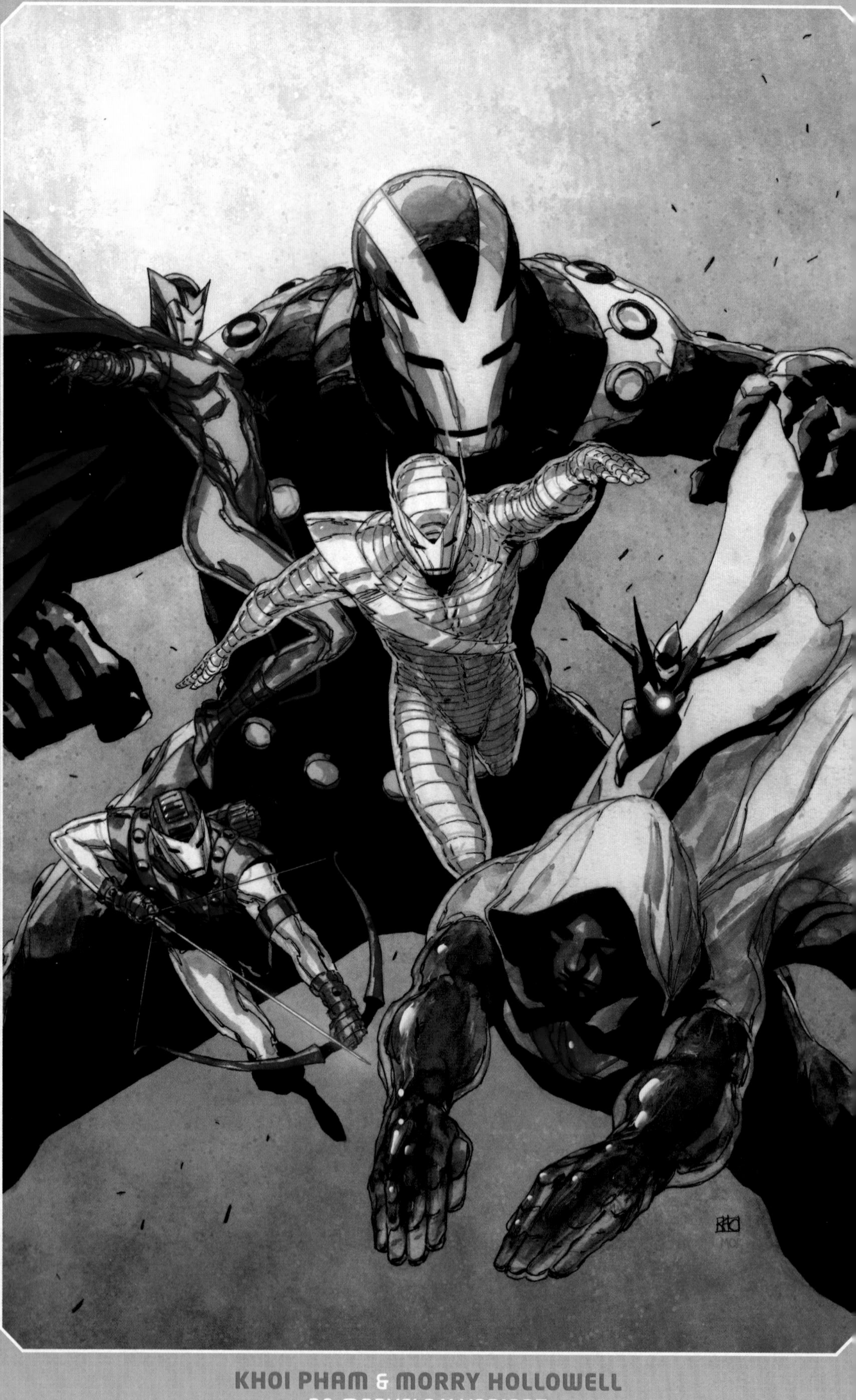

KHOI PHAM & MORRY HOLLOWELL
30 MARVELS X VARIANT